Homework

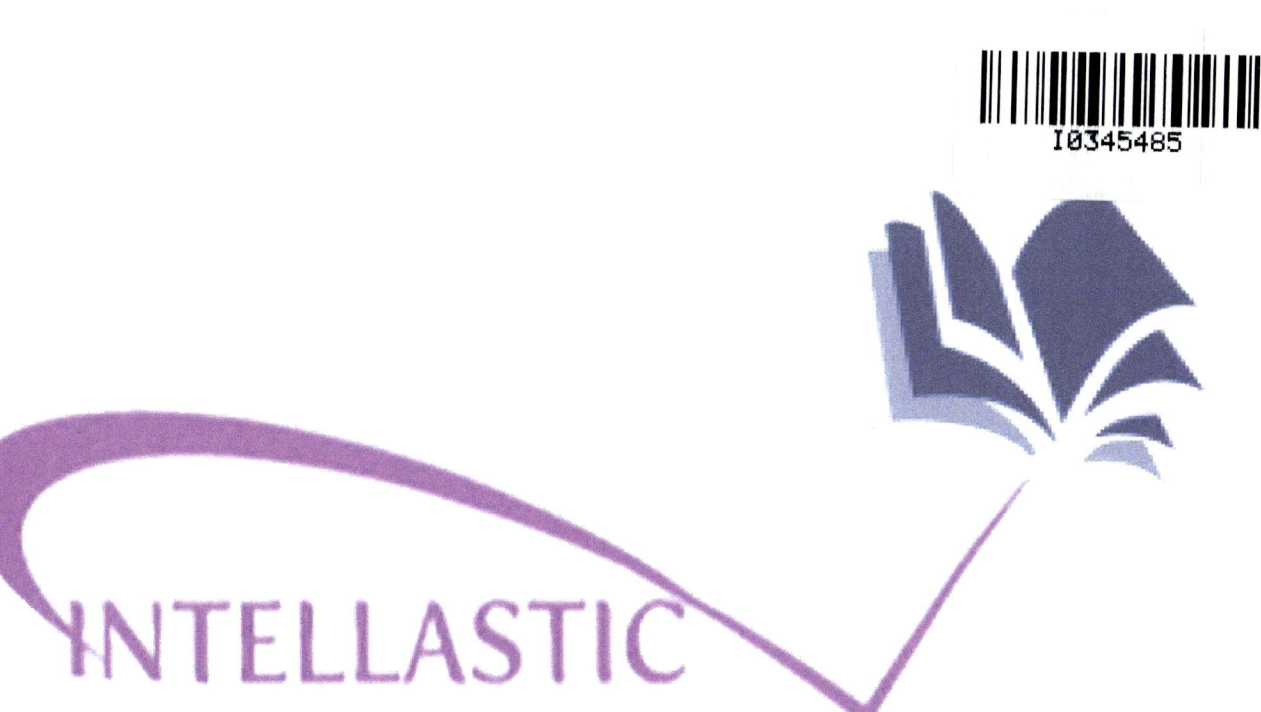

Learn To Read English With Directions In Haitian Creole
Answer Key
Homework
Color Edition

Homework

ISBN 978-1-945738-57-9
© 2022 – Wendy A. Charles & Alexander J. Charles
All Rights Reserved
Baldwin, New York
www.intellastic.com

All rights reserved. No portion of this book may be reproduced, stored in a retrieval system, or transmitted in any form or by any means – electronic, mechanical, photocopy, recording, video presentation, private instruction, scanning or other – except for brief quotations in critical reviews or articles, without the prior written permission of the writers.

All Rights Reserved. Printed in the USA.

Homework

Table of Contents

Unit A		
Lesson 1.1	Reading Words with the Letter A/a	1
Lesson 1.2	Reading Words with the Short Vowel "a" Sound	2
Lesson 1.2	Reading & Writing Words with the Short Vowel "a" Sound	3
Lesson 1.3	Reading Words with the Long Vowel "a" Sound	4
Lesson 1.3	Reading & Writing Words with the Long Vowel "a" Sound	5
Lessons 1.2 & 1.3	Reading Short Vowel and Long Vowel Words	6
Lesson 1.4	Reading Words with the "age" Letter Combination	7
Lesson 1.5	Reading Words with the "ai" Vowel Pair	8
Lesson 1.6	Reading Letter "a" Words with the Schwa Sound	9
Lesson 1.7	Reading Words with the "ar" Letter Combination	10
Lesson 1.7	Reading Words with the "ar" Letter Combination	11
Lesson 1.8	Reading Words with a Silent Letter "a"	12
Unit Review	Reading Words with Vowel "a" Sounds: /ă/,/ā/,/ə/ & Silent	13
Lesson 1.9	Reading Multisyllable Words	14
Lesson 1.9	Reading Multisyllable Words	15
Lesson 1.10	Proper and Common Nouns and Adjectives	16

Unit B		
Lesson 2.1	Reading Words with the Letter B/b	17
Lesson 2.2	Reading Words with the "br" Letter Combination	18
Lesson 2.3	Reading Words with the "bl" Letter Combination	19
Lesson 2.3	Reading Words with the "ble" Letter Combination	20
Lesson 2.4	Reading Words with the "mb" Letter Combination	21
Lesson 2.4	Reading Words with the "bt" Letter Combination	22
Lesson 2.5	Reading Words with a Silent Letter "b"	23
Lesson 2.6	Reading Multisyllable Words	24
Lesson 2.6	Reading Multisyllable Words	25
Lesson 2.7	Proper and Common Nouns and Adjectives	26

Homework

Unit C

Lesson 3.1	Reading Words with the Letter C/c	27
Lesson 3.1	Reading Words with the Hard Letter "c"	28
Lesson 3.2	Reading Words with the Soft Letter "c"	29
Lessons 3.1 & 3.2	Reading Hard Letter "c" and Soft Letter "c" Words	30
Lesson 3.3	Reading Words with the "cr" Letter Combination	31
Lesson 3.4	Reading Words with the "cl" Letter Combination	32
Lesson 3.4	Reading Words with the "cle" Letter Combination	33
Lesson 3.5	Reading Words with the "ct" Letter Combination	34
Lesson 3.6	Reading Soft Letter "c" Words	35
Lesson 3.6	Reading Soft Letter "c" Words	36
Lesson 3.7	Reading Words with the "ch" Letter Combination	37
Lesson 3.8	Reading Words with the "cc" Letter Combination	38
Lesson 3.9	Reading Words with a Silent Letter "c"	39
Lesson 3.10	Reading Multisyllable Words	40
Lesson 3.10	Reading Multisyllable Words	41
Lesson 3.11	Proper and Common Nouns and Adjectives	42

Unit D

Lesson 4.1	Reading Words with the Letter D/d	43
Lesson 4.2	Reading Letter "d" Words with the /d/ Sound & /j/ Sound	44
Lesson 4.2	Reading Words with the "dr" Letter Combination	45
Lesson 4.3	Reading Words with the "ed" Suffix/ Past Tense Verbs	46
Lesson 4.4	Reading Words with a Silent Letter "d"	47
Lesson 4.5	Reading Multisyllable Words	48
Lesson 4.5	Reading Multisyllable Words	49
Lesson 4.6	Proper and Common Nouns and Adjectives	50

Unit E

Lesson 5.1	Reading Words with the Letter E/e	51
Lesson 5.2	Reading Words with the Short Vowel "e" Sound	52
Lesson 5.2	Reading & Writing Words with the Short Vowel "e" Sound	53

Homework

Lesson 5.3	Reading Words with the Long Vowel "e" Sound	54
Lesson 5.3	Reading & Writing Words with the Long Vowel "e" Sound	55
Lessons 5.2 & 5.3	Reading Short Vowel and Long Vowel Words	56
Lesson 5.4	Reading Words with Letter "e" Vowel Pairs	57
Lesson 5.5	Reading Words with the Final Letter "e"	58
Lesson 5.6	Reading Letter "e" Words with the Schwa Vowel Sound	59
Lesson 5.7	Reading Words with the "er" Letter Combination	60
Lesson 5.8	Reading Words with the "eu" and "ew" Letter Combinations	61
Lesson 5.9	Reading Words with the "ey" Letter Combination	62
Lesson 5.10	Reading Words with a Silent Letter "e"	63
Unit Review	Reading Words with Vowel "e" Sounds: /ĕ/, /ē/, /ə/ & Silent	64
Lesson 5.11	Reading Multisyllable Words	65
Lesson 5.11	Reading Multisyllable Words	66
Lesson 5.12	Proper and Common Nouns and Adjectives	67

Unit F

Lesson 6.1	Reading Words with the Letter F/f	68
Lesson 6.2	Reading Words with the "fr" Letter Combination	69
Lesson 6.3	Reading Words with the "fl" Letter Combination	70
Lesson 6.3	Reading Words with the "fle" Letter Combination	71
Lesson 6.4	Reading Words with the "ft," "lf" and "ff" Letter Combinations	72
Lesson 6.5	Reading Words with a Silent Letter "f"	73
Lesson 6.6	Reading Singular and Plural forms of Words Ending in "-f" & "-fe"	74
Lesson 6.7	Reading Multisyllable Words	75
Lesson 6.7	Reading Multisyllable Words	76
Lesson 6.8	Proper and Common Nouns and Adjectives	77

Unit G

Lesson 7.1	Reading Words with the Letter G/g	78
Lesson 7.1	Reading Words with the Hard Letter "g"	79
Lesson 7.2	Reading Words with the Soft Letter G/g	80
Lessons 7.1 & 7.2	Reading Hard Letter "g" and Soft Letter "g" Words	81

Homework

Lessons 7.1 & 7.2	Reading Hard Letter "g" and Soft Letter "g" Words	82
Lesson 7.3	Reading Words with the "gr" Letter Combination	83
Lesson 7.4	Reading Words with the "gl" Letter Combination	84
Lesson 7.4	Reading Words with the "gle" Letter Combination	85
Lesson 7.5	Reading Words with the "gh" Letter Combination	86
Lesson 7.6	Reading Words with the "gn" Letter Combination	87
Lesson 7.7	Reading Words with a Silent Letter "g"	88
Lesson 7.8	Reading Multisyllable Words	89
Lesson 7.8	Reading Multisyllable Words	90
Lesson 7.9	Proper and Common Nouns and Adjectives	91

Unit H

Lesson 8.1	Reading Words with the Letter H/h	92
Lesson 8.2	Reading Words with the Letter "h" Combinations: "sh," "wh," "ch," "th," "rh," "ph" and "gh"	93
Lesson 8.2	Reading Words with the Letter "h" Combinations: "sh," "wh," "ch," "th," "rh," "ph," "gh" and "sch"	94
Lesson 8.3	Reading Words with a Silent Letter "h"	95
Lesson 8.4	Reading Multisyllable Words	96
Lesson 8.4	Reading Multisyllable Words	97
Lesson 8.5	Proper and Common Nouns and Adjectives	98

Unit I

Lesson 9.1	Reading Words with the Letter I/i	99
Lesson 9.2	Reading Words with the Short Vowel "i" Sound	100
Lesson 9.2	Reading & Writing Words with the Short Vowel "i" Sound	101
Lesson 9.3	Reading Words with the Long Vowel "i" Sound	102
Lesson 9.3	Reading & Writing Words with the Long Vowel "i" Sound	103
Lessons 9.2 & 9.3	Reading Short Vowel and Long Vowel Words	104
Lesson 9.4	Reading Words with Letter "i" Vowel Pairs	105
Lesson 9.5	Reading Words with the Final Letter "i"	106
Lesson 9.6	Reading Letter "i" Words with the Schwa Vowel Sound	107

Lesson 9.7	Reading Words with the "ir" Letter Combination	108
Lesson 9.8	Reading Letter "i" Words with the Long Vowel "e" Sound	109
Lesson 9.9	Reading Words with a Silent Letter "i"	110
Unit Review	Reading Words with Vowel "i" Sounds: /ĭ/, /ī/, /ə/ & Silent	111
Lesson 9.10	Reading Multisyllable Words	112
Lesson 9.10	Reading Multisyllable Words	113
Lesson 9.11	Proper and Common Nouns and Adjectives	114

Unit J

Lesson 10.1	Reading Words with the Letter J/j	115
Lesson 10.2	Reading Multisyllable Words	116
Lesson 10.2	Reading Multisyllable Words	117
Lesson 10.3	Proper and Common Nouns and Adjectives	118

Unit K

Lesson 11.1	Reading Words with the Letter K/k	119
Lesson 11.2	Reading Words with the Letter "k" and "ck" Letter Combination	120
Lesson 11.3	Reading Words with the "kle" Letter Combination	121
Lesson 11.4	Reading Words with a Silent Letter "k"	122
Lesson 11.5	Reading Multisyllable Words	123
Lesson 11.5	Reading Multisyllable Words	124
Lesson 11.6	Proper and Common Nouns and Adjectives	125

Unit L

Lesson 12.1	Reading Words with the Letter L/l	126
Lesson 12.2	Reading Words with the Letter "l" Combinations: "fl," "pl" & "sl"	127
Lesson 12.3	Reading Words with a Silent Letter "l"	128
Lesson 12.4	Reading Multisyllable Words	129
Lesson 12.4	Reading Multisyllable Words	130
Lesson 12.5	Proper and Common Nouns and Adjectives	131

Homework

Unit M

Lesson 13.1	Reading Words with the Letter M/m	132
Lesson 13.2	Reading Words with a Silent Letter "m"	133
Lesson 13.3	Reading Multisyllable Words	134
Lesson 13.3	Reading Multisyllable Words	135
Lesson 13.4	Proper and Common Nouns and Adjectives	136

Unit N

Lesson 14.1	Reading Words with the Letter N/n	137
Lesson 14.2	Reading Words with the "ng" Letter Combination	138
Lesson 14.3	Reading Words with a Silent Letter "n"	139
Lesson 14.4	Reading Multisyllable Words	140
Lesson 14.4	Reading Multisyllable Words	141
Lesson 14.5	Proper and Common Nouns and Adjectives	142

Unit O

Lesson 15.1	Reading Words with the Letter O/o	143
Lesson 15.2	Reading Words with the Short Vowel "o" Sound	144
Lesson 15.2	Reading & Writing Words with the Short Vowel "o" Sound	145
Lesson 15.3	Reading Words with the Long Vowel "o" Sound	146
Lesson 15.3	Reading & Writing Words with the Long Vowel "o" Sound	147
Lessons 15.2 & 15.3	Reading Short Vowel and Long Vowel Words	148
Lesson 15.4	Reading Words with Letter "o" Vowel Pairs	149
Lesson 15.5	Reading Words with the Final Letter "o"	150
Lesson 15.6	Reading Letter "o" Words with the Schwa Vowel Sound	151
Lesson 15.7	Reading Words with Vowel "o" Sounds: /ŏ/, /ō/ & /o͞o/	152
Lesson 15.8	Reading Words with the "or" Letter Combination	153
Lesson 15.8	Reading Words with the "or" Letter Combination	154
Lesson 15.9	Reading Words with a Silent Letter "o"	155
Unit Review	Reading Words with Vowel "o" Sounds: /ŏ/, /ō/, /ə/ & Silent	156
Lesson 15.10	Reading Multisyllable Words	157
Lesson 15.10	Reading Multisyllable Words	158

Lesson 15.11	Proper and Common Nouns and Adjectives	159
Unit P		
Lesson 16.1	Reading Words with the Letter P/p	160
Lesson 16.2	Reading Words with the "ph" Letter Combination	161
Lesson 16.3	Reading Words with the "pr" Letter Combination	162
Lesson 16.4	Reading Words with the "pl" Letter Combination	163
Lesson 16.4	Reading Words with the "ple" Letter Combination	164
Lesson 16.5	Reading Words with a Silent Letter "p"	165
Lesson 16.6	Reading Multisyllable Words	166
Lesson 16.6	Reading Multisyllable Words	167
Lesson 16.7	Proper and Common Nouns and Adjectives	168
Unit Q		
Lesson 17.1	Reading Words with the Letter Q/q	169
Lesson 17.2	Reading Words with the Letter "q" and "qu" Letter Combination	170
Lesson 17.2	Reading Words with the "qu" Letter Combination	171
Lesson 17.3	Reading Multisyllable Words	172
Lesson 17.3	Reading Multisyllable Words	173
Lesson 17.4	Proper and Common Nouns and Adjectives	174
Unit R		
Lesson 18.1	Reading Words with the Letter R/r	175
Lesson 18.2	Reading Words with the Letter "r" Combinations: "br," "cr," "dr," "fr," "gr," "pr" and "tr"	176
Lesson 18.3	Reading Multisyllable Words	177
Lesson 18.3	Reading Multisyllable Words	178
Lesson 18.4	Proper and Common Nouns and Adjectives	179
Unit S		
Lesson 19.1	Reading Words with the Letter S/s	180
Lesson 19.1	Reading Words with the Letter S/s	181

Homework

Lesson 19.2	Reading Words with the "sion," "sial" & "scious" Suffixes	182
Lesson 19.3	Reading Words with the "sch" Letter Combination	183
Lesson 19.4	Reading Words with the "scr," "shr," "spr" & "str" Letter Combinations	184
Lesson 19.5	Reading Words with the "sl" & "sle" Letter Combinations	185
Lesson 19.5	Reading Words with the "sle" Letter Combination	186
Lesson 19.6	Reading Words with the "sm" Letter Combination	187
Lesson 19.7	Reading Words with the "ss" Letter Combination	188
Lesson 19.8	Reading Words with a Silent Letter "s"	189
Lesson 19.9	Reading Multisyllable Words	190
Lesson 19.9	Reading Multisyllable Words	191
Lesson 19.10	Proper and Common Nouns and Adjectives	192

Unit T

Lesson 20.1	Reading Words with the Letter T/t	193
Lesson 20.2	Reading Words with the "thm" Letter Combination	194
Lesson 20.3	Reading Words with the "tion," "tial" & "tious" Suffixes	195
Lesson 20.4	Reading Words with the "tr" Letter Combination	196
Lesson 20.5	Reading Words with the "tle" Letter Combination	197
Lesson 20.6	Reading Words with the Letter "t" Sounds	198
Lesson 20.7	Reading Words with a Silent Letter "t"	199
Lesson 20.8	Reading Multisyllable Words	200
Lesson 20.8	Reading Multisyllable Words	201
Lesson 20.9	Proper and Common Nouns and Adjectives	202

Unit U

Lesson 21.1	Reading Words with the Letter U/u	203
Lesson 21.2	Reading Words with the Short Vowel "u" Sound	204
Lesson 21.2	Reading & Writing Words with the Short Vowel "u" Sound	205
Lesson 21.3	Reading Words with the Long Vowel "u" Sound	206
Lesson 21.3	Reading & Writing Words with the Long Vowel "u" Sound	207
Lessons 21.2 & 21.3	Reading Short Vowel and Long Vowel Words	208
Lesson 21.4	Reading Words with Letter "u" Vowel Pairs	209

Homework

Lesson 21.5	Reading Words with the Final Letter "u"	210
Lesson 21.6	Reading Letter "u" Words with the Schwa Vowel Sound	211
Lesson 21.7	Reading Words with the "ur" Letter Combination	212
Lesson 21.8	Reading Words with a Silent Letter "u"	213
Unit Review	Reading Words with Vowel "u" Sounds: /ŭ/, /o͞o/, /ə/ & Silent	214
Lesson 21.9	Reading Multisyllable Words	215
Lesson 21.9	Reading Multisyllable Words	216
Lesson 21.10	Proper and Common Nouns and Adjectives	217

Unit V

Lesson 22.1	Reading Words with the Letter V/v	218
Lesson 22.2	Reading Multisyllable Words	219
Lesson 22.2	Reading Multisyllable Words	220
Lesson 22.3	Proper and Common Nouns and Adjectives	221

Unit W

Lesson 23.1	Reading Words with the Letter W/w	222
Lesson 23.2	Reading Words with a Vowel before the Letter "w"	223
Lesson 23.3	Reading Words with a Silent "w" and "wr" Letter Combination	224
Lesson 23.3	Reading Words with a Silent Letter "w"	225
Lesson 23.4	Reading Multisyllable Words	226
Lesson 23.4	Reading Multisyllable Words	227
Lesson 23.5	Proper and Common Nouns and Adjectives	228

Unit X

Lesson 24.1	Reading Words with the Letter X/x	229
Lesson 24.1	Reading Words with the Letter X/x	230
Lesson 24.2	Reading Multisyllable Words	231
Lesson 24.2	Reading Multisyllable Words	232
Lesson 24.3	Proper and Common Nouns and Adjectives	233

Homework

Unit Y

Lesson 25.1	Reading Words with the Letter Y/y	234
Lesson 25.1	Reading Words with the Letter Y/y	235
Lesson 25.2	Reading Words with a Vowel before the Letter "y"	236
Lesson 25.3	Reading Words with the "cy" Letter Combination	237
Lesson 25.4	Reading Words with the Final Letter "y"	238
Lesson 25.5	Reading Words with the "yr" Letter Combination	239
Lesson 25.6	Reading Letter "y" Words with the Schwa Sound	240
Lesson 25.7	Reading Words with a Silent Letter "y"	241
Lesson 25.8	Reading Multisyllable Words	242
Lesson 25.8	Reading Multisyllable Words	243
Lesson 25.9	Proper and Common Nouns and Adjectives	244

Unit Z

Lesson 26.1	Reading Words with the Letter Z/z	245
Lesson 26.1	Reading Words with the Letter Z/z	246
Lesson 26.2	Reading Words with a Silent Letter "z"	247
Lesson 26.3	Reading Multisyllable Words	248
Lesson 26.3	Reading Multisyllable Words	249
Lesson 26.4	Proper and Common Nouns and Adjectives	250

Appendix

Appendix 1.0	Introduction of the Letter A/a	251
Appendix 2.0	Introduction of the Letter B/b	252
Appendix 2.0	Letter Recognition B/b	253
Appendix 3.0	Introduction of the Letter C/c	254
Appendix 3.0	Letter Recognition C/c	255
Appendix 4.0	Introduction of the Letter D/d	256
Appendix 4.0	Letter Recognition D/d	257
Appendix 5.0	Introduction of the Letter E/e	258
Appendix 6.0	Introduction of the Letter F/f	259
Appendix 6.0	Letter Recognition F/f	260

Appendix 7.0	Introduction of the Letter G/g	261
Appendix 7.0	Letter Recognition G/g	262
Appendix 8.0	Introduction of the Letter H/h	263
Appendix 8.0	Letter Recognition H/h	264
Appendix 9.0	Introduction of the Letter I/i	265
Appendix 10.0	Introduction of the Letter J/j	266
Appendix 10.0	Letter Recognition J/j	267
Appendix 11.0	Introduction of the Letter K/k	268
Appendix 11.0	Letter Recognition K/k	269
Appendix 12.0	Introduction of the Letter L/l	270
Appendix 12.0	Letter Recognition L/l	271
Appendix 13.0	Introduction of the Letter M/m	272
Appendix 13.0	Letter Recognition M/m	273
Appendix 14.0	Introduction of the Letter N/n	274
Appendix 14.0	Letter Recognition N/n	275
Appendix 15.0	Introduction of the Letter O/o	276
Appendix 16.0	Introduction of the Letter P/p	277
Appendix 16.0	Letter Recognition P/p	278
Appendix 17.0	Introduction of the Letter Q/q	279
Appendix 17.0	Letter Recognition Q/q	280
Appendix 18.0	Introduction of the Letter R/r	281
Appendix 18.0	Letter Recognition R/r	282
Appendix 19.0	Introduction of the Letter S/s	283
Appendix 19.0	Letter Recognition S/s	284
Appendix 20.0	Introduction of the Letter T/t	285
Appendix 20.0	Letter Recognition T/t	286
Appendix 21.0	Introduction of the Letter U/u	287
Appendix 22.0	Introduction of the Letter V/v	288
Appendix 22.0	Letter Recognition V/v	289
Appendix 23.0	Introduction of the Letter W/w	290
Appendix 23.0	Letter Recognition W/w	291

Homework

Appendix 24.0	Introduction of the Letter X/x	292
Appendix 24.0	Letter Recognition X/x	293
Appendix 25.0	Introduction of the Letter Y/y	294
Appendix 25.0	Letter Recognition Y/y	295
Appendix 26.0	Introduction of the Letter Z/z	296
Appendix 26.0	Letter Recognition Z/z	297

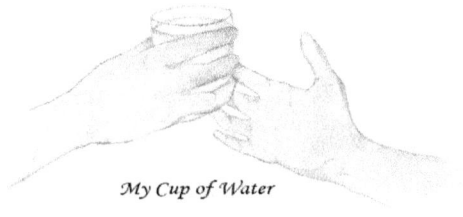

My Cup of Water

Homework

 Name: _____ Date:___/___/_____ Score:_____

Lesson 1.1

Reading Words with the Letter A/a

✓ **Lesson Check Point**

 Directions: Read each target word. Find the letter "a" and put a check (✓) in the column that identifies its position: beginning, within or end.
Direksyons: Li chak mo objektif. Jwenn lèt "a" a epi mete yon tchèck (✓) nan kolòn ki idantifye pozisyon li an: nan kòmansman, ladan oubyen nan finisman.

Target Words	Beginning (First Letter)	Within	End (Last Letter)
1. sofa			✓
2. basic		✓	
3. April	✓		
4. thankful		✓	
5. formula			✓

 Directions: Read each target word. Read the words in the row and circle the word that has a different vowel "a" sound.
Direksyons: Li chak mo objektif. Li mo yo ki nan ranje a epi antoure mo a ki bay yon son vwayèl "a" ki diferan an.

Target Words				
6. clan	mass	(play)	can't	camp
7. plant	task	back	ants	(plane)
8. grass	hand	(flame)	nap	ask
9. stand	(gate)	rank	bass	has
10. bran	had	sand	raft	(sauce)

Homework

 Name: _____ Date:___/___/_____ Score:_____

Lesson 1.2

Reading Words with the Short Vowel "a" Sound

✓ **Lesson Check Point**

 Directions: Read the words in the four boxes. Circle two words with the short vowel /ă/ sound. The anchor word for the short vowel /ă/ sound is <u>apple</u>.

Direksyons: Li mo yo ki nan kat ti bwat yo. Antoure de mo ki genyen son vwayèl kout /ă/ a. Mo referans pou son vwayèl kout /ă/ a se mo, <u>apple</u>.

sake	(track)	lay	(pack)	(lad)	(rattle)
(wax)	nail	(pack)	(pad)	plane	car

(tap)	(ram)	(hat)	calm	place	(tan)
ball	yarn	shape	(van)	sale	(and)

 **Directions:** Read the words in the four boxes. Circle two words that rhyme. Rhyming words have the same ending sound, such as <u>tap</u> and <u>map</u>.

Direksyons: Li mo yo ki nan kat ti bwat yo. Antoure de mo ki rime. De mo oubyen plizyè mo ki rime genyen menm son nan finisman yo, tankou <u>tap</u> ak <u>map</u>.

ape	(fan)	(snack)	ball	palm	aunt
mall	(can)	tape	(crack)	(mass)	(grass)

(tax)	day	law	(fast)	(glass)	(class)
(wax)	straw	(past)	rain	tall	pause

Homework

 Name: _____ Date: ___/___/_____ Score: _____

Lesson 1.2

Reading & Writing Words with the Short Vowel "a" Sound

✓ **Lesson Check Point**

Directions: Read each sentence and underline three words with the short vowel /ă/ sound. Then, write the underlined words on the lines below. The anchor word for the short vowel /ă/ sound is <u>apple</u>.

Direksyons: Li chak fraz epi soulinye twa mo ki genyen son vwayèl kout /ă/ a. Answit, ekri mo soulinye yo sou trè sa yo ki anba. Mo referans pou son vwayèl kout /ă/ a se mo, <u>apple</u>.

Model

<u>Ann</u> raised her <u>hand</u> in <u>class</u>.

    Ann   hand   class

1. The large <u>map</u> is in the <u>black</u> <u>sack</u>.

    map   black   sack

2. My father's crystal <u>glasses</u> <u>have</u> <u>cracks</u>.

    glasses   have   cracks

3. I <u>can</u> walk <u>faster</u> on the <u>grass</u> in the park.

    can   faster   grass

4. The <u>man</u> <u>has</u> a large, tasty cake in his <u>bag</u>.

    man   has   bag

5. My awesome <u>math</u> teacher gave <u>snacks</u> to the <u>class</u>.

    math   snacks   class

Homework

 Name:, _____ Date:___/___/_____ Score: _____

Lesson 1.3

Reading Words with the Long Vowel "a" Sound

✓ **Lesson Check Point**

 **Directions:** Read the words in the four boxes. Circle two words with the long vowel /ā/ sound. The anchor word for the long vowel /ā/ sound is <u>ape</u>.

Direksyons: Li mo yo ki nan kat ti bwat yo. Antoure de mo ki genyen son vwayèl long /ā/ a. Mo referans pou son vwayèl long /ā/ a se mo, <u>ape</u>.

fat	father	soda	(hale)	(pages)	nap
(tape)	(ray)	man	(date)	comma	(bake)

grass	(rate)	(wail)	sand	(state)	(cape)
(pale)	plant	(scale)	map	yam	taps

 **Directions:** Read the words in the four boxes. Circle two words that rhyme. Rhyming words have the same ending sound, such as <u>wait</u> and <u>date</u>.

Direksyons: Li mo ki nan kat ti bwat yo. Antoure de mo ki rime. De mo oubyen plizyè mo ki rime genyen menm son nan finisman yo, tankou <u>wait</u> ak <u>date</u>.

idea	(may)	at	(cake)	(taste)	(waste)
fast	(sway)	(take)	alike	had	lack

(face)	sad	(pain)	asks	and	ago
(trace)	can't	am	(Dane)	(game)	(tame)

Homework

Name: _____ Date: ___/___/_____ Score: _____

Lesson 1.3

Reading & Writing Words with the Long Vowel "a" Sound

✓ **Lesson Check Point**

Directions: Read each sentence and underline three words with the long vowel /ā/ sound. Then, write the underlined words on the lines below. The anchor word for the long vowel /ā/ sound is ape.

Direksyons: Li chak fraz epi soulinye twa mo ki genyen son vwayèl long /ā/ a. Answit, ekri mo soulinye yo sou trè sa yo ki anba. Mo referans pou son vwayèl long /ā/ a se mo, ape.

Model

Ann has grapes and cake on her plate.

    grapes   cake   plate

1. She said, "It rained all day in Maine."

    rained   day   Maine

2. Diane ate two large bagels with grape jam.

    ate   bagels   grape

3. Dave was brave to go into the dark cave alone.

    Dave   brave   cave

4. It is not safe to wait on the train platform after dark.

    safe   wait   train

5. Late last night, Alex baked large cakes in square pans.

    Late   baked   cakes

 Learn To Read English With Directions In Haitian Creole

Homework

Name: _____ Date: ___/___/_____ Score: _____

Review Lessons 1.2 & 1.3
Reading Short Vowel and Long Vowel Words

 Directions: Read the target words in the word box. In the first column, write the words that have the short vowel /ă/ sound, as in the word <u>apple</u>. In the second column, write the words that have the long vowel /ā/ sound, as in the word <u>ape</u>.

Direksyons: Li mo yo objektif yo ki nan bwat mo a. Nan premye kolòn nan, ekri mo ki bay son vwayèl kout /ă/ yo, tankou li ye nan mo <u>apple</u> la. Nan dezyèm kolòn nan, ekri mo ki bay son vwayèl long /ā/ yo, tankou li ye nan mo <u>ape</u> la.

Target Word Box				
trap	plane	gram	tape	asked
plant	same	land	snacks	paid
label	packs	cake	safe	late
crack	shape	pass	male	cap

Letter "a" has the /ă/ sound as in the word <u>apple</u>

Letter "a" has the /ā/ sound as in the word <u>ape</u>

cap	male
gram	tape
asked	same
plant	paid
land	label
trap	cake
packs	safe
crack	late
pass	plane
snacks	shape

Homework

 Name: _____ Date: ___/___/_____ Score: _____

Lesson 1.4

Reading Words with the "age" Letter Combination

✓ Lesson Check Point

 Directions: Read each target word. Find the "age" letter combination and put a check (✓) in the column that correctly identifies its sounds.
Direksyons: Li chak mo objektif. Jwenn konbinezon lèt "age" la epi mete yon tchèk (✓) nan kolòn nan ki idantifye son li yo kòrèkteman.

Target Words	"age" has the /ā/ + /j/ sounds as in the word stage	"age" has the /ĭ/ + /j/ sounds as in the word package	"age" has the /ä/ + /j/ or /ä/ + /zh/ sounds as in the word massage
1. pages	✓		
2. fuselage			✓
3. average		✓	
4. upstage	✓		
5. entourage			✓

 Directions: Read each sentence and underline the word that has an "age" letter combination that has the /ĭ/ + /j/ sounds, as in the word package.
Direksyons: Li chak fraz epi soulinye mo a ki genyen konbinezon lèt "age" la ki bay son /ĭ/ + /j/ a, tankou li ye nan mo package la.

6. At my school, teenage students wear <u>vintage</u> shirts.

7. The teenage star and his entourage ate <u>sausages</u> and rice.

8. My agent <u>encouraged</u> everyone to have a relaxing massage.

9. The stage <u>manager</u> scheduled three performances in New York.

10. The search team found the airplane's fuselage in <u>Anchorage</u>, Alaska.

Homework

 Name: _____ Date:___/___/_____ Score: _____

Lesson 1.5

Reading Words with the "ai" Vowel Pair

✓ Lesson Check Point

  Directions: Read each target word. Circle the word in the column that has the same "ai" sound as the target word.

Direksyons: Li chak mo objektif. Antoure mo a ki nan kolòn nan ki bay menm son "ai" la tankou mo objektif la.

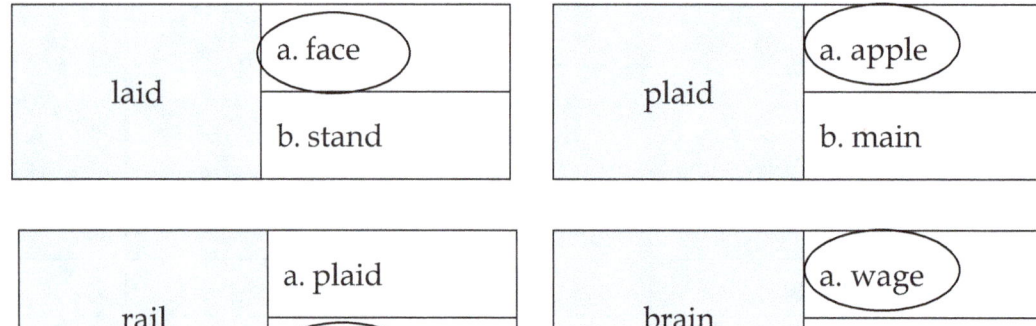

  Directions: Read each target word. Put a check (✓) under the correct column heading.

Direksyons: Li chak mo objektif. Mete yon tchèk (✓) anba antèt kolòn ki kòrèk la.

Target Words	Words have the long "a" sound as in the word <u>sail</u>	Words do not have the long "a" sound
1. plaid		✓
2. gain	✓	
3. said		✓
4. train	✓	

Learn To Read English With Directions In Spanish

Homework

 Name: _____ Date:___/___/_____ Score: _____

Lesson 1.6

Reading Letter "a" Words with the Schwa Vowel Sound

✓ **Lesson Check Point**

 Directions: Read each target word. Circle the word in the column that has the same "a" sound as the target word.
Direksyons: Li chak mo objektif. Antoure mo a ki nan kolòn nan ki bay menm son "a" a tankou mo ojektif la.

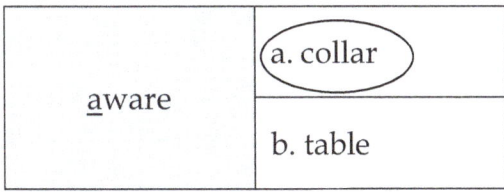
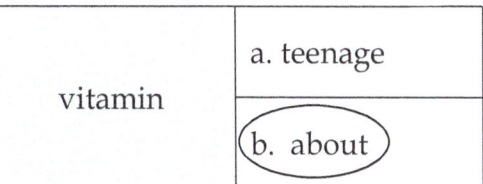
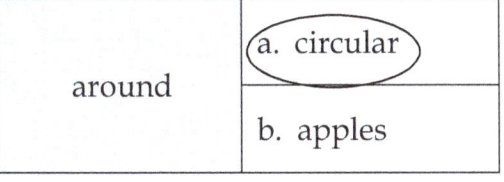
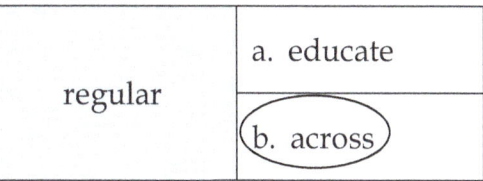

 Directions: Read each sentence and underline the letter "a" word that has the schwa vowel /ə/ sound. The anchor word for the letter "a" schwa vowel sound is <u>sofa</u>.
Direksyons: Li chak fraz epi soulinye mo ki genyen lèt "a" a ki bay son schwa /ə/. Mo referans pou son schwa lèt "a" a se mo, <u>sofa</u>.

1. The large snakes are from <u>Kenya</u>.

2. Alex always adds <u>sugar</u> to his tea.

3. The artist will draw the map of <u>Africa</u>.

4. This Sunday, I will walk in the <u>parade</u>.

5. At the <u>plaza</u>, the cars are tan and black.

6. Mrs. Ansel's math class is very <u>popular</u>.

Homework

 Name: _____ Date: ___/___/_____ Score: _____

Lesson 1.7

Reading Words with the "ar" Letter Combination

✓ Lesson Check Point

 Directions: Read each target word. Circle the word in the column that has the same "a" + "r" sounds as the target word.

Direksyons: Li chak mo objektif. Antoure mo a ki nan kolòn nan ki bay menm son "a" + "r" yo tankou mo ojektif la.

yarn	a. regular
	b. (chart)

sugar	a. warn
	b. (dollar)

carrot	a. (arrow)
	b. cedar

scholar	a. (grammar)
	b. artist

 Directions: Read each target word. Put a check (✓) under the correct column heading.

Direksyons: Li chak mo objektif. Mete yon tchèk (✓) anba antèt kolòn ki kòrèk la.

Target Words	"ar" has the /ă/ + /r/ sounds as in the word baron	"ar" has the /ə/ + /r/ sounds as in the word dollar	"ar" has the /ä/ + /r/ sounds as in the word car	"ar" has the /ô/ + /r/ sounds as in the word war
1. yarn			✓	
2. sugar		✓		
3. carrot	✓			
4. scholar		✓		

Homework

Name: _____ Date: ___/___/_____ Score: _____

Lesson 1.7

Reading Words with the "ar" Letter Combination

Dictionary Skills/ Vocabulary

✓ **Lesson Check Point**

Directions: Read each target word and its definition. Write the target word on the line in front of its meaning. Use a dictionary or the Internet to check your answers.

Direksyons: Li chak mo objektif ak definisyon yo chak. Ekri mo objektif la sou trè ki devan definisyon li an. Itilize yon diksyonè oubyen entènèt pou tcheke repons ou yo.

Target Word Box				
Argentina	park	married	part	carriage

1. <u>Argentina</u>   a large South American country
2. <u>carriage</u>   a vehicle that is pulled by a horse
3. <u>married</u>   to have been joined in marriage
4. <u>part</u>   an assigned role in a performance
5. <u>park</u>   a place with trees, playgrounds and benches

Directions: Read each sentence and write the target word that correctly completes the sentence.

Direksyons: Li chak fraz epi ekri mo objektif ki konplete fraz la kòrèkteman.

6. Arnold is having a family barbecue at the __park__.

7. Arsenio and I are getting __married__ on March 31st.

8. The couple will have a __carriage__ ride around the park.

9. My classmate, Arty, has a major __part__ in the musical drama.

10. Do you know that Spanish is the official language of __Argentina__?

Homework

Name: _____ Date: ___/___/_____ Score: _____

Lesson 1.8

Reading Words with a Silent Letter "a"

Directions: Read the target words in the word box. Write the words that have a silent letter "a" in the first column. Write the words that do not have a silent letter "a" in the second column.

Direksyons: Li mo objektif yo ki nan ti bwat mo a. Ekri mo yo ki genyen lèt "a" ki pa pwononse a nan premye kolòn nan. Ekri mo yo ki pa genyen lèt "a" ki pa pwononse a nan dezyèm kolòn nan.

Target Word Box				
heating	landing	chart	breadbox	many
assist	beautify	East	floating	oatmeal
camp	hand	coat	ready	teams
boar	flake	cars	half	sand

Letter "a" is silent

boar
coat
East
teams
ready
floating
oatmeal
beautify
heating
breadbox

Letter "a" has a letter "a" sound

cars
chart
half
many
camp
hand
flake
sand
assist
landing

Learn To Read English With Directions In Spanish

Homework

 Name: _____ Date:___/___/_____ Score: _____

Unit Review - A/a

Reading Words with Vowel "a" Sounds: /ă/, /ā/, /ə/ & Silent

✓ **Lesson Check Point**

 Directions: Read each target word. Circle the word in the column that has the same "a" sound as the target word.

Direksyons: Li chak mo objektif. Antoure mo a ki nan kolòn nan ki bay menm son "a" a tankou mo ojektif la.

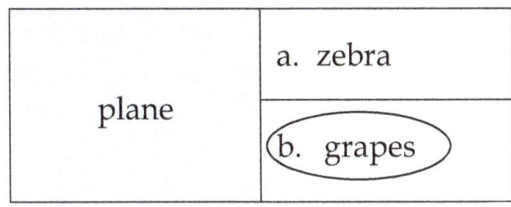
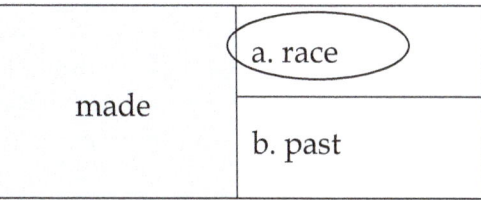
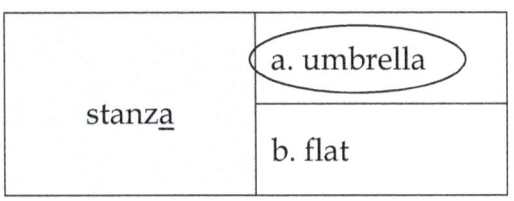
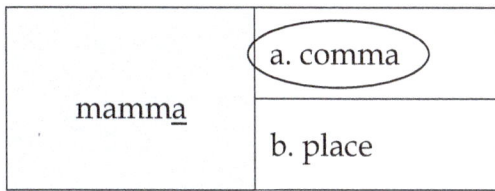

 Directions: Read each target word. Put a check (✓) under the correct column heading.

Direksyons: Li chak mo objektif. Mete yon tchèk (✓) anba antèt kolòn ki kòrèk la.

Target Words	"a" has the /ă/ sound as in the word <u>apple</u>	"a" has the /ā/ sound as in the word <u>ate</u>	"a" has the /ə/ sound as in the word <u>sofa</u>	"a" is silent as in the word <u>boat</u>
1. plane		✓		
2. made		✓		
3. stanz<u>a</u>			✓	
4. mamm<u>a</u>			✓	

Homework

 Name: _____ Date: ___/___/_____ Score: _____

The Reading Challenge

Lesson 1.9

Reading Multisyllable Words

✓ Lesson Check Point

 **Directions:** Read and divide each target word into syllables. Write each word and place a hyphen (-) between the syllables in the second column. Write the number of syllables in the third column. Use a dictionary or the Internet to check your answers.

Direksyons: Li epi divize chak mo objektif an silab. Ekri chak mo epi mete yon tirè (-) ant silab yo nan dezyèm kolòn nan. Ekri kantite silab ke yo genyen an nan twazyèm kolòn nan. Itilize yon diksyonè oubyen entènèt pou tcheke repons ou yo.

Target Words	Words Divided into Syllables	Number of Syllables
1. giant	gi-ant	2
2. constantly	con-stant-ly	3
3. observant	ob-ser-vant	3
4. pregnancy	preg-nan-cy	3
5. mousetrap	mouse-trap	2
6. eyelashes	eye-lash-es	3
7. implanted	im-plant-ed	3
8. democrat	dem-o-crat	3
9. eggplant	egg-plant	2
10. servant	ser-vant	2

Homework

 Name: _____ Date: ___/___/_____ Score: _____

The Reading Challenge

Lesson 1.9

Reading Multisyllable Words

✓ **Lesson Check Point**

 Directions: Read each target word. Circle the word in the row that is divided correctly into syllables. Use a dictionary or the Internet to check your answers.

Direksyons: Li chak mo objektif. Antoure mo a ki nan ranje a ki divize an silab korèkteman yo. Itilize yon diksyonè oubyen entènèt pou tcheke repons ou yo.

Model

| important | a. im-por-tant (circled) | b. im-port-ant | c. im-porta-nt |

1. abundant	a. a-bun-dant (circled)	b. ab-un-dant	c. ab-und-ant
2. contestant	a. con-tes-tant (circled)	b. cont-es-tant	c. con-test-ant
3. advocate	a. ad-vo-cate (circled)	b. a-dvoc-ate	c. ad-voc-ate
4. dependent	a. dep-en-dent	b. de-pen-dent (circled)	c. de-pend-ent
5. elegant	a. e-leg-ant	b. el-e-gant (circled)	c. e-le-gant
6. answering	a. ans-wer-ing	b. a-nswe-ring	c. an-swer-ing (circled)
7. flamboyant	a. flam-boy-ant (circled)	b. flam-bo-yant	c. flam-boya-nt
8. ascendant	a. a-scen-dant	b. asc-en-dant	c. as-cen-dant (circled)

Learn To Read English With Directions In Haitian Creole

Homework

Name: _____ Date: ___/___/_____ Score: _____

Lesson 1.10

Reading and Writing

Proper and Common Nouns and Adjectives

Directions: Read the words in the word box. Put an (X) on the line next to each word that is written incorrectly. Remember that all proper nouns and proper adjectives are capitalized. Use a dictionary or the Internet to check your answers.

Direksyons: Li chak mo yo ki nan bwat mo a. Met yon (X) sou ti trè a ki bò kote mo ki pa kri byen yo. Sonje ke tout non pwòp ak adjektif pwop ekri avèk yon lèt majiskil nan kòmansman yo. Itilize yon diksyonè oubyen entènèt pou tcheke repons ou yo.

Word Box					
X	africa	X	april	X	Alarming
X	apple Inc.		airport	X	alabama
	angel		attraction		American
	Afghanistan	_	Australian	X	Above

Directions: Read each unedited sentence and underline the word that is written incorrectly. Write each sentence correctly on the line.

Direksyons: Li chak fraz ki pa edite yo epi soulinye mo ki pa ekri byen an. Ekri chak fraz korèkteman sou liy lan.

Model
Andrew has a view of the <u>atlantic</u> Ocean from his apartment.
<u>Andrew has a view of the Atlantic Ocean from his apartment.</u>

1. Anna always <u>Asks</u> challenging questions about Asia.
<u>Anna always asks challenging questions about Asia.</u>

2. The <u>Author</u> wrote a book about ants and alligators.
<u>The author wrote a book about ants and alligators.</u>

3. Our amazing, <u>All-star</u> athletes are competing in Athens.
<u>Our amazing, all-star athletes are competing in Athens.</u>

4. My <u>Aunt</u> said, "Many animals live in the Amazon Rainforest."
<u>My aunt said, "Many animals live in the Amazon Rainforest."</u>

Homework

 Name: _____ Date:___/___/_____ Score: _____

Lesson 2.1

Reading Words with the Letter B/b

✓ Lesson Check Point

 Directions: Read each target word. Find the letter "b" and put a check (✓) in the column that identifies its position: beginning, within or end.
Direksyons: Li chak mo objektif. Jwenn lèt "b" a epi mete yon tchèck (✓) nan kolòn ki idantifye pozisyon li an: nan kòmansman, ladan oubyen nan finisman.

Target Words	Beginning (First Letter)	Within	End (Last Letter)
1. tab			✓
2. limb			✓
3. bring	✓		
4. about		✓	
5. husband		✓	

 Directions: Read each sentence and underline the words that begin with the letter "b." Write all the underlined words in alphabetical order on the lines below.
Direksyons: Li chak fraz epi soulinye mo ki kòmanse avèk lèt "b" yo. Ekri tout mo ki soulinye yo nan lòd alfabetik sou trè sa yo ki anba.

6. Adam has a <u>big</u> <u>bat</u>.

7. Ann has a <u>black</u> <u>bag</u>.

8. Andy's <u>boats</u> are <u>blue</u>.

9. The <u>buds</u> have <u>bloomed</u>.

10. The fat <u>bees</u> are <u>by</u> the flowers.

bag_____   bat_____   bees_____
big_____   black_____ bloomed_____
blue_____   boats_____ buds_____
               by_____

Homework

 Name: _____ Date:___/___/_____ Score:_____

Lesson 2.2

Reading Words with the "br" Letter Combination

Dictionary Skills/ Vocabulary

✓ Lesson Check Point

 Directions: Read each target word and its definition. Write the letter of the definition on the line of each target word. Use a dictionary or the Internet to check your answers.
Direksyons: Li chak mo objektif ak definisyon yo chak. Ekri lèt la ki koresponn ak definisyon an sou trè chak mo objektif yo. Itilize yon diksyonè oubyen entènèt pou tcheke repons ou yo.

Target Words	Definitions
1. _e_ brakes	a. shiny, glowing reflection of light
2. _a_ bright	b. baked food product that is made from wheat
3. _d_ brook	c. separated into pieces as a result of a strong force
4. _c_ broke	d. a place where water flows along a small path
5. _b_ bread	e. device that slows down and stops a vehicle

 Directions: Read each sentence. Underline the word in the parentheses that correctly completes each sentence. Then, write the underlined word on the line.
Direksyons: Li chak fraz. Soulinye mo a ki nan parantèz yo ki konplete chak fraz kòrèkteman. Answit, ekri mo soulinye a sou trè a.

6. Bret ___broke___ the baseball bat. (bright, broke)

7. My bike's ___brakes___ are bad. (brakes, bright)

8. The sun at the bay is ___bright___. (bread, bright)

9. Brian is sitting by the ___brook___. (brook, brakes)

10. Brad always eats ___bread___ for breakfast. (brook, bread)

Homework

 Name: _____ Date:___/___/_____ Score: _____

Lesson 2.3

Reading Words with the "bl" Letter Combination

Dictionary Skills/ Vocabulary

✓ **Lesson Check Point**

 Directions: Read each target word and its definition. Write the target word on the line in front of its meaning. Use a dictionary or the Internet to check your answers.
Direksyons: Li chak mo objektif ak definisyon yo chak. Ekri mo objektif la sou trè ki devan definisyon li an. Itilize yon diksyonè oubyen entènèt pou tcheke repons ou yo.

Target Word Box				
blames	blouse	blind	blueberry	blanket

1. <u>blames</u>   to assign fault
2. <u>blueberry</u>   a sweet fruit
3. <u>blouse</u>   a long loosely fitting shirt
4. <u>blind</u>   a person or animal's inability to see things
5. <u>blanket</u>   a large cloth covering used to cover a bed

 Directions: Read each sentence. Underline the word in the parentheses that correctly completes each sentence. Then, write the underlined word on the line.
Direksyons: Li chak fraz. Soulinye mo a ki nan parantèz yo ki konplete chak fraz kòrèkteman. Answit, ekri mo soulinye a sou trè a.

6. The <u>blind</u> boys have Braille books. (blueberry, <u>blind</u>)

7. Bill's <u>blanket</u> has pictures of bats on it. (blind, <u>blanket</u>)

8. Beth washed her <u>blouse</u> with bleach. (blames, <u>blouse</u>)

9. Bob <u>blames</u> me for eating the bananas. (<u>blames</u>, blanket)

10. The boys ate <u>blueberry</u> bread at brunch. (blouse, <u>blueberry</u>)

Homework

 Name: _____ Date: ___/___/_____ Score: _____

Lesson 2.3

Reading Words with the "ble" Letter Combination

✓ **Lesson Check Point**

Directions: Read each target word. Find the "ble" letter combination and put a check (✓) in the column that identifies its position: beginning, within or end.

Direksyons: Li chak mo objektif. Jwenn konbinezon lèt "ble" a epi mete yon tchèk (✓) nan kolòn nan ki idantifye pozisyon li an: nan kòmansman, ladan oubyen nan finisman.

Target Words	Beginning (First 3 Letters)	Within	End (Last 3 Letters)
1. blew	✓		
2. doublet		✓	
3. capable			✓
4. terrible			✓
5. assembled		✓	

Directions: Read each target word. Put a check (✓) in the "yes" column if the "ble" letter combination has the /b/ + /ə/ + /l/ sounds. Put a check (✓) in the "no" column if the "ble" letter combination does not have the /b/ + /ə/ + /l/ sounds.

Direksyons: Li chak mo objektif. Mete yon tchèk (✓) nan kolòn "yes" an si konbinezon let "ble" a bay sons /b/ + /ə/ + /l/. Mete yon tchèk (✓) nan kolòn "no" an si konbinezon let "ble" a pa bay sons /b/ + /ə/ + /l/.

Target Words	Yes	No
6. cable	✓	
7. tablet		✓
8. emblem		✓
9. enjoyable	✓	
10. convertible	✓	

Learn To Read English With Directions In Spanish

 Homework

Name: _____ Date:___/___/_____ Score:_____

Lesson 2.4

Reading Words with the "mb" Letter Combination

✓ **Lesson Check Point**

 Directions: Read each target word. Circle the word in the column that has the same "mb" sound(s) as the target word.

Direksyons: Li chak mo objektif. Antoure mo a ki nan kolòn nan ki bay menm son "mb" la (yo) tankou mo ojektif la.

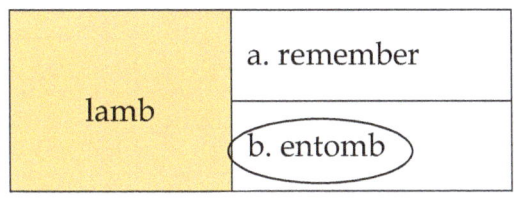
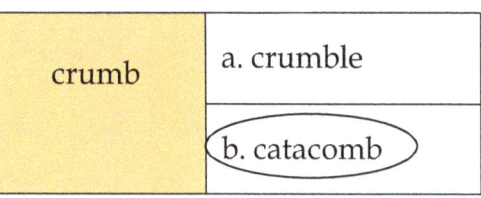
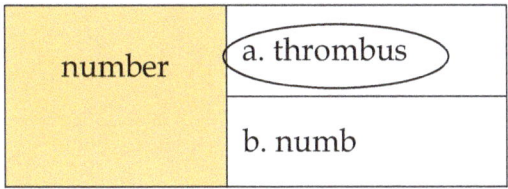
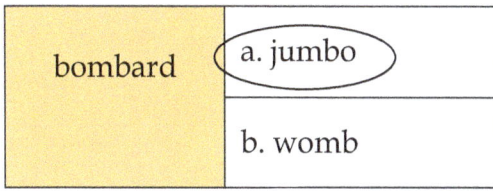

 Directions: Read each target word. In the second column, write the number of letters in the word. In the third column, write the number of letters heard in the word.

Direksyons: Li chak mo objektif. Nan dezyèm kolòn nan, ekri kantite lèt ki nan mo a. Nan twazyèm kolòn nan, ekri kantite lèt ou tande nan mo a.

Target Words	Number of letters in the word	Number of letters heard
1. lamb	4	3
2. crumb	5	4
3. number	6	6
4. bombard	7	7

Learn To Read English With Directions In Haitian Creole

Homework

 Name: _____ Date:___/___/_____ Score: _____

Lesson 2.4

Reading Words with the "bt" Letter Combination

✓ Lesson Check Point

 Directions: Read each target word. Circle the word in the column that has the same "bt" sound(s) as the target word.

Direksyons: Li chak mo objektif. Antoure mo a ki nan kolòn nan ki bay menm son "bt" la (yo) tankou mo ojektif la.

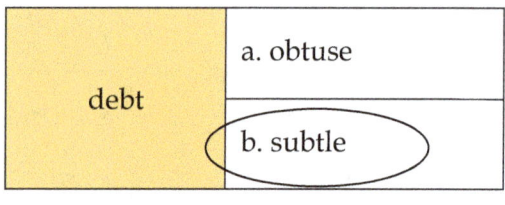
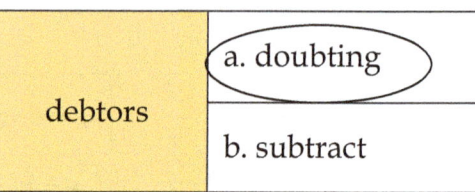
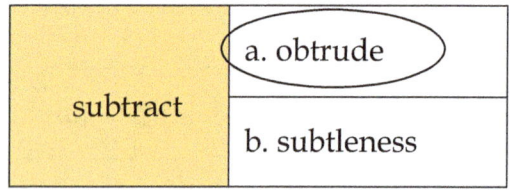
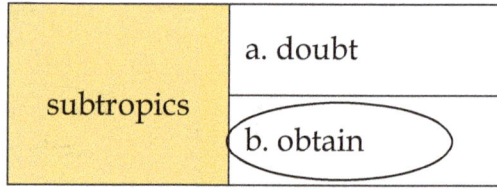

 Directions: Read each target word. In the second column, write the number of letters in the word. In the third column, write the number of letters heard in the word.

Direksyons: Li chak mo objektif. Nan dezyèm kolòn nan, ekri kantite lèt ki nan mo a. Nan twazyèm kolòn na, ekri kantite lèt ou tande nan mo a.

Target Words	Number of letters in the word	Number of letters heard
1. debt	4	3
2. debtors	7	6
3. subtract	8	8
4. subtropics	10	10

Homework

 Name: _____ Date: ___/___/_____ Score: _____

Lesson 2.5

Reading Words with a Silent "b"

✓ Lesson Check Point

Directions: Read the target words in the word box. Write the words that have a silent letter "b" in the first column. Write the words that do not have a silent letter "b" in the second column.

Direksyons: Li mo objektif yo ki nan ti bwat mo a. Ekri mo yo ki genyen lèt "b" ki pa pwononse a nan premye kolòn nan. Ekri mo yo ki pa genyen lèt "b" ki pa pwononse a nan dezyèm kolòn nan.

Target Word Box				
crumbs	indebted	behave	laboratory	combing
doubt	rebate	plumbing	burger	quibble
basket	beagle	lamb	subtlety	bonding
public	climbers	balance	thumb	beaver

Letter "b" is silent	Letter "b" has the /b/ sound
lamb	behave
indebted	beaver
thumb	rebate
doubt	burger
crumbs	basket
quibble	beagle
combing	public
subtlety	balance
climbers	bonding
plumbing	laboratory

Learn To Read English With Directions In Haitian Creole

Homework

 Name: _____ Date:___/___/_____ Score:_____

The Reading Challenge

Lesson 2.6

Reading Multisyllable Words

✓ Lesson Check Point

 Directions: Read and divide each target word into syllables. Write each word and place a hyphen (-) between the syllables in the second column. Write the number of syllables in the third column. Use a dictionary or the Internet to check your answers.

Direksyons: Li epi divize chak mo objektif an silab. Ekri chak mo epi mete yon tirè (-) ant silab yo nan dezyèm kolòn nan. Ekri kantite silab ke yo genyen an nan twazyèm kolòn nan. Itilize yon diksyonè oubyen entènèt pou tcheke repons ou yo.

Target Words	Words Divided into Syllables	Number of Syllables
1. absent	ab-sent	2
2. submit	sub-mit	2
3. table	ta-ble	2
4. tablet	tab-let	2
5. absolutely	ab-so-lute-ly	4
6. somebody	some-bod-y	3
7. habitat	hab-i-tat	3
8. fabulous	fab-u-lous	3
9. observing	ob-serv-ing	3
10. subtracting	sub-tract-ing	3

Homework

 Name: _____ Date: ___/___/_____ Score: _____

The Reading Challenge

Lesson 2.6

Reading Multisyllable Words

✓ **Lesson Check Point**

 Directions: Read each target word. Circle the word in the row that is divided correctly into syllables. Use a dictionary or the Internet to check your answers.

Direksyons: Li chak mo objektif. Antoure mo a ki nan ranje a ki divize an silab korèkteman yo. Itilize yon diksyonè oubyen entènèt pou tcheke repons ou yo.

Model

| because | (a. be-cause) | b. beca-use | c. b-ecause |

1. barbecue	a. bar-b-ecue	b. bar-becue	(c. bar-be-cue)
2. brainstorm	(a. brain-storm)	b. brai-nst-orm	c. br-ain-storm
3. belated	a. belat-ed	(b. be-lat-ed)	c. b-ela-ted
4. barber	a. barb-er	(b. bar-ber)	c. ba-rber
5. biweekly	a. bi-wee-kly	b. biw-eek-ly	(c. bi-week-ly)
6. bathroom	(a. bath-room)	b. ba-throom	c. bathr-oom
7. beagle	a. beag-le	(b. bea-gle)	c. be-agle
8. background	(a. back-ground)	b. backgr-ound	c. ba-ckground

Unit B
Lesson 2.6

Learn To Read English With Directions In Haitian Creole   25   Copyrighted Material

Homework

Name: _____ Date: ___/___/_____ Score: _____

Lesson 2.7

Reading and Writing

Proper and Common Nouns and Adjectives

Directions: Read the words in the word box. Put an (X) on the line next to each word that is written incorrectly. Remember that all proper nouns and proper adjectives are capitalized. Use a dictionary or the Internet to check your answers.

Direksyons: Li chak mo yo ki nan bwat mo a. Met yon (X) sou ti trè a ki bò kote mo ki pa kri byen yo. Sonje ke tout non pwòp ak adjektif pwop ekri avèk yon lèt majiskil nan kòmansman yo. Itilize yon diksyonè oubyen entènèt pou tcheke repons ou yo.

Word Box					
__	Bronx	_X_	brazilian	__	British
_X_	bathtaB	__	biology	_X_	bulgaria
_X_	bangladesh	_X_	Bonanza	_X_	botswana
__	bittersweet	__	Brother Bob	__	Bonaparte

Directions: Read each unedited sentence and underline the word that is written incorrectly. Write each sentence correctly on the line.

Direksyons: Li chak fraz ki pa edite yo epi soulinye mo ki pa ekri byen an. Ekri chak fraz korèkteman sou liy lan.

Model
<u>brandon's</u> books are about big boats.
<u>Brandon's books are about big boats.</u>

1. Bess and Beth are at the <u>Beach</u>.
<u>Bess and Beth are at the beach.</u>

2. The <u>Boy's</u> bike is blue and brown.
<u>The boy's bike is blue and brown.</u>

3. <u>bugs</u> and birds are flying by the bay.
<u>Bugs and birds are flying by the bay.</u>

4. <u>baby</u> Ben has a big bear and a black boat.
<u>Baby Ben has a big bear and a black boat.</u>

Homework

 Name: _____ Date: ___/___/_____ Score: _____

Lesson 3.1

Reading Words with the Letter C/c

✓ **Lesson Check Point**

 Directions: Read each target word. Find the letter "c" and put a check (✓) in the column that identifies its position: beginning, within or end.
Direksyons: Li chak mo objektif. Jwenn lèt "c" a epi mete yon tchèck (✓) nan kolòn ki idantifye pozisyon li an: nan kòmansman, ladan oubyen nan finisman.

Target Words	Beginning (First Letter)	Within	End (Last Letter)
1. zinc			✓
2. carrot	✓		
3. fabric			✓
4. impacted		✓	
5. protractor		✓	

 Directions: Read each sentence and underline the words that begin with the letter "c." Write all the underlined words in alphabetical order on the lines below.
Direksyons: Li chak fraz epi soulinye mo ki kòmanse avèk lèt "c" yo. Ekri tout mo ki soulinye yo nan lòd alfabetik sou trè sa yo ki anba.

6. The <u>clock</u> is on a big <u>chain</u>.

7. Andrew is <u>counting</u> the <u>cats</u>.

8. Bobby will <u>climb</u> up the <u>cliff</u>.

9. All the <u>coins</u> add up to ten <u>cents</u>.

10. Al said, "The <u>chair</u> is by my baby's <u>crib</u>."

<u>cats_____</u>   <u>cents_____</u>   <u>chain_____</u>

<u>chair_____</u>   <u>cliff_____</u>   <u>climb_____</u>

<u>clock_____</u>   <u>coins_____</u>   <u>counting_____</u>

                       <u>crib_____</u>

Homework

Name: _____ Date: ___/___/_____ Score: _____

Lesson 3.1

Reading Words with the Hard Letter "c"

✓ **Lesson Check Point**

Directions: Read each target word. Put a check (✓) under the correct column heading.

Direksyons: Li chak mo objektif. Mete yon tchèk (✓) anba antèt kolòn ki kòrèk la.

Target Words	Hard "c" has the /k/ sound as in the word <u>cat</u>	Soft "c" has the /s/ sound as in the word <u>cell</u>
1. cavity	✓	
2. central		✓
3. century		✓
4. camping	✓	
5. covering	✓	

Directions: Read each sentence and underline the words that have the hard "c" sound, as in the word <u>cat</u>. Write all the underlined words in alphabetical order on the lines below.

Direksyons: Li chak fraz epi souliye mo ki gen son "c" difisil, tankou nan mo <u>cat</u> la. Ekri tout mo ki soulinye yo nan lòd alfabetik sou trè sa yo ki anba.

6. Cindy likes to eat <u>cake</u> and <u>candy</u>.

7. Cyril is the <u>coolest</u> kid in his <u>class</u>.

8. The <u>climbers</u> did not see the icy <u>cliff</u>.

9. The experienced <u>chemists</u> <u>can</u> study animal cells.

10. My <u>college</u> <u>campus</u> has four large buildings in the city.

<u>cake</u>_____   <u>campus</u>_____   <u>can</u>_____

<u>candy</u>_____   <u>chemists</u>_____   <u>class</u>_____

<u>cliff</u>_____   <u>climbers</u>_____   <u>college</u>_____

                              <u>coolest</u>_____

Homework

Name: _____ Date: ___/___/_____ Score: _____

Lesson 3.2

Reading Words with the Soft Letter "c"

Directions: Read each target word. Put a check (✓) under the correct column heading.

Direksyons: Li chak mo objektif. Mete yon tchèk (✓) anba antèt kolòn ki kòrèk la.

Target Words	Hard "c" has the /k/ sound as in the word <u>cat</u>	Soft "c" has the /s/ sound as in the word <u>cell</u>
1. cub	✓	
2. cab	✓	
3. city		✓
4. grace		✓
5. recite		✓

Directions: Read each sentence and underline the words that have the soft "c" sound, as in the word <u>cell</u>. Write all the underlined words in alphabetical order on the lines below.

Direksyons: Li chak fraz epi soulinye mo ki bay son dous "c" yo, tankou li ye nan mo <u>cell</u> la. Ekri tout mo ki soulinye yo nan lòd alfabetik sou trè sa yo ki anba.

6. A <u>cyclone</u> is a strong wind that moves in a <u>circle</u>.

7. We will <u>celebrate</u> <u>Cindy's</u> birthday in the country.

8. While in the <u>city</u>, I ate cranberry and <u>cinnamon</u> candy.

9. The <u>ceramic</u> dishes and <u>cereal</u> bowls are in the cabinets.

10. We can repair the <u>ceilings</u> in the <u>Central</u> Street apartments.

<u>ceilings</u>_____   <u>celebrate</u>_____   <u>Central</u>_____

<u>ceramic</u>_____   <u>cereal</u>_____   <u>Cindy's</u>_____

<u>cinnamon</u>_____   <u>city</u>_____   <u>circle</u>_____

<u>cyclone</u>_____

Learn To Read English With Directions In Haitian Creole

Homework

Name: _____ Date: ___/___/_____ Score: _____

Review Lessons 3.1 & 3.2

Reading Hard Letter "c" and Soft Letter "c" Words

Directions: Read the target words in the word box. In the first column, write the words with the letter "c" that have the /k/ sound, as in the word <u>cat</u>. In the second column, write the words with the letter "c" that have the /s/ sound, as in the word <u>cell</u>.

Direksyons: Li mo objektif yo ki nan bwat mo a. Nan premye kolòn nan, ekri mo yo ki genyen lèt "c" ki bay son /k/ yo, tankou li ye nan mo <u>cat</u>. Nan dezyèm kolòn nan, ekri mo yo ki genyen lèt "c" ki bay son /s/ yo, tankou li ye nan mo <u>cell</u>.

Target Word Box				
cyst	car	cold	fence	icy
cider	places	candy	lacy	color
can	curl	come	cute	Tracy
face	cents	curb	cinch	camel

Hard letter "c" has the /k/ sound as in the word <u>cat</u>

- car
- can
- curl
- curb
- cold
- cute
- come
- color
- camel
- candy

Soft letter "c" has the /s/ sound as in the word <u>cell</u>

- icy
- cyst
- face
- lacy
- cents
- cider
- Tracy
- fence
- cinch
- places

Learn To Read English With Directions In Spanish

Homework

 Name: _____ Date:___/___/_____ Score:_____

Lesson 3.3

Reading Words with the "cr" Letter Combination

Dictionary Skills/ Vocabulary

✓ Lesson Check Point

Directions: Read each target word and its definition. Write the letter of the definition on the line of each target word. Use a dictionary or the Internet to check your answers.

Direksyons: Li chak mo objektif ak definisyon yo chak. Ekri lèt la ki koresponn ak definisyon an sou trè chak mo objektif yo. Itilize yon diksyonè oubyen entènèt pou tcheke repons ou yo.

Target Words	Definitions
1. <u>b</u> crabs	a. to have collided violently with another vehicle
2. <u>a</u> crashed	b. shelled animals that live by and in water
3. <u>e</u> creek	c. brittle texture of something that is easily broken
4. <u>c</u> crispy	d. to have walked from one side to the other side
5. <u>d</u> crossed	e. a stream of water that is smaller than a river

Directions: Read each sentence. Underline the word in the parentheses that correctly completes each sentence. Then, write the underlined word on the line.

Direksyons: Li chak fraz. Soulinye mo a ki nan parantèz yo ki konplete chak fraz kòrèkteman. Answit, ekri mo soulinye a sou trè a.

6. The children _____crossed_____ the street. (<u>crossed</u>, creek)

7. My mommy's cookies are _____crispy_____. (<u>crispy</u>, crashed)

8. Cindy and Chad had a picnic by the ___creek___. (crispy, <u>creek</u>)

9. The big ___crabs___ live in a cold water creek. (crossed, <u>crabs</u>)

10. In the city, the cars __crashed__ into one another. (<u>crashed</u>, crabs)

Homework

☑ Name: _____ Date:___/___/_____ Score:_____

Lesson 3.4

Reading Words with the "cl" Letter Combination

Dictionary Skills/ Vocabulary

✓ Lesson Check Point

Directions: Read each target word and its definition. Write the target word on the line in front of its meaning. Use a dictionary or the Internet to check your answers.

Direksyons: Li chak mo objektif ak definisyon yo chak. Ekri mo objektif la sou trè ki devan definisyon li an. Itilize yon diksyonè oubyen entènèt pou tcheke repons ou yo.

Target Word Box				
clapped	cleans	clock	close	clothes

1. close_____   a near position
2. clock_____   a device used to indicate and display time
3. clapped____   to have hit the palms of one's hands together
4. cleans_____   the process of removing dirt off of something
5. clothes_____   garments used to cover and adorn a person's body

Directions: Read each sentence. Underline the word in the parentheses that correctly completes each sentence. Then, write the underlined word on the line.

Direksyons: Li chak fraz. Soulinye mo a ki nan parantèz yo ki konplete chak fraz kòrèkteman. Answit, ekri mo soulinye a sou trè a.

6. Cecil _____cleans_____ the cabinets with bleach. (clock, cleans)

7. Cindy hangs her _____clothes_____ in the closet. (clothes, close)

8. The audience _____clapped_____ for the choir. (clapped, clothes)

9. Chad lives _____close_____ to the country's capital. (cleans, close)

10. The _____clock_____ in the cabin tells the correct time. (clock, clapped)

Homework

 Name: _____ Date: ___/___/_____ Score: _____

Lesson 3.4

Reading Words with the "cle" Letter Combination

✓ **Lesson Check Point**

 Directions: Read each target word. Find the "cle" letter combination and put a check (✓) in the column that identifies its position: beginning, within or end.

Direksyons: Li chak mo objektif. Jwenn konbinezon lèt "cle" a epi mete yon tchèk (✓) nan kolòn nan ki idantifye pozisyon li an: nan kòmansman, ladan oubyen nan finisman.

Target Words	Beginning (First 3 Letters)	Within	End (Last 3 Letters)
1. clerk	✓		
2. cleave	✓		
3. vehicle			✓
4. bicycle			✓
5. inclemently		✓	

 Directions: Read each target word. Put a check (✓) in the "yes" column if the "cle" letter combination has the /k/ + /ə/ + /l/ sounds. Put a check (✓) in the "no" column if the "cle" letter combination does not have the /k/ + /ə/ + /l/ sounds.

Direksyons: Li chak mo objektif. Mete yon tchèk (✓) nan kolòn "yes" an si konbinezon let "cle" a bay sons /k/ + /ə/ + /l/. Mete yon tchèk (✓) nan kolòn "no" an si konbinezon let "cle" a pa bay sons /k/ + /ə/ + /l/.

Target Words	Yes	No
6. clerk		✓
7. cleave		✓
8. vehicle	✓	
9. bicycle	✓	
10. inclemently		✓

Homework

 Name: _____ Date: ___/___/_____ Score: _____

Lesson 3.5

Reading Words with the "ct" Letter Combination

✓ **Lesson Check Point**

 Directions: Read each target word. Circle the word in the column that has the same "ct" sound(s) as the target word.

Direksyons: Li chak mo objektif. Antoure mo a ki nan kolòn nan ki bay menm son "ct" la (yo) tankou mo objektif la.

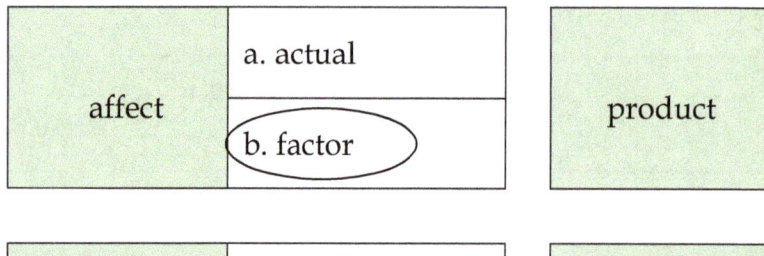

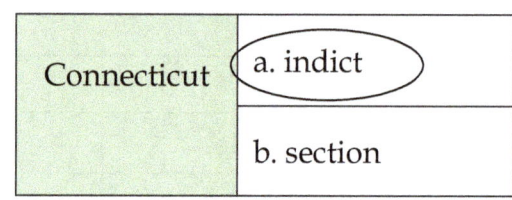

 Directions: Read each target word. Put a check (✓) under the correct column heading.

Direksyons: Li chak mo objektif. Mete yon tchèk (✓) anba antèt kolòn ki kòrèk la.

Target Words	"ct" has the /k/ + /t/ sounds as in the word <u>fact</u>	"ct" has the silent "c" + /t/ sound as in the word <u>indict</u>
1. affect	✓	
2. product	✓	
3. practicing	✓	
4. Connecticut		✓

Learn To Read English With Directions In Spanish

Homework

 Name: _____ Date:___/___/_____ Score:_____

Lesson 3.6

Reading Soft Letter "c" Words

✓ Lesson Check Point

 Directions: Read each target word. Circle the word in the column that has the same "cean," "cian," "cial," "cious" or "cient" sound as the target word.

Direksyons: Li chak mo objektif. Antoure mo a ki nan kolòn nan ki bay menm son "cean," "cian," "cial," "cious" oubyen "cient" yo tankou mo objektif la.

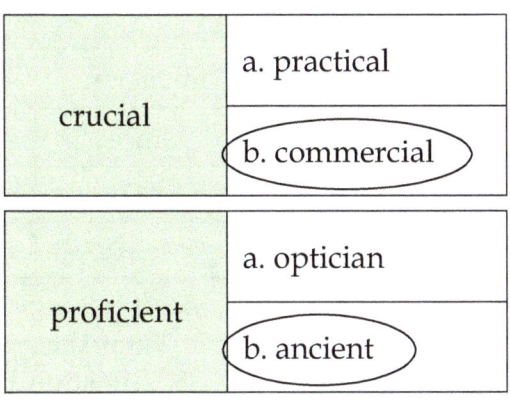

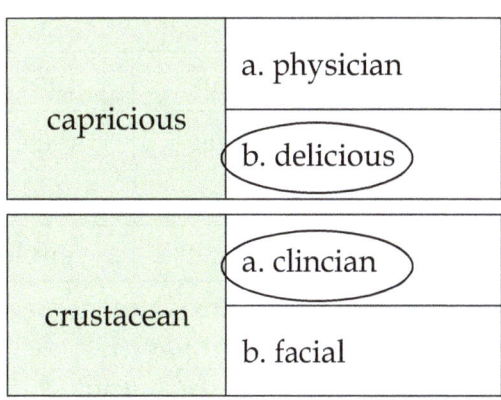

 Directions: Read each target word. Put a check (✓) in the column that identifies the same "cean," "cian," "cial," "cious" or "cient" sound within the target word.

Direksyons: Li chak mo objektif. Mete yon tchèk (✓) nan kolòn nan ki idantifye menm son "cean," "cian," "cial," "cious" oubyen "cient" yo nan mo objektif la.

Target Words	"cean" has the /sh/+/ə/+/n/ sounds as in the word <u>ocean</u>	"cial" has the /sh/+/ə/+/l/ sounds as in the word <u>special</u>	"cious" has the /sh/+/ə/+/s/ sounds as in the word <u>delicious</u>	"cient" has the /sh/+/ə/+/n/+/t/ sounds as in the word <u>ancient</u>
1. crucial		✓		
2. capricious			✓	
3. proficient				✓
4. crustacean	✓			

Homework

Name: _____ Date: ___/___/_____ Score: _____

Lesson 3.6

Reading Soft Letter "c" Words

Directions: Read the target words in the word box. In the first column, write the words with the letter "c" that have the /s/ sound, as in the word <u>cell</u>. In the second column, write the words with the letter "c" that have the /sh/ sound, as in the word <u>ocean</u>.

Direksyons: Li mo objektif yo ki nan bwat la. Nan premye kolòn nan, ekri mo yo ki avèk lèt "c" ki bay son /s/ yo, tankou li ye nan mo <u>cell</u>. Nan dezyèm kolòn nan, ekri mo ki avèk lèt "c" ki bay son /sh/ yo, tankou li ye nan mo <u>ocean</u>.

Target Word Box				
politician	fancy	deficie	musician	cider
ferocious	special	fence	nice	social
bicycle	excited	spicy	facial	cents
crustacean	circle	sufficie	city	magician

Soft letter "c" has the /s/ sound as in the word cell

- city
- nice
- fence
- cider
- circle
- fancy
- spicy
- cents
- bicycle
- excited

Soft letter "c" has the /sh/ sound as in the word ocean

- social
- facial
- special
- deficient
- musician
- magician
- sufficient
- ferocious
- politician
- crustacean

Learn To Read English With Directions In Spanish

Homework

 Name: _____ Date: ___/___/_____ Score: _____

Lesson 3.7

Reading Words with the "ch" Letter Combination

✓ **Lesson Check Point**

   Directions: Read each target word. Circle the word in the column that has the same "ch" sound as the target word.

Direksyons: Li chak mo objektif. Antoure mo a ki nan kolòn nan ki bay menm son "ch" a tankou mo objektif la.

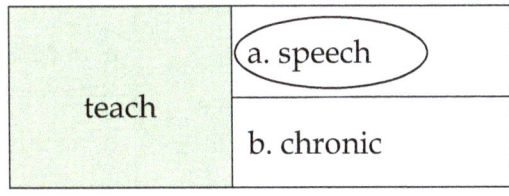
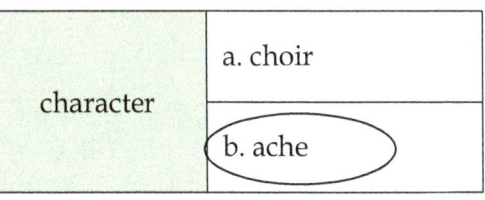
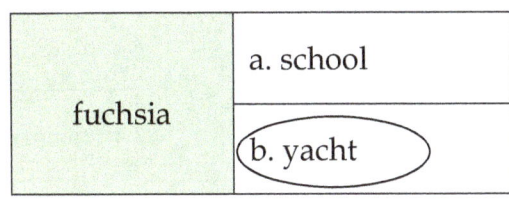
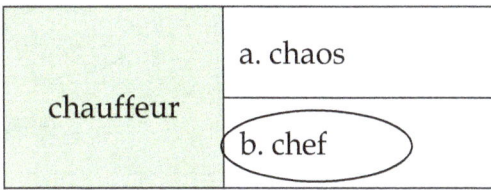

   Directions: Read each target word. Put a check (✓) under the correct column heading.

Direksyons: Li chak mo objektif. Mete yon tchèk (✓) anba antèt kolòn ki kòrèk la.

Target Words	"ch" has the /ch/ sound as in the word <u>chain</u>	"ch" has the /sh/ sound as in the word <u>chef</u>	"ch" has the /k/ sound as in the word <u>chaos</u>	"ch" is silent as in the word <u>yacht</u>
1. teach	✓			
2. character			✓	
3. fuchsia				✓
4. chauffeur		✓		

Homework

Name: _____ Date: ___/___/_____ Score: _____

Lesson 3.8

Reading Words with the "cc" Letter Combination

✓ Lesson Check Point

Directions: Read each target word. Circle the word in the column that has the same "cc" sound(s) as the target word.

Direksyons: Li chak mo objektif. Antoure mo a ki nan kolòn nan ki bay menm son "cc" la (yo) tankou mo objektif la.

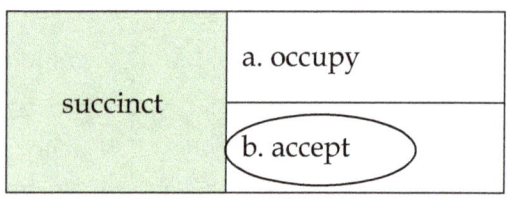

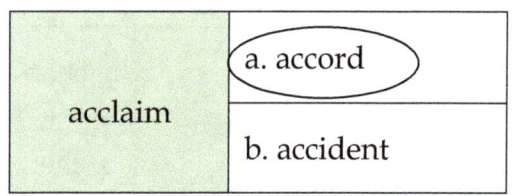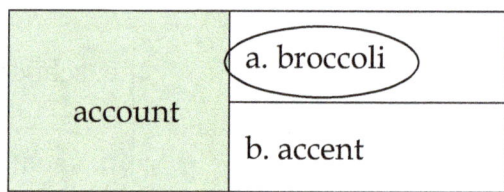

Directions: Read each target word. Put a check (✓) under the correct column heading.

Direksyons: Li chak mo objektif. Mete yon tchèk (✓) anba antèt kolòn ki kòrèk la.

Target Words	"cc" has the /k/ sound as in the word <u>soccer</u>	"cc" has the /k/ + /s/ sounds as in the word <u>accept</u>
1. succinct		✓
2. success		✓
3. acclaim	✓	
4. account	✓	

Homework

 Name: _____ Date: ___/___/_____ Score: _____

Lesson 3.9

Reading Words with a Silent Letter "c"

✓ Lesson Check Point

 Directions: Read the target words in the word box. Write the words that have a silent letter "c" in the first column. Write the words that do not have a silent letter "c" in the second column.

Direksyons: Li mo objektif yo ki nan ti bwat mo a. Ekri mo yo ki genyen lèt "c" ki pa pwononse a nan premye kolòn nan. Ekri mo yo ki pa genyen lèt "c" ki pa pwononse a nan dezyèm kolòn nan.

Target Word Box				
corner	scuba	scent	cycle	score
essence	domestic	clocks	collar	acquit
abscess	descend	fascinate	ascent	scene
adolescent	escalator	disciple	recruit	fuchsia

Letter "c" is silent

- scene
- scent
- acquit
- ascent
- abscess
- fuchsia
- descend
- disciple
- fascinate
- adolescent

Letter "c" has a /k/, /s/ or /sh/ sound

- score
- cycle
- collar
- clocks
- scuba
- corner
- recruit
- essence
- domestic
- escalator

Homework

 Name: _____ Date:___/___/_____ Score:_____

The Reading Challenge

Lesson 3.10

Reading Multisyllable Words

✓ Lesson Check Point

 Directions: Read and divide each target word into syllables. Write each word and place a hyphen (-) between the syllables in the second column. Write the number of syllables in the third column. Use a dictionary or the Internet to check your answers.

Direksyons: Li epi divize chak mo objektif an silab. Ekri chak mo epi mete yon tirè (-) ant silab yo nan dezyèm kolòn nan. Ekri kantite silab ke yo genyen an nan twazyèm kolòn nan. Itilize yon diksyonè oubyen entènèt pou tcheke repons ou yo.

Target Words	Words Divided into Syllables	Number of Syllables
1. cardinal	car-di-nal	3
2. chamber	cham-ber	2
3. cockroach	cock-roach	2
4. cauliflower	cau-li-flow-er	4
5. cylinder	cyl-in-der	3
6. conjunction	con-junc-tion	3
7. casual	ca-su-al	3
8. complexion	com-plex-ion	3
9. category	cat-e-go-ry	4
10. California	Cal-i-for-nia	4

Homework

 Name: _____ Date:___/___/_____ Score:_____

The Reading Challenge

Lesson 3.10

Reading Multisyllable Words

✓ Lesson Check Point

 Directions: Read each target word. Circle the word in the row that is divided correctly into syllables. Use a dictionary or the Internet to check your answers.

Direksyons: Li chak mo objektif. Antoure mo a ki nan ranje a ki divize an silab korèkteman yo. Itilize yon diksyonè oubyen entènèt pou tcheke repons ou yo.

Model

| calculus | a. calcu-lus | (b. cal-cu-lus) | c. cal-culus |

1. clinical	(a. clin-i-cal)	b. clini-cal	c. clin-ic-al
2. cockatoo	a. co-ck-atoo	(b. cock-a-too)	c. cocka-too
3. coconut	a. coco-nut	b. co-conut	(c. co-co-nut)
4. clerical	(a. cler-i-cal)	b. cleri-cal	c. cle-ri-cal
5. citizen	a. cit-izen	(b. cit-i-zen)	c. ci-tiz-en
6. condition	(a. con-di-tion)	b. cond-i-tion	c. co-ndi-tion
7. congruent	a. co-ngru-ent	(b. con-gru-ent)	c. con-g-ruent
8. constitute	a. cons-tit-ute	b. const-i-tute	(c. con-sti-tute)

Unit C Lesson 3.10

Homework

Name: _____ Date:___/___/_____ Score:_____

Lesson 3.11

Reading and Writing

Proper and Common Nouns and Adjectives

Directions: Read the words in the word box. Put an (X) on the line next to each word that is written incorrectly. Remember that all proper nouns and proper adjectives are capitalized. Use a dictionary or the Internet to check your answers.

Direksyons: Li chak mo yo ki nan bwat mo a. Met yon (X) sou ti trè a ki bò kote mo ki pa kri byen yo. Sonje ke tout non pwòp ak adjektif pwop ekri avèk yon lèt majiskil nan kòmansman yo. Itilize yon diksyonè oubyen entènèt pou tcheke repons ou yo.

Word Box					
_X_	City	___	closet	_X_	Curtain
___	capital	_X_	CriCket	_X_	Cutting
___	Columbus	___	canyon	___	Costa Rica
___	Cousin Charles	_X_	cherokee	_X_	carson city

Directions: Read each unedited sentence and underline the word that is written incorrectly. Write each sentence correctly on the line.

Direksyons: Li chak fraz ki pa edite yo epi soulinye mo ki pa ekri byen an. Ekri chak fraz korèkteman sou liy lan.

Model
The <u>Camp</u> in Cleveland is closed.
<u>The camp in Cleveland is closed.</u>

1. <u>chad</u> is carrying his bag of rice.
<u>Chad is carrying his bag of rice.</u>

2. The climate in <u>central</u> America is not cold.
<u>The climate in Central America is not cold.</u>

3. The <u>Coffee</u> and cocoa in our cups are cold.
<u>The coffee and cocoa in our cups are cold.</u>

4. Charles and Cecil are <u>Characters</u> in my cool book.
<u>Charles and Cecil are characters in my cool book.</u>

Homework

 Name: _____ Date: ___/___/_____ Score: _____

Lesson 4.1

Reading Words with the Letter D/d

✓ Lesson Check Point

 Directions: Read each target word. Find the letter "d" and put a check (✓) in the column that identifies its position: beginning, within or end.
Direksyons: Li chak mo objektif. Jwenn lèt "d" a epi mete yon tchèck (✓) nan kolòn ki idantifye pozisyon li an: nan kòmansman, ladan oubyen nan finisman.

Target Words	Beginning (First Letter)	Within	End (Last Letter)
1. hold			✓
2. dollar	✓		
3. holiday		✓	
4. darling	✓		
5. kingdom		✓	

 Directions: Read each sentence and underline the words that begin with the letter "d." Write all the underlined words in alphabetical order on the lines below.
Direksyons: Li chak fraz epi soulinye mo ki kòmanse avèk lèt "d" yo. Ekri tout mo ki soulinye yo nan lòd alfabetik sou trè sa yo ki anba.

6. My <u>daughter</u> is an excellent <u>doctor</u>.

7. Fred ate <u>deep-fried</u> chicken for <u>dinner</u>.

8. The <u>detective</u> <u>drives</u> his blue car to the city.

9. My mom <u>drove</u> <u>directly</u> to the college campus.

10. I asked about the <u>dangers</u> of the hot <u>desert</u> sun.

<u>dangers</u>   <u>daughter</u>   <u>deep-fried</u>
<u>desert</u>   <u>detective</u>   <u>dinner</u>
<u>directly</u>   <u>doctor</u>   <u>drives</u>
    <u>drove</u>

Homework

 Name: _____ Date:____/____/_____ Score:_____

Lesson 4.2

Reading Letter "d" Words with the /d/ Sound & /j/ Sound

✓ Lesson Check Point

 Directions: Read each target word. Circle the word in the column that has the same "d" sound as the target word.

Direksyons: Li chak mo objektif. Antoure mo a ki nan kolòn nan ki bay menm son "d" a tankou mo objektif la.

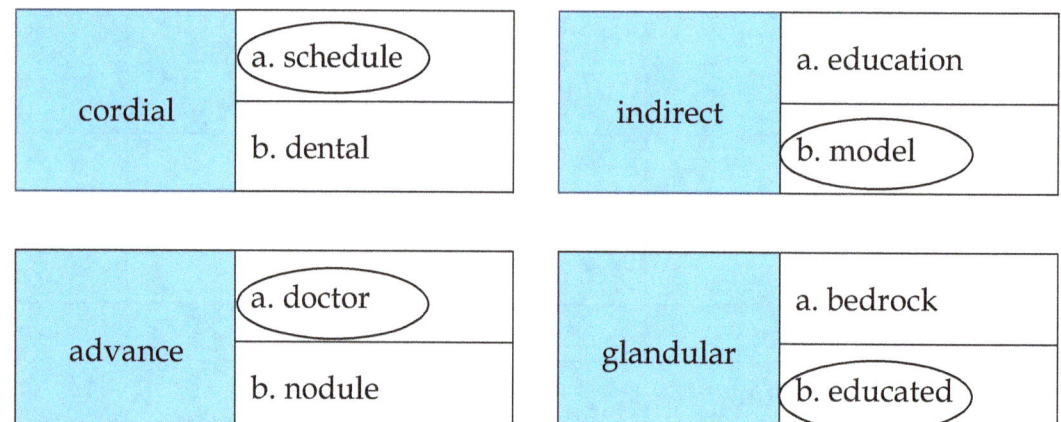

 Directions: Read each target word. Put a check (✓) under the correct column heading.

Direksyons: Li chak mo objektif. Mete yon tchèk (✓) anba antèt kolòn ki kòrèk la.

Target Words	"d" has the /d/ sound as in the word <u>doctor</u>	"d" has the /j/ sound as in the word <u>educate</u>
1. cordial		✓
2. indirect	✓	
3. advance	✓	
4. glandular		✓

Homework

 Name: _____ Date:___/___/_____ Score:_____

Lesson 4.2

Reading Words with the "dr" Letter Combination

Dictionary Skills/ Vocabulary

✓ **Lesson Check Point**

 Directions: Read each target word and its definition. Write the letter of the definition on the line of each target word. Use a dictionary or the Internet to check your answers.
Direksyons: Li chak mo objektif ak definisyon yo chak. Ekri lèt la ki koresponn ak definisyon an sou trè chak mo objektif yo. Itilize yon diksyonè oubyen entènèt pou tcheke repons ou yo.

Target Words	Definitions
1. _d_ dress up	a. a musical instrument
2. _b_ drive	b. to operate a car, train or bus
3. _a_ drum	c. pictures made with an artist's tool
4. _e_ dramatic	d. to wear fancy clothes for a special event
5. _c_ drawings	e. the act of showing feelings during a performance

 Directions: Read each sentence. Underline the word in the parentheses that correctly completes each sentence. Then, write the underlined word on the line.
Direksyons: Li chak fraz. Soulinye mo a ki nan parantèz yo ki konplete chak fraz kòrèkteman. Answit, ekri mo soulinye a sou trè a.

6. We will _____drive_____ out of the driveway. (dress up, <u>drive</u>)

7. Danny's _____drawings_____ were skillfully done. (drive, <u>drawings</u>)

8. David played the _____drum_____ at the concert. (<u>drum</u>, dramatic)

9. At the show, Diana did a _____dramatic_____ dance. (<u>dramatic</u>, drive)

10. Everyone in my class will dress up for the dance. (<u>dress up</u>, drawings)

Homework

Name: _____ Date: ___/__/_____ Score: _____

Lesson 4.3

Reading Words with the "ed" Suffix/ Past Tense Verbs

✓ **Lesson Check Point**

Directions: Read each target word. Circle the word in the column that has the same "ed" sound(s) as the target word.
Direksyons: Li chak mo objektif. Antoure mo a ki nan kolòn nan ki bay menm son "ed" a tankou mo objektif la.

fixed	a. framed
	b. (ripped)

saved	a. cooked
	b. (tamed)

started	a. (plotted)
	b. produced

stopped	a. rested
	b. (licked)

Directions: Read each target word. Put a check (✓) under the correct column heading.
Direksyons: Li chak mo objektif. Mete yon tchèk (✓) anba antèt kolòn ki kòrèk la.

Target Words	"ed" has the /i/ + /d/ sounds as in the word <u>rested</u>	"ed" has the /d/ sound as in the word <u>hugged</u>	"ed" has the /t/ sound as in the word <u>tipped</u>
1. fixed			✓
2. saved		✓	
3. started	✓		
4. stopped			✓

Homework

 Name: _____ Date: ___/___/_____ Score: _____

Lesson 4.4

Reading Words with a Silent Letter "d"

✓ Lesson Check Point

 Directions: Read the target words in the word box. Write the words that have a silent letter "d" in the first column. Write the words that do not have a silent letter "d" in the second column.

Direksyons: Li mo objektif yo ki nan ti bwat mo a. Ekri mo yo ki genyen yon lèt "d" ki pa pwononse a nan premye kolòn nan. Ekri mo yo ki pa genyen yon lèt "d" ki pa pwononse a nan dezyèm kolòn nan.

Target Word Box				
sedge	candy	saddle	fridge	fade
dollar	deck	radiant	radish	drink
bridge	denim	adjective	doctor	nudge
cartridge	pendant	knowledge	Windsor	Wednesday

Letter "d" is silent

- nudge
- bridge
- fridge
- sedge
- saddle
- Windsor
- adjective
- cartridge
- knowledge
- Wednesday

Letter "d" has the /d/ sound

- fade
- deck
- drink
- denim
- candy
- dollar
- doctor
- radish
- radiant
- pendant

Homework

 Name: _____   Date: ___/___/_____   Score: _____

The Reading Challenge

Lesson 4.5

Reading Multisyllable Words

✓ Lesson Check Point

 Directions: Read and divide each target word into syllables. Write each word and place a hyphen (-) between the syllables in the second column. Write the number of syllables in the third column. Use a dictionary or the Internet to check your answers.

Direksyons: Li epi divize chak mo objektif an silab. Ekri chak mo epi mete yon tirè (-) ant silab yo nan dezyèm kolòn nan. Ekri kantite silab ke yo genyen an nan twazyèm kolòn nan. Itilize yon diksyonè oubyen entènèt pou tcheke repons ou yo.

Target Words	Words Divided into Syllables	Number of Syllables
1. dentistry	den-tist-ry	3
2. dialect	di-a-lect	3
3. development	de-vel-op-ment	4
4. disembark	dis-em-bark	3
5. denominate	de-nom-i-nate	4
6. department	de-part-ment	3
7. description	de-scrip-tion	3
8. demanding	de-mand-ing	3
9. designer	de-sign-er	3
10. dependent	de-pen-dent	3

Learn To Read English With Directions In Spanish

Homework

 Name: _____ Date: ___/___/_____ Score: _____

The Reading Challenge

Lesson 4.5

Reading Multisyllable Words

✓ Lesson Check Point

 Directions: Read each target word. Circle the word in the row that is divided correctly into syllables. Use a dictionary or the Internet to check your answers.

Direksyons: Li chak mo objektif. Antoure mo a ki nan ranje a ki divize an silab korèkteman yo. Itilize yon diksyonè oubyen entènèt pou tcheke repons ou yo.

Model

| dictionary | a. di-ction-ary | b. dic-tion-ar-y (circled) | c. dic-tiona-ry |

| 1. deception | a. dec-ep-tion | b. de-cep-tion (circled) | c. de-ce-ption |

| 2. database | a. da-ta-base (circled) | b. dat-a-base | c. da-tab-ase |

| 3. delinquent | a. del-in-quent | b. de-lin-quent (circled) | c. delin-qu-ent |

| 4. disengage | a. dis-en-gage (circled) | b. di-sen-gage | c. dis-eng-age |

| 5. drapery | a. dra-pe-ry | b. drap-er-y (circled) | c. drape-r-y |

| 6. decided | a. de-cide-d | b. de-ci-ded | c. de-cid-ed (circled) |

| 7. duplicate | a. du-pli-cate (circled) | b. dup-li-cate | c. du-plic-ate |

| 8. diagnosis | a. dia-gno-sis | b. di-ag-no-sis (circled) | c. diagn-o-sis |

Unit D
Lesson 4.5

Learn To Read English With Directions In Haitian Creole

Homework

Name: _____ Date: ___/___/_____ Score: _____

Lesson 4.6

Reading and Writing

Proper and Common Nouns and Adjectives

Directions: Read the words in the word box. Put an (X) on the line next to each word that is written incorrectly. Remember that all proper nouns and proper adjectives are capitalized. Use a dictionary or the Internet to check your answers.

Direksyons: Li chak mo yo ki nan bwat mo a. Met yon (X) sou ti trè a ki bò kote mo ki pa kri byen yo. Sonje ke tout non pwòp ak adjektif pwop ekri avèk yon lèt majiskil nan kòmansman yo. Itilize yon diksyonè oubyen entènèt pou tcheke repons ou yo.

Word Box					
X	dr.	X	Dove	X	Desk
X	dutch	__	Delhi	__	driver
__	Detroit	__	Dominica	__	distant
X	Dessert	X	december	__	Damascus

Directions: Read each unedited sentence and underline the word that is written incorrectly. Write each sentence correctly on the line.

Direksyons: Li chak fraz ki pa edite yo epi soulinye mo ki pa ekri byen an. Ekri chak fraz korèkteman sou liy lan.

Model
Dan said, "My daughter's name is <u>donna</u>."
Dan said, "My daughter's name is Donna."

1. After dinner, I ate <u>dad's</u> donuts.
After dinner, I ate Dad's donuts.

2. <u>dina</u> designed a cute denim dress.
Dina designed a cute denim dress.

3. Daniel dug a <u>Ditch</u> by the bushes.
Daniel dug a ditch by the bushes.

4. <u>detroit</u> Diner has delicious dishes.
Detroit Diner has delicious dishes.

Unit D Lesson 4.6

Learn To Read English With Directions In Spanish

Homework

 Name: _____ Date: ___/___/_____ Score: _____

Lesson 5.1

Reading Words with the Letter E/e

✓ Lesson Check Point

Directions: Read each target word. Find the letter "e" and put a check (✓) in the column that identifies its position: beginning, within or end.
Direksyons: Li chak mo objektif. Jwenn lèt "e" a epi mete yon tchèck (✓) nan kolòn ki idantifye pozisyon li an: nan kòmansman, ladan oubyen nan finisman.

Target Words	Beginning (First Letter)	Within	End (Last Letter)
1. east	✓		
2. alive			✓
3. exact	✓		
4. heater		✓	
5. annex		✓	

Directions: Read each target word. Read the words in the row and circle the word that has a different vowel "e" sound.
Direksyons: Li chak mo objektif. Li mo yo ki nan ranje a epi antoure mo a ki bay yon son vwayèl "e" ki diferan an.

Target Words					
6. help	tend	(he)	sell	rent	
7. check	bell	rest	cent	(she)	
8. shell	west	clef	(me)	step	
9. bless	(be)	get	red	sent	
10. French	self	(the)	dent	desk	

Learn To Read English With Directions In Haitian Creole

Homework

 Name: _____ Date: ___/___/_____ Score: _____

Lesson 5.2

Reading Words with the Short Vowel "e" Sound

✓ Lesson Check Point

 Directions: Read the words in the four boxes. Circle two words with the short vowel /ĕ/ sound. The anchor word for the short vowel /ĕ/ sound is <u>egg</u>.

Direksyons: Li mo yo ki nan kat ti bwat yo. Antoure de mo ki genyen son vwayèl kout /ĕ/ a. Mo referans pou son vwayel kout /ĕ/a se mo, <u>egg</u>.

| were | (send) | | great | dean | | please | (bred) |
| (dwell) | scheme | | (peg) | (belt) | | we | (spend) |

| (blend) | sea | | (bet) | these | | (spell) | (Ted) |
| (rend) | she | | take | (den) | | leaf | be |

 Directions: Read the words in the four boxes. Circle two words that rhyme. Rhyming words have the same ending sound, such as <u>set</u> and <u>wet</u>.

Direksyons: Li mo yo ki nan kat ti bwat yo. Antoure de mo ki rime. De mo oubyen plizyè mo ki rime genyen menm son nan finisman yo, tankou <u>set</u> ak <u>wet</u>.

| (Ben) | leap | | lead | they | | (nest) | heat |
| her | (ten) | | (wreck) | (peck) | | (west) | break |

| meal | (sell) | | (tend) | (send) | | smell | (melt) |
| (tell) | where | | these | bent | | bend | (felt) |

Homework

Name: _____ Date: ___/___/_____ Score: _____

Lesson 5.2

Reading & Writing Words with the Short Vowel "e" Sound

✓ **Lesson Check Point**

Directions: Read each sentence and underline three words with the short vowel /ĕ/ sound. Then, write the underlined words on the lines below. The anchor word for the short vowel /ĕ/ sound is egg.

Direksyons: Li chak fraz epi soulinye twa mo ki genyen son vwayèl kout /ĕ/ a. Answit, ekri mo soulinye yo sou trè sa yo ki anba. Mo referans pou son vwayèl kout /ĕ/ a se mo, egg.

Model

She placed her legs on the wet deck.

    legs   wet   deck

1. At the campsite, he fell into the deep red well.

    fell   red   well

2. Do you know whether Beth ironed her blue dress?

    whether   Beth   dress

3. At Mr. Eastman's house, the pets made a mess in the den.

    pets   mess   den

4. On Tuesday, the men slept in the green and orange tents.

    men   slept   tents

5. In December, I saw Lewis with ten extremely large emblems.

    December   ten   emblems

Homework

 Name: _____ Date:___/___/_____ Score: _____

Lesson 5.3

Reading Words with the Long Vowel "e" Sound

✓ **Lesson Check Point**

 Directions: Read the words in the four boxes. Circle two words with the long vowel /ē/ sound. The anchor word for the long vowel /ē/ sound is <u>me</u>.

Direksyons: Li mo yo ki nan kat ti bwat yo. Antoure de mo ki genyen son vwayèl long /ē/ a. Mo referans pou son vwayèl long /ē/ a se mo, <u>me</u>.

pelt	text		great	(weak)		best	(crease)
(tree)	(meat)		wet	(three)		(peace)	fear

(grease)	belt		(knee)	peck		(eels)	(team)
pearl	(cleave)		bear	(teal)		spell	lent

 Directions: Read the words in the four boxes. Circle two words that rhyme. Rhyming words have the same ending sound, such as <u>beep</u> and <u>reap</u>.

Direksyons: Li mo yo ki nan kat ti bwat yo. Antoure de mo ki rime. De mo oubyen plizyè mo ki rime genyen menm son nan finisman yo, tankou <u>beep</u> ak <u>reap</u>.

(peak)	crest		speck	apples		blest	(cream)
beard	(seek)		(real)	(peel)		heart	(dream)

(meal)	spent		(please)	(ease)		lets	(cheat)
(deal)	tear		smell	head		(treat)	stress

Homework

Name: _____ Date: ___/___/_____ Score: _____

Lesson 5.3

Reading & Writing Words with the Long Vowel "e" Sound

✓ **Lesson Check Point**

Directions: Read each sentence and underline three words with the long vowel /ē/ sound. Then, write the underlined words on the lines below. The anchor word for the long vowel /ē/ sound is <u>me</u>.

Direksyons: Li chak fraz epi soulinye twa mo ki genyen son vwayèl long /ē/ a. Answit, ekri mo soulinye yo sou trè sa yo ki anba. Mo referans pou son vwayèl long /ē/ a se mo, <u>me</u>.

Model

<u>We</u> are <u>reading</u> an article entitled, "<u>Eagles</u> Bird of Prey."

    We   reading   Eagles

1. The <u>dean</u> is <u>speaking</u> about our ten athletic <u>teams</u>.

    dean   speaking   teams

2. At <u>three</u> o'clock, <u>she</u> began to <u>eat</u> bread and eggs.

    three   she   eat

3. <u>Sheila</u> and <u>Peter</u> are <u>reading</u> interesting articles.

    Sheila   Peter   reading

4. <u>Steve</u> said, "One pound of <u>meat</u> has more <u>protein</u> than ten eggs."

    Steve   meat   protein

5. My <u>teacher</u> began her lesson with <u>three</u> facts about the planet <u>Venus</u>.

    teacher   three   Venus

Homework

Name: _____ Date: ___/___/_____ Score: _____

Review Lessons 5.2 & 5.3

Reading Short Vowel and Long Vowel Words

Directions: Read the target words in the word box. In the first column, write the words that have the short vowel /ĕ/ sound, as in the word <u>egg</u>. In the second column, write the words that have the long vowel /ē/ sound, as in the word <u>me</u>.

Direksyons: Li mo objektif yo ki nan bwat mo a. Nan premye kolòn nan, ekri mo ki bay son vwayèl kout /ĕ/ yo, tankou li ye nan mo <u>egg</u> la. Nan dezyèm kolòn nan, ekri mo ki bay son vwayèl long /ē/ yo, tankou li ye nan mo <u>me</u> la.

Target Word Box				
defeat	stem	supreme	stream	press
coffee	never	flesh	between	stress
help	speech	next	dress	ceiling
ever	complete	deplete	check	asleep

Letter "e" has the /ĕ/ sound as in the word <u>egg</u>

Letter "e" has the /ē/ sound as in the word <u>me</u>

help	defeat
ever	coffee
stem	speech
never	complete
flesh	supreme
next	deplete
dress	stream
check	between
press	ceiling
stress	asleep

Learn To Read English With Directions In Spanish

Homework

 Name: _____ Date:___/___/_____ Score:_____

Lesson 5.4

Reading Words with Letter "e" Vowel Pairs

✓ **Lesson Check Point**

 Directions: Read each target word. Circle the word in the column that has the same vowel "ea," "ee," "ei," "eo" or "eu" sound as the target word.
Direksyons: Li chak mo objektif. Antoure mo a ki nan kolòn nan ki bay menm son vwayèl "ea," "ee," "ei," "eo" oubyen "eu" a tankou mo objektif la.

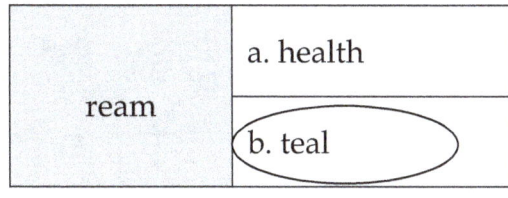
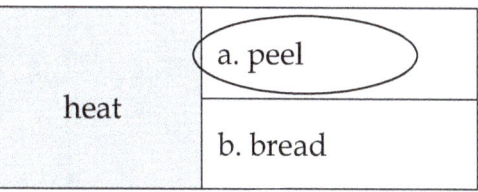
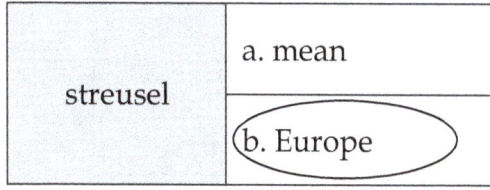

ream	a. health
	b. teal (circled)

heat	a. peel (circled)
	b. bread

protein	a. asleep (circled)
	b. hear

streusel	a. mean
	b. Europe (circled)

 Directions: Read each target word. Put a check (✓) under the correct column heading.
Direksyons: Li chak mo objektif. Mete yon tchèk (✓) anba antèt kolòn ki kòrèk la.

Target Words	Words have the long "e" sound as in the word <u>tea</u>	Words do not have the long "e" sound
1. ream	✓	
2. heat	✓	
3. protein	✓	
4. streusel		✓

Homework

 Name: _____ Date:___/___/_____ Score: _____

Lesson 5.5

Reading Words with the Final Letter "e"

✓ **Lesson Check Point**

 Directions: Read each target word. Find the letter "e" and put a check (✓) in the column that identifies its position within the syllable.

Direksyons: Li chak mo objektif. Jwenn lèt "e" a epi mete yon tchèk (✓) nan kolòn ki idantifye pozisyon li an nan silab la.

Target Words	"e" is at the end of a one syllable word	"e" is at the end of the first syllable	"e" is at the end of a multi-syllable word
1. he	✓		
2. me	✓		
3. hero		✓	
4. r<u>e</u>fresh		✓	
5. becom<u>e</u>			✓

 Directions: Read each target word. Put a check (✓) under the correct column heading.

Direksyons: Li chak mo objektif. Mete yon tchèk (✓) anba antèt kolòn ki kòrèk la.

Target Words	"e" has the /ĕ/ sound as in the word <u>egg</u>	"e" has the /ē/ sound as in the word <u>me</u>	"e" has the /ə/ sound as in the word <u>item</u>	"e" is silent as in the word <u>great</u>
6. either		✓		
7. pollen			✓	
8. resting	✓			
9. Europe				✓
10. urgently			✓	

Homework

 Name: _____ Date:__/___/_____ Score: _____

Lesson 5.6

Reading Letter "e" Words with the Schwa Vowel Sound

✓ **Lesson Check Point**

 Directions: Read each target word. Circle the word in the column that has the same "e" sound as the target word.

Direksyons: Li chak mo objektif. Antoure mo a ki nan kolòn nan ki bay menm son "e" a tankou mo objektif la.

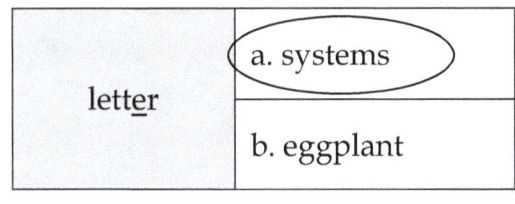
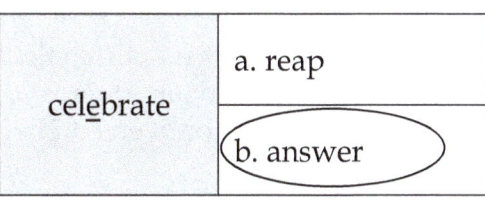
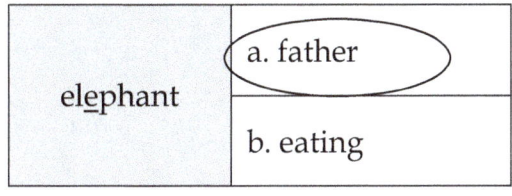
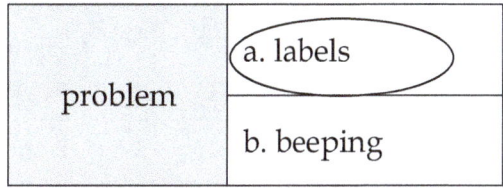

 Directions: Read each sentence and underline the letter "e" word that has the schwa vowel /ə/ sound. The anchor word for the letter "e" schwa vowel sound is <u>item</u>.

Direksyons: Li chak fraz epi soulinye mo ki genyen lèt "e" ki bay son schwa /ə/ a. Mo referans pou son schwa lèt "e" a se mo, <u>item</u>.

1. You will <u>benefit</u> from reading this book.

2. Today, Emma began to <u>shiver</u> from fear.

3. Curried <u>chicken</u> with rice tastes very good.

4. My friend, Pete, made a profound <u>statement</u>.

5. Eddie painted an <u>elephant</u> for his art project.

6. There is <u>oxygen</u> in the large blue and white tank.

Homework

Name: _____ Date: ___/___/_____ Score: _____

Lesson 5.7

Reading Words with the "er" Letter Combination

Dictionary Skills/ Vocabulary

✓ **Lesson Check Point**

Directions: Read each target word and its definition. Write the letter of the definition on the line of each target word. Use a dictionary or the Internet to check your answers.

Direksyons: Li chak mo objektif ak definisyon yo chak. Ekri lèt la ki koresponn ak definisyon an sou trè chak mo objektif yo. Itilize yon diksyonè oubyen entènèt pou tcheke repons ou yo.

Target Words	Definitions
1. _c_ ferry	a. sweet fruit
2. _e_ brother	b. meal eaten in the evening
3. _d_ periscope	c. a boat that sails across a body of water
4. _b_ supper	d. a viewing instrument that has a system of lenses
5. _a_ blackberries	e. a male person who has the same parent(s) as another

Directions: Read each sentence and write the target word that correctly completes the sentence.
Direksyons: Li chak fraz epi ekri mo objektif ki konplete fraz la kòrèkteman.

6. The _____ferry_____ is floating under the city bridge.

7. Are you going to put _____blackberries_____ on your cereal?

8. Jerry always looks through his big _____periscope_____.

9. My sister and _____brother_____ like to eat sweet cherries.

10. Tonight, we are going to have herring for _____supper_____.

Homework

 Name: _____ Date: ___/___/_____ Score: _____

Lesson 5.8

Reading Words with the "eu" and "ew" Letter Combinations

✓ **Lesson Check Point**

Directions: Read each sentence and underline the word that has a silent letter "e."

Direksyons: Li chak fraz epi soulinye mo a ki genyen lèt "e" ki pa pwononse a.

Model
My father said, "The apricot <u>streusel</u> is very tasty."

1. The <u>eulogy</u> at Eddie's funeral was very touching.

2. <u>Lieutenant</u> Glen has been a soldier for ten years.

3. Eleven of my friends went to <u>Europe</u> for an exciting vacation.

4. Prior to the wedding, Edwina will sew my <u>white</u> bridal gown.

Directions: Read each sentence and underline the word with an "eu" or "ew" letter combination that has the long vowel /y$\overline{oo}$/ or /$\overline{oo}$/ sound, as in the words <u>feud</u> and <u>flew</u>.

Direksyons: Li chak fraz epi soulinye mo a ki genyen yon konbinezon lèt "eu" oubyen "ew" ki bay son vwayèl long /y$\overline{oo}$/ oubyen /$\overline{oo}$/ a, tankou li ye nan mo <u>feud</u> ak <u>flew</u>.

5. Emily likes to wear <u>neutral</u> colors.

6. Edward <u>chews</u> his baked granola bar very slowly.

7. The artist <u>drew</u> a picture of an eagle and her eaglets.

8. <u>Eugene's</u> favorite television show is "The Price is Right."

9. The patients in the hospital are being treated for <u>rheumatic</u> fever.

10. Dr. Edmond said that Annie's <u>rheumatism</u> is a very painful condition.

Homework

 Name: _____ Date: ___/___/_____ Score: _____

Lesson 5.9

Reading Words with the "ey" Letter Combination

✓ **Lesson Check Point**

 Directions: Read each target word. Put a check (✓) under the correct column heading.

Direksyons: Li chak mo objektif. Mete yon tchèk (✓) anba antèt kolòn ki kòrèk la.

Target Words	"ey" has the long /ē/ sound as in the word honey	"ey" has the long /ā/ sound as in the word hey
1. they're		✓
2. journey	✓	
3. odyssey	✓	
4. obeyed		✓

 Directions: Read each sentence and underline the word with the "ey" letter combination. Put a check (✓) under the correct column heading.
Direksyons: Li chak fraz epi soulinye mo a ki genyen konbinezon lèt "ey" la. Mete yon tchèk (✓) anba antèt kolòn ki kòrèk la.

	"ey" has the long /ē/ sound as in the word honey	"ey" has the long /ā/ sound as in the word hey
5. I completed an extremely long <u>survey</u>.		✓
6. He should <u>obey</u> the class rules.		✓
7. <u>They</u> like to eat eggs for breakfast.		✓
8. The new <u>medley</u> sounds very good.	✓	
9. I like <u>parsley</u> flakes on my sandwich.	✓	
10. It is difficult to <u>convey</u> the message.		✓

Homework

 Name: _____ Date:___/___/_____ Score:_____

Lesson 5.10

Reading Words with a Silent Letter "e"

✓ **Lesson Check Point**

 Directions: Read the target words in the word box. Write the words that have a silent letter "e" in the first column. Write the words that do not have a silent letter "e" in the second column.

Direksyons: Li mo objektif yo ki nan ti bwat mo a. Ekri mo yo ki genyen yon lèt "e" ki pa pwononse a nan premye kolòn nan. Ekri mo yo ki pa genyen yon lèt "e" ki pa pwononse a nan dezyèm kolòn nan.

Target Word Box				
beat	intake	water	cube	denting
ate	tea	blue	mule	life
bone	wife	the	lively	reading
sea	me	space	meat	elephant

Letter "e" is silent

- ate
- cube
- life
- blue
- mule
- wife
- bone
- space
- lively
- intake

Letter "e" has a letter /e/ sound

- me
- sea
- the
- tea
- beat
- meat
- water
- denting
- reading
- elephant

Learn To Read English With Directions In Haitian Creole

Homework

 Name: _____ Date:___/___/_____ Score: _____

Unit Review – E/e

Reading Words with Vowel "e" Sounds: /ĕ/, /ē/, /ə/ & Silent

✓ **Lesson Check Point**

 Directions: Read each target word. Circle the word in the column that has the same "e" sound as the target word.

Direksyons: Li chak mo objektif. Antoure mo a ki nan kolòn nan ki bay menm son "e" a tankou mo objektif la.

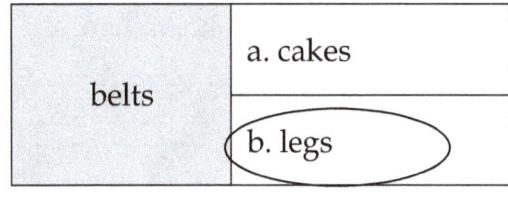

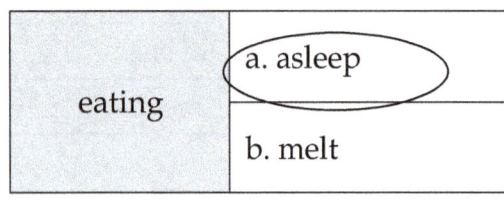 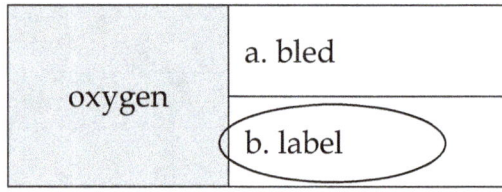

 Directions: Read each target word. Put a check (✓) under the correct column heading.

Direksyons: Li chak mo objektif. Mete yon tchèk (✓) anba antèt kolòn ki kòrèk la.

Target Words	"e" has the /ĕ/ sound as in the word <u>egg</u>	"e" has the /ē/ sound as in the word <u>me</u>	"e" has the /ə/ sound as in the word <u>item</u>	"e" is silent as in the word <u>great</u>
1. belts	✓			
2. peanuts		✓		
3. eating		✓		
4. oxygen			✓	

Learn To Read English With Directions In Spanish

Homework

 Name: _____ Date:___/___/_____ Score:_____

The Reading Challenge

Lesson 5.11

Reading Multisyllable Words

✓ **Lesson Check Point**

 Directions: Read and divide each target word into syllables. Write each word and place a hyphen (-) between the syllables in the second column. Write the number of syllables in the third column. Use a dictionary or the Internet to check your answers.

Direksyons: Li epi divize chak mo objektif an silab. Ekri chak mo epi mete yon tirè (-) ant silab yo nan dezyèm kolòn nan. Ekri kantite silab ke yo genyen an nan twazyèm kolòn nan. Itilize yon diksyonè oubyen entènèt pou tcheke repons ou yo.

Target Words	Words Divided into Syllables	Number of Syllables
1. nutshell	nut-shell	2
2. increasing	in-creas-ing	3
3. emblem	em-blem	2
4. stairwell	stair-well	2
5. exceeding	ex-ceed-ing	3
6. airmen	air-men	2
7. drunken	drunk-en	2
8. eggshell	egg-shell	2
9. repeated	re-peat-ed	3
10. fasten	fas-ten	2

Unit E
Lesson 5.11

Homework

 Name: _____ Date: ___/___/_____ Score: _____

The Reading Challenge

Lesson 5.11

Reading Multisyllable Words

✓ **Lesson Check Point**

 Directions: Read each target word. Circle the word in the row that is divided correctly into syllables. Use a dictionary or the Internet to check your answers.

Direksyons: Li chak mo objektif. Antoure mo a ki nan ranje a ki divize an silab korèkteman yo. Itilize yon diksyonè oubyen entènèt pou tcheke repons ou yo.

Model

| megabyte | a. me-ga-byte | b. meg-a-byte (circled) | c. me-gaby-te |

| 1. ecosystem | a. eco-sys-tem | b. e-co-sys-tem (circled) | c. eco-syst-em |

| 2. segregate | a. se-gre-gate | b. se-greg-ate | c. seg-re-gate (circled) |

| 3. countrymen | a. coun-trym-en | b. count-ry-men | c. coun-try-men (circled) |

| 4. woodpecker | a. wood-peck-er (circled) | b. wood-pec-ker | c. woo-dpeck-er |

| 5. gardening | a. gard-en-ing | b. gar-de-ning | c. gar-den-ing (circled) |

| 6. legislate | a. leg-is-late (circled) | b. le-gis-late | c. leg-isl-ate |

| 7. comprehend | a. comp-re-hend | b. com-preh-end | c. com-pre-hend (circled) |

| 8. dividend | a. div-i-dend (circled) | b. di-vid-end | c. div-id-end |

Homework

Name: _____ Date: ___/___/_____ Score: _____

Lesson 5.12

Reading and Writing

Proper and Common Nouns and Adjectives

Directions: Read the words in the word box. Put an (X) on the line next to each word that is written incorrectly. Remember that all proper nouns and proper adjectives are capitalized. Use a dictionary or the Internet to check your answers.

Direksyons: Li chak mo yo ki nan bwat mo a. Met yon (X) sou ti trè a ki bò kote mo ki pa kri byen yo. Sonje ke tout non pwòp ak adjektif pwop ekri avèk yon lèt majiskil nan kòmansman yo. Itilize yon diksyonè oubyen entènèt pou tcheke repons ou yo.

Word Box					
X	EssEx	__	edition	__	elbow
__	English	__	elaborate	X	ecuador
__	Eskimo	__	Egyptology	X	Education
X	eastern european	X	erie Channel	X	Middle east

Directions: Read each unedited sentence and underline the word that is written incorrectly. Write each sentence correctly on the line.

Direksyons: Li chak fraz ki pa edite yo epi soulinye mo ki pa ekri byen an. Ekri chak fraz korèkteman sou liy lan.

Model
All my friends are <u>Excited</u> about the class trip to Europe.
<u>All my friends are excited about the class trip to Europe.</u>

1. My friend, Elias, speaks <u>english</u> extremely well.
<u>My friend, Elias, speaks English extremely well.</u>

2. Mr. <u>edison</u> developed a battery for the electric car.
<u>Mr. Edison developed a battery for the electric car.</u>

3. This evening, Dr. Edwards <u>Examined</u> Elliot's eyes.
<u>This evening, Dr. Edwards examined Elliot's eyes.</u>

4. Eileen's e-ticket to <u>edinburgh</u> will expire on April eleventh.
<u>Eileen's e-ticket to Edinburgh will expire on April eleventh.</u>

Homework

Name: _____ Date:___/___/_____ Score: _____

Lesson 6.1

Reading Words with the Letter F/f

✓ **Lesson Check Point**

Directions: Read each target word. Find the letter "f" and put a check (✓) in the column that identifies its position: beginning, within or end.
Direksyons: Li chak mo objektif. Jwenn lèt "f" a epi mete yon tchèck (✓) nan kolòn ki idantifye pozisyon li an: nan kòmansman, ladan oubyen nan finisman.

Target Words	Beginning (First Letter)	Within	End (Last Letter)
1. leaf			✓
2. fresh	✓		
3. flipped	✓		
4. comfort		✓	
5. defrost		✓	

Directions: Read each sentence and underline the words that begin with the letter "f." Write all the underlined words in alphabetical order on the lines below.
Direksyons: Li chak fraz epi soulinye mo ki kòmanse avèk lèt "f" yo. Ekri tout mo ki soulinye yo nan lòd alfabetik sou trè sa yo ki anba.

6. Did you know the <u>fox</u> had <u>fleas</u>?

7. Annie said, "The <u>field</u> is <u>far</u> away."

8. Last January, Bobby ate a lot of <u>fast</u> <u>food</u>.

9. The children like to have <u>fun</u> at the <u>fountain</u>.

10. In the afternoon, the <u>flock</u> of birds <u>flew</u> away.

<u>far</u>_____ <u>fast</u>_____ <u>field</u>_____
<u>fleas</u>_____ <u>flew</u>_____ <u>flock</u>_____
<u>food</u>_____ <u>fountain</u>_____ <u>fox</u>_____
           <u>fun</u>_____

Homework

Name: _____ Date: ___/___/_____ Score: _____

Lesson 6.2

Reading Words with the "fr" Letter Combination

Dictionary Skills/ Vocabulary

✓ Lesson Check Point

Directions: Read each target word and its definition. Write the letter of the definition on the line of each target word. Use a dictionary or the Internet to check your answers.
Direksyons: Li chak mo objektif ak definisyon yo chak. Ekri lèt la ki koresponn ak definisyon an sou trè chak mo objektif yo. Itilize yon diksyonè oubyen entènèt pou tcheke repons ou yo.

Target Words	Definitions
1. e frames	a. facial expression indicating displeasure
2. b French	b. language spoken in France
3. c front	c. the first or forward position
4. a frowns	d. something made solid by extreme cold
5. d frozen	e. borders around an object, such as a picture

Directions: Read each sentence. Underline the word in the parentheses that correctly completes each sentence. Then, write the underlined word on the line.
Direksyons: Li chak fraz. Soulinye mo a ki nan parantèz yo ki konplete chak fraz kòrèkteman. Answit, ekri mo soulinye a sou trè a.

6. The food in the freezer is _____frozen_____. (frame, <u>frozen</u>)

7. Flo puts her drawings in beautiful _____frames_____. (<u>frames</u>, frozen)

8. Freda speaks _____French_____ and Finnish fluently. (frowns, <u>French</u>)

9. The whiteboard is in _____front_____ of the classroom. (<u>front</u>, French)

10. Happy clowns do not have _____frowns_____ on their faces. (<u>frowns</u>, frames)

Homework

Name: _____ Date: ___/___/_____ Score: _____

Lesson 6.3

Reading Words with the "fl" Letter Combination

Dictionary Skills/ Vocabulary

✓ **Lesson Check Point**

Directions: Read each target word and its definition. Write the target word on the line in front of its meaning. Use a dictionary or the Internet to check your answers.

Direksyons: Li chak mo objektif ak definisyon yo chak. Ekri mo objektif la sou trè ki devan definisyon li an. Itilize yon diksyonè oubyen entènèt pou tcheke repons ou yo.

Target Word Box				
flag	flavor	flu	flute	flying

1. __flavor__   the taste of food
2. __flute__   a woodwind instrument
3. __flying__   to travel through the air with wings
4. __flu__   a sickness caused by an acute viral infection
5. __flag__   a designed fabric used as a country's symbol

Directions: Read each sentence. Underline the word in the parentheses that correctly completes each sentence. Then, write the underlined word on the line.

Direksyons: Li chak fraz. Soulinye mo a ki nan parantèz yo ki konplete chak fraz kòrèkteman. Answit, ekri mo soulinye a sou trè a.

6. Fred is in bed with the bad _____flu_____. (flag, <u>flu</u>)

7. Francis enjoys _____flying_____ in the airplane. (<u>flying</u>, flavor)

8. The Japanese _____flag_____ is white and red. (<u>flag</u>, flute)

9. Flossy is learning to play the _____flute_____ in class. (<u>flute</u>, flu)

10. Flex's fried chicken is full of _____flavor_____. (<u>flavor</u>, flying)

Homework

 Name: _____ Date:___/___/_____ Score: _____

Lesson 6.3

Reading Words with the "fle" Letter Combination

✓ Lesson Check Point

 Directions: Read each target word. Find the "fle" letter combination and put a check (✓) in the column that identifies its position: beginning, within or end.
Direksyons: Li chak mo objektif. Jwenn konbinezon lèt "fle" a epi mete yon tchèk (✓) nan kolòn nan ki idantifye pozisyon li an: nan kòmansman, ladan oubyen nan finisman.

Target Words	Beginning (First 3 Letters)	Within	End (Last 3 Letters)
1. fled	✓		
2. baffle			✓
3. waffle			✓
4. deflect		✓	
5. inflexed		✓	

 Directions: Read each target word. Put a check (✓) in the "yes" column if the "fle" letter combination has the /f/ + /ə/ + /l/ sounds. Put a check (✓) in the "no" column if the "fle" letter combination does not have the /f/ + /ə/ + /l/ sounds.
Direksyons: Li chak mo objektif. Mete yon tchèk (✓) nan kolòn "yes" an si konbinezon lèt "fle" a bay sons /f/ + /ə/ + /l/. Mete yon tchèk (✓) nan kolòn "no" an si konbinezon lèt "fle" a pa bay sons /f/ + /ə/ + /l/.

Target Words	Yes	No
6. fled		✓
7. baffle	✓	
8. waffle	✓	
9. deflect		✓
10. inflexed		✓

Homework

Name: _____ Date: ___/___/_____ Score: _____

Lesson 6.4

Reading Words with the "ft," "lf" and "ff" Letter Combinations

Dictionary Skills/ Vocabulary

✓ **Lesson Check Point**

Directions: Read each target word and its definition. Write the letter of the definition on the line of each target word. Use a dictionary or the Internet to check your answers.

Direksyons: Li chak mo objektif ak definisyon yo chak. Ekri lèt la ki koresponn ak definisyon an sou trè chak mo objektif yo. Itilize yon diksyonè oubyen entènèt pou tcheke repons ou yo.

Target Words	Definitions
1. _c_ staff	a. not hard or firm
2. _b_ golf	b. an athletic game
3. _e_ cliff	c. people who work for a company
4. _a_ soft	d. vehicles driving along the road
5. _d_ traffic	e. a high and steep area of overhanging soil and rock

Directions: Read each sentence and write the target word that correctly completes the sentence.
Direksyons: Li chak fraz epi ekri mo objektif ki konplete fraz la kòrèkteman.

6. My family enjoys sleeping on _____soft_____ beds.

7. The _____traffic_____ on the road is backed up to Main Street.

8. My dad's company is hiring new _____staff_____ members.

9. Fred and Francis are playing _____golf_____ on the course.

10. During the camping trip, the boys climbed up a high ____cliff____.

Homework

 Name: _____ Date:___/___/_____ Score:_____

Lesson 6.5

Reading Words with a Silent Letter "f"

✓ Lesson Check Point

 Directions: Read the target words in the word box. Write the words that have a silent letter "f" in the first column. Write the words that do not have a silent letter "f" in the second column.

Direksyons: Li mo objektif yo ki nan ti bwat mo a. Ekri mo yo ki genyen lèt "f" ki pa pwononse a nan premye kolòn nan. Ekri mo yo ki pa genyen lèt "f" ki pa pwononse a nan dezyèm kolòn nan.

Target Word Box				
effort	infant	off	friend	afraid
buffer	before	stiff	figure	rainfall
official	graffiti	waffle	confront	stuffy
suffer	effect	fitting	filter	refer

Letter "f" is silent

- off
- stiff
- buffer
- effort
- suffer
- waffle
- official
- effect
- stuffy
- graffiti

Letter "f" has the /f/ sound

- refer
- filter
- afraid
- before
- figure
- infant
- friend
- fitting
- rainfall
- confront

Learn To Read English With Directions In Haitian Creole

Homework

☑ Name: _____ Date:___/___/_____ Score:_____

Lesson 6.6

Reading Singular and Plural forms of Words Ending in "-f" & "-fe"

✓ **Lesson Check Point**

Directions: Read each target word. Put a check (✓) in the second column if the plural form of the target word ends with "-ves." Put a check (✓) in the third column if the plural form of the target word ends with "-s" or "-es."
Direcciones: Lee cada palabra objetivo. Coloca un signo de verificación (✓) en la segunda columna si la forma plural de la palabra objetivo termina con "-ves". Coloca un signo de verificación (✓) en la tercera columna si la forma plural de la palabra objetivo termina con "-s" o "-es."

Target Words	The plural form of the target word ends with "-ves"	The plural form of the target word ends with "-s" or "-es"
1. roof		✓
2. calf	✓	
3. knife	✓	
4. chief		✓
5. belief		✓

Directions: Read each sentence. Complete each sentence by writing the plural form of the word on the line.
Direksyons: Li chak fraz. Konplete chak fraz pandan ou ap ekri fòm pliryèl korèk mo a sou trè a.

6. In autumn, the _____leaves_____ change color. (leaf)

7. The two dull _____knives_____ cannot cut the bread. (knife)

8. On Friday, five bold _____thieves_____ robbed the bank. (thief)

9. Lifeguards are stationed by the pool to save _____lives_____. (life)

10. During the storm, the shingles on the ____roofs____ blew away. (roof)

Homework

 Name: _____ Date: ___/___/_____ Score: _____

The Reading Challenge

Lesson 6.7

Reading Multisyllable Words

✓ **Lesson Check Point**

 Directions: Read and divide each target word into syllables. Write each word and place a hyphen (-) between the syllables in the second column. Write the number of syllables in the third column. Use a dictionary or the Internet to check your answers.

Direksyons: Li epi divize chak mo objektif an silab. Ekri chak mo epi mete yon tirè (-) ant silab yo nan dezyèm kolòn nan. Ekri kantite silab ke yo genyen an nan twazyèm kolòn nan. Itilize yon diksyonè oubyen entènèt pou tcheke repons ou yo.

Target Words	Words Divided into Syllables	Number of Syllables
1. finalist	fi-nal-ist	3
2. facade	fa-cade	2
3. flowery	flow-er-y	3
4. folding	fold-ing	2
5. formula	for-mu-la	3
6. failure	fail-ure	2
7. fluctuate	fluc-tu-ate	3
8. foolish	fool-ish	2
9. freedom	free-dom	2
10. frequency	fre-quen-cy	3

Homework

Name: _____ Date:___/___/_____ Score:_____

The Reading Challenge

Lesson 6.7

Reading Multisyllable Words

✓ Lesson Check Point

Directions: Read each target word. Circle the word in the row that is divided correctly into syllables. Use a dictionary or the Internet to check your answers.

Direksyons: Li chak mo objektif. Antoure mo a ki nan ranje a ki divize an silab korèkteman yo. Itilize yon diksyonè oubyen entènèt pou tcheke repons ou yo.

Model

| factory | a. fac-tor-y | b. fac-to-ry ⭕ | c. fa-cto-ry |

1. forgetful	a. for-get-ful ⭕	b. fo-rget-ful	c. forg-et-ful
2. faculty	a. fac-u-lty	b. fa-cult-y	c. fac-ul-ty ⭕
3. fabulous	a. fab-u-lous ⭕	b. fa-bul-ous	c. fab-ulo-us
4. financial	a. fi-nan-cial ⭕	b. fin-an-cial	c. fin-anc-ial
5. foliage	a. fo-li-age ⭕	b. fol-i-age	c. fo-lia-ge
6. foreigner	a. fore-ign-er	b. fore-ig-ner	c. for-eign-er ⭕
7. focusing	a. fo-cus-ing ⭕	b. foc-us-ing	c. foc-u-sing
8. falsify	a. fal-sif-y	b. fals-i-fy	c. fal-si-fy ⭕

Homework

Name: _____ Date: ___/___/_____ Score: _____

Lesson 6.8

Reading and Writing

Proper and Common Nouns and Adjectives

Directions: Read the words in the word box. Put an (X) on the line next to each word that is written incorrectly. Remember that all proper nouns and proper adjectives are capitalized. Use a dictionary or the Internet to check your answers.

Direksyons: Li chak mo yo ki nan bwat mo a. Met yon (X) sou ti trè a ki bò kote mo ki pa kri byen yo. Sonje ke tout non pwòp ak adjektif pwop ekri avèk yon lèt majiskil nan kòmansman yo. Itilize yon diksyonè oubyen entènèt pou tcheke repons ou yo.

Word Box					
X	Farmer	__	frog	X	france
X	Friend	__	female	__	fingers
X	french	X	frankfort	X	finnish
__	Fort Lee	__	Franklin	__	Fred's Diner

Directions: Read each unedited sentence and underline the word that is written incorrectly. Write each sentence correctly on the line.

Direksyons: Li chak fraz ki pa edite yo epi soulinye mo ki pa ekri byen an. Ekri chak fraz korèkteman sou liy lan.

Model
Fiji is my <u>Florist's</u> favorite holiday destination.
<u>Fiji is my florist's favorite holiday destination.</u>

1. Flo said, "China is in the <u>far</u> East."
<u>Flo said, "China is in the Far East.</u>

2. Frank is visiting Aunt <u>flossy</u> in Florida.
<u>Frank is visiting Aunt Flossy in Florida.</u>

3. <u>franklin</u> and Francis were born in Frankfort.
<u>Franklin and Francis were born in Frankfort.</u>

4. On <u>friday</u>, Florence wore a fancy dress to the dance.
<u>On Friday, Florence wore a fancy dress to the dance.</u>

Homework

Name: _____ Date: ___/___/_____ Score: _____

Lesson 7.1

Reading Words with the Letter G/g

✓ **Lesson Check Point**

Directions: Read each target word. Find the letter "g" and put a check (✓) in the column that identifies its position: beginning, within or end.

Direksyons: Li chak mo objektif. Jwenn lèt "g" a epi mete yon tchèck (✓) nan kolòn ki idantifye pozisyon li an: nan kòmansman, ladan oubyen nan finisman.

Target Words	Beginning (First Letter)	Within	End (Last Letter)
1. judge		✓	
2. loving			✓
3. sibling			✓
4. grammar	✓		
5. hamburger		✓	

Directions: Read each sentence and underline the words that begin with the letter "g." Write all the underlined words in alphabetical order on the lines below.

Direksyons: Li chak fraz epi soulinye mo ki kòmanse avèk lèt "g" yo. Ekri tout mo ki soulinye yo nan lòd alfabetik sou trè sa yo ki anba.

6. The <u>goldfish</u> is in a <u>glass</u> bowl.

7. On Saturday, I am <u>going</u> to the art <u>gallery</u>.

8. On Sundays, <u>Grace</u> enjoys singing <u>gospel</u> music.

9. Annie is <u>growing</u> beautiful flowers in her <u>garden</u>.

10. The <u>graphic</u> designer drew a <u>great</u> logo for my business card.

gallery _____   garden _____   glass _____
going _____   goldfish _____   gospel _____
Grace _____   graphic _____   great _____
                   growing _____

Homework

 Name: _____ Date: ___/___/_____ Score: _____

Lesson 7.1

Reading Words with the Hard Letter "g"

✓ Lesson Check Point

Directions: Read each target word. Put a check (✓) under the correct column heading.

Direksyons: Li chak mo objektif. Mete yon tchèk (✓) anba antèt kolòn ki kòrèk la.

Target Words	Hard "g" has the /g/ sound as in the word gum	Soft "g" has the /j/ sound as in the word gem
1. girls	✓	
2. giant		✓
3. glossy	✓	
4. gender		✓
5. garden	✓	

Directions: Read each sentence and underline the words that have the hard "g" sound. The anchor word for the hard "g" sound is gum. Write all the underlined words in alphabetical order on the lines below.

Direksyons: Li chak fraz epi soulinye mo yo ki bay son "g" di a. Mo referans pou son "g" di a se mo, gum. Ekri tout mo ki soulinye yo nan lòd alfabetik sou trè sa yo ki anba.

6. Ginny's gift was a colorful globe.

7. George is guilty of grabbing the balloons.

8. The giant likes to eat grapes and garlic cloves.

9. In Guyana, the skilled gymnasts are very gracious.

10. Two groups of students are going to visit Germany.

garlic   gift   globe
going   grabbing   gracious
grapes   groups   guilty
                Guyana

Homework

Name: _____ Date:___/___/_____ Score:_____

Lesson 7.2

Reading Words with the Soft Letter "g"

Directions: Read each target word. Put a check (✓) under the correct column heading.

Direksyons: Li chak mo objektif. Mete yon tchèk (✓) anba antèt kolòn ki kòrèk la.

Target Words	Soft "g" has the /j/ or /zh/ sound as in the words gem & massage	Hard "g" has the /g/ sound as in the word gum	Both soft "g" and hard "g" sounds as in the word gauge
1. give		✓	
2. emerge	✓		
3. apology	✓		
4. garages			✓
5. geographical			✓

Directions: Read each sentence and underline the words that have the soft "g" sound. The anchor word for the soft "g" sound is gem. Write all the underlined words in alphabetical order on the lines below.

Direksyons: Li chak fraz epi soulinye mo yo ki bay son "g" dous lan. Mo referans pou son "g" dous lan se mo, gem. Ekri tout mo ki soulinye yo nan lòd alfabetik sou trè sa yo ki anba.

6. The <u>gentle giant</u> did not break the gate.

7. Gilbert gave me two <u>oranges</u> and a big <u>gyro</u>.

8. Mr. Green said, "The two geese are in a <u>huge cage</u>."

9. My guest took a guided tour of <u>Genie's gymnasium</u>.

10. There is a picture of a <u>gigantic</u> gorilla on the next <u>page</u>.

cage_____	huge_____	Genie's_____
gentle_____	giant_____	gigantic_____
gymnasium_____	gyro_____	oranges_____
	page_____	

Homework

Name: _____ Date: ___/___/_____ Score: _____

Review Lessons 7.1 & 7.2

Reading Hard Letter "g" and Soft Letter "g" Words

Directions: Read each target word. Put a check (✓) under the correct column heading.

Direksyons: Li chak mo objektif. Mete yon tchèk (✓) anba antèt kolòn ki kòrèk la.

Target Words	Soft "g" has the /j/ or /zh/ sound as in the words gem & massage	Hard "g" has the /g/ sound as in the word gum	Both soft "g" and hard "g" sounds as in the word gauge
1. griddle		✓	
2. change	✓		
3. analogy	✓		
4. girlfriend		✓	
5. geography			✓

Directions: Read each sentence and underline the words that have the hard "g" sound. The anchor word for the hard "g" sound is gum. Write all the underlined words in alphabetical order on the lines below.

Direksyons: Li chak fraz epi soulinye mo yo ki bay son "g" di a. Mo referans pou son "g" di a se mo, gum. Ekri tout mo ki souliye yo nan lòd alfabetik sou trè sa yo ki anba.

6. George gave each child a toy kangaroo.

7. Gina designed a great maze in the garden.

8. Geron received golf clubs as a birthday gift.

9. Gene is allergic to an ingredient in orange gum.

10. Grandma said, "The magic gel is in a gold bottle."

garden _____ gave _____ gift _____
gold _____ golf _____ Grandma _____
great _____ gum _____ ingredient _____
　　　　　　　　kangaroo _____

Homework

Name: _____ Date: ___/___/_____ Score: _____

Review Lessons 7.1 & 7.2

Reading Hard Letter "g" and Soft Letter "g" Words

Directions: Read the target words in the word box. In the first column, write the words with the letter "g" that have the /g/ sound, as in the word <u>gum</u>. In the second column, write the words with the letter "g" that have the /j/ sound, as in the word <u>gem</u>.

Direksyons: Li mo objektif yo ki nan bwat mo a. Nan premye kolòn nan, ekri mo yo ki genyen lèt "g" ki bay son /g/ a, tankou li ye nan mo <u>gum</u> nan. Nan dezyèm kolòn nan, ekri mo yo ki genyen lèt "g" ki bay son/j/ a, tankou li ye nan mo <u>gem</u> nan.

Target Word Box				
page	gesture	good	gene	green
garden	gills	ginger	gift	gentle
cage	ago	orange	gypsy	grade
gulp	bag	large	figure	German

Hard letter "g" has the /g/ sound as in the word <u>gum</u>

- gills
- gulp
- ago
- bag
- good
- gift
- green
- grade
- figure
- garden

Soft letter "g" has the /j/ sound as in the word <u>gem</u>

- page
- cage
- gesture
- ginger
- large
- gene
- gypsy
- orange
- gentle
- German

Unit G
Review Lessons 7.1 & 7.2

Homework

Name: _____ Date:___/___/_____ Score:_____

Lesson 7.3

Reading Words with the "gr" Letter Combination

Dictionary Skills/ Vocabulary

✓ Lesson Check Point

Directions: Read each target word and its definition. Write the letter of the definition on the line of each target word. Use a dictionary or the Internet to check your answers.

Direksyons: Li chak mo objektif ak definisyon yo chak. Ekri lèt la ki koresponn ak definisyon an sou trè chak mo objektif yo. Itilize yon diksyonè oubyen entènèt pou tcheke repons ou yo.

Target Words	Definitions
1. _e_ grilled	a. the color of leaves and plant stems
2. _c_ gravity	b. characteristic of distinction and importance
3. _b_ great	c. force that keeps things grounded
4. _a_ green	d. kindness and politeness in a person's character
5. _d_ gracious	e. to have cooked food on parallel bars over a fire

Directions: Read each sentence. Underline the word in the parentheses that correctly completes each sentence. Then, write the underlined word on the line.

Direksyons: Li chak fraz. Soulinye mo a ki nan parantèz yo ki konplete chak fraz kòrèkteman. Answit, ekri mo soulinye a sou trè a.

6. The _____green_____ grass is growing. (grilled, green)

7. At the barbecue, my dad ___grilled___ the chicken. (great, grilled)

8. Gloria is always ___gracious___ and charming. (gracious, green)

9. The ___great___ citizens received service awards. (gravity, great)

10. Gravity___ stops things from floating upward. (Gracious, Gravity)

Homework

Name: _____ Date: ___/___/_____ Score: _____

Lesson 7.4

Reading Words with the "gl" Letter Combination

Dictionary Skills/ Vocabulary

✓ Lesson Check Point

Directions: Read each target word and its definition. Write the target word on the line in front of its meaning. Use a dictionary or the Internet to check your answers.
Direksyons: Li chak mo objektif ak definisyon yo chak. Ekri mo objektif la sou trè ki devan definisyon li an. Itilize yon diksyonè oubyen entènèt pou tcheke repons ou yo.

Target Word Box				
glamorous	glass	glasses	gloves	glows

1. <u>glamorous</u> having glamour
2. <u>gloves</u> protective coverings for hands
3. <u>glows</u> to reflect light through an object
4. <u>glass</u> a container used for drinking hot or cold beverages
5. <u>glasses</u> a pair of lenses fitted into a frame that a person wears to see

Directions: Read each sentence. Underline the word in the parentheses that correctly completes each sentence. Then, write the underlined word on the line.
Direksyons: Li chak fraz. Soulinye mo a ki nan parantèz yo ki konplete chak fraz kòrèkteman. Answit, ekri mo soulinye a sou trè a.

6. My doctor always wears latex ____<u>gloves</u>____. (glows, <u>gloves</u>)

7. The computer screen ____<u>glows</u>____ in the dark. (gloves, <u>glows</u>)

8. Greg wears ____<u>glasses</u>____ to see things at a distance. (<u>glasses</u>, glass)

9. Gloria likes to drink her coffee with a crystal ____<u>glass</u>____. (glows, <u>glass</u>)

10. The girls bought ____<u>glamorous</u>____ dresses for the concert. (<u>glamorous</u>, glasses)

Homework

 Name: _____ Date:___/___/_____ Score:_____

Lesson 7.4

Reading Words with the "gle" Letter Combination

✓ Lesson Check Point

Directions: Read each target word. Find the "gle" letter combination and put a check (✓) in the column that identifies its position: beginning, within or end.

Direksyons: Li chak mo objektif. Jwenn konbinezon lèt "gle" a epi mete yon tchèk (✓) nan kolòn nan ki idantifye pozisyon li an: nan kòmansman, ladan oubyen nan finisman.

Target Words	Beginning (First 3 Letters)	Within	End (Last 3 Letters)
1. ringlet		✓	
2. dangle			✓
3. bungle			✓
4. gleamed	✓		
5. Glenwood	✓		

Directions: Read each target word. Put a check (✓) in the "yes" column if the "gle" letter combination has the /g/ + /ə/ + /l/ sounds. Put a check (✓) in the "no" column if the "gle" letter combination does not have the /g/ + /ə/ + /l/ sounds.

Direksyons: Li chak mo objektif. Mete yon tchèk (✓) nan kolòn "yes" an si konbinezon let "gle" a bay sons /g/ + /ə/ + /l/. Mete yon tchèk (✓) nan kolòn "no" an si konbinezon let "gle" a pa bay sons /g/ + /ə/ + /l/.

Target Words	Yes	No
6. ringlet		✓
7. dangle	✓	
8. bungle	✓	
9. gleamed		✓
10. Glenwood		✓

Homework

Name: _____ Date:___/___/_____ Score:_____

Lesson 7.5

Reading Words with the "gh" Letter Combination

✓ Lesson Check Point

Directions: Read each target word. Circle the word in the column that has the same "gh" sound as the target word.

Direksyons: Li chak mo objektif. Antoure mo a ki nan kolòn nan ki bay menm son "gh" la tankou mo objektif la.

ghost	(a. ghastly)
	b. rough

weight	a. enough
	(b. thigh)

insight	a. laughing
	(b. weigh)

coughing	a. mighty
	(b. tougher)

Directions: Read each target word. Put a check (✓) under the correct column heading.

Direksyons: Li chak mo objektif. Mete yon tchèk (✓) anba antèt kolòn ki kòrèk la.

Target Words	"gh" has the /g/ sound as in the word <u>ghetto</u>	"gh" has the /f/ sound as in the word <u>laugh</u>	"gh" is silent as in the word <u>light</u>
1. ghost	✓		
2. weight			✓
3. insight			✓
4. coughing		✓	

Homework

 Name: _____ Date: ___/___/_____ Score: _____

Lesson 7.6

Reading Words with the "gn" Letter Combination

✓ **Lesson Check Point**

 Directions: Read each target word. Circle the word in the column that has the same "gn" sound(s) as the target word.

Direksyons: Li chak mo objektif. Antoure mo a ki nan kolòn nan ki bay menm son "gn" la (yo) tankou mo objektif la.

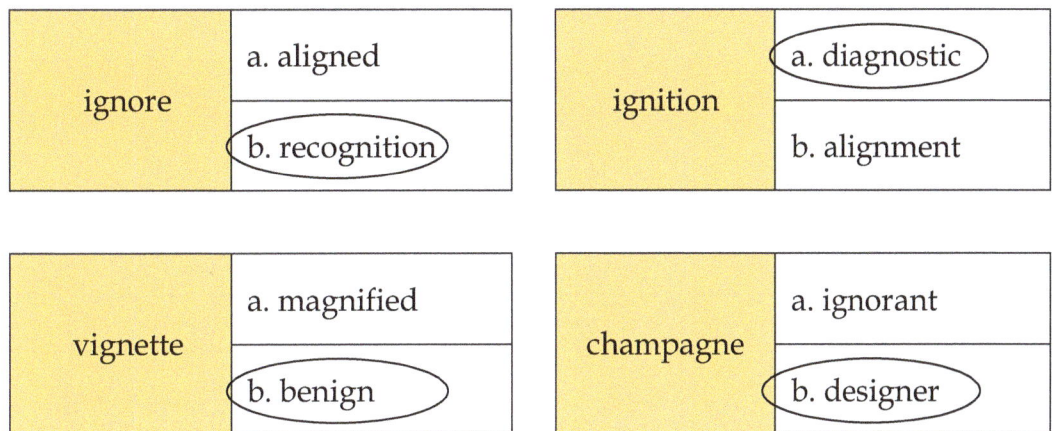

 Directions: Read each target word. Put a check (✓) under the correct column heading.

Direksyons: Li chak mo objektif. Mete yon tchèk (✓) anba antèt kolòn ki kòrèk la.

Target Words	"gn" has the /g/ + /n/ sounds as in the word <u>ignite</u>	"gn" has the silent "g" + /n/ sound as in the word <u>sign</u>
1. ignore	✓	
2. ignition	✓	
3. vignette		✓
4. champagne		✓

Homework

 Name: _____ Date: ___/___/_____ Score: _____

Lesson 7.7

Reading Words with a Silent Letter "g"

✓ Lesson Check Point

 Directions: Read the target words in the word box. Write the words that have a silent letter "g" in the first column. Write the words that do not have a silent letter "g" in the second column.

Direksyons: Li mo objektif yo ki nan ti bwat mo a. Ekri mo yo ki genyen lèt "g" ki pa pwononse a nan premye kolòn nan. Ekri mo yo ki pa genyen lèt "g" ki pa pwononse a nan dezyèm kolòn nan.

Target Word Box				
signal	ago	Ghana	goat	campaign
clog	thigh	bright	gloves	foreign
design	program	magic	sign	tight
bologna	good	goggle	smug	snuggle

Letter "g" is silent

- sign
- tight
- thigh
- bright
- design
- foreign
- goggle
- bologna
- snuggle
- campaign

Letter "g" has the /g/ or /j/ sound

- ago
- clog
- goat
- good
- smug
- gloves
- magic
- Ghana
- signal
- program

Homework

 Name: _____ Date: ___/___/_____ Score: _____

The Reading Challenge

Lesson 7.8

Reading Multisyllable Words

✓ **Lesson Check Point**

 Directions: Read and divide each target word into syllables. Write each word and place a hyphen (-) between the syllables in the second column. Write the number of syllables in the third column. Use a dictionary or the Internet to check your answers.

Direksyons: Li epi divize chak mo objektif an silab. Ekri chak mo epi mete yon tirè (-) ant silab yo nan dezyèm kolòn nan. Ekri kantite silab ke yo genyen an nan twazyèm kolòn nan. Itilize yon diksyonè oubyen entènèt pou tcheke repons ou yo.

Target Words	Words Divided into Syllables	Number of Syllables
1. goalkeeper	goal-keep-er	3
2. government	gov-ern-ment	3
3. gasoline	gas-o-line	3
4. guarantee	guar-an-tee	3
5. gelatin	gel-a-tin	3
6. glorified	glo-ri-fied	3
7. gathering	gath-er-ing	3
8. Grenada	Gre-na-da	3
9. generalize	gen-er-al-ize	4
10. glamorous	glam-or-ous	3

Homework

 Name: _____ Date:___/___/_____ Score:_____

The Reading Challenge

Lesson 7.8

Reading Multisyllable Words

✓ **Lesson Check Point**

 Directions: Read each target word. Circle the word in the row that is divided correctly into syllables. Use a dictionary or the Internet to check your answers.

Direksyons: Li chak mo objektif. Antoure mo a ki nan ranje a ki divize an silab korèkteman yo. Itilize yon diksyonè oubyen entènèt pou tcheke repons ou yo.

Model

galaxy	a. ga-lax-y	b. gal-ax-y ⭕	c. gal-a-xy

1. generate	a. ge-ner-ate	b. gen-er-ate ⭕	c. gen-era-te

2. gigabyte	a. gig-a-byte ⭕	b. gi-ga-byte	c. gig-aby-te

3. gardenia	a. ga-rde-nia	b. gar-de-nia ⭕	c. gar-den-ia

4. gondola	a. go-ndo-la	b. go-ndol-a	c. gon-do-la ⭕

5. generous	a. gen-er-ous ⭕	b. ge-ner-ous	c. gen-ero-us

6. gradual	a. grad-u-al ⭕	b. gra-du-al	c. grad-ua-l

7. gasoline	a. gas-o-line ⭕	b. ga-soline	c. gas-oli-ne

8. gestation	a. gest-a-tion	b. ge-stat-ion	c. ges-ta-tion ⭕

Homework

Name: _____ Date: ___/___/_____ Score: _____

Lesson 7.9

Reading and Writing

Proper and Common Nouns and Adjectives

Directions: Read the words in the word box. Put an (X) on the line next to each word that is written incorrectly. Remember that all proper nouns and proper adjectives are capitalized. Use a dictionary or the Internet to check your answers.

Direksyons: Li chak mo yo ki nan bwat mo a. Met yon (X) sou ti trè a ki bò kote mo ki pa kri byen yo. Sonje ke tout non pwòp ak adjektif pwop ekri avèk yon lèt majiskil nan kòmansman yo. Itilize yon diksyonè oubyen entènèt pou tcheke repons ou yo.

Word Box					
__	Guyana	__	Greek	X	guam
X	georgia	X	Glacier	__	great
X	Gesture	__	guardian	X	Guitar
__	Grandfather	X	Gentleman	__	Germany

Directions: Read each unedited sentence and underline the word that is written incorrectly. Write each sentence correctly on the line.

Direksyons: Li chak fraz ki pa edite yo epi soulinye mo ki pa ekri byen an. Ekri chak fraz korèkteman sou liy lan.

Model
Ginger and <u>gene</u> are going to Georgetown, Guyana.
<u>Ginger and Gene are going to Georgetown, Guyana.</u>

1. The <u>Gorgeous</u> gymnast is from Gibraltar.
<u>The gorgeous gymnast is from Gibraltar.</u>

2. On Friday, <u>gina</u> was gossiping about Gene.
<u>On Friday, Gina was gossiping about Gene.</u>

3. Ginger bought a glamorous <u>Gold</u> ring from Guatemala.
<u>Ginger bought a glamorous gold ring from Guatemala.</u>

4. I saw a gracious gazelle at the famous Golden <u>gate</u> Zoo.
<u>I saw a gracious gazelle at the famous Golden Gate Zoo.</u>

Homework

Name: _____ Date:___/___/_____ Score:_____

Lesson 8.1

Reading Words with the Letter H/h

✓ **Lesson Check Point**

Directions: Read each target word. Find the letter "h" and put a check (✓) in the column that identifies its position: beginning, within or end.
Direksyons: Li chak mo objektif. Jwenn lèt "h" a epi mete yon tchèck (✓) nan kolòn ki idantifye pozisyon li an: nan kòmansman, ladan oubyen nan finisman.

Target Words	Beginning (First Letter)	Within	End (Last Letter)
1. Utah			✓
2. teach			✓
3. horse	✓		
4. helper	✓		
5. Fahrenheit		✓	

Directions: Read each sentence and underline the words that begin with the letter "h." Write all the underlined words in alphabetical order on the lines below.
Direksyons: Li chak fraz epi soulinye mo ki kòmanse avèk lèt "h" yo. Ekri tout mo ki soulinye yo nan lòd alfabetik sou trè sa yo ki anba.

6. Pat's <u>high</u> chair is very <u>heavy</u>.

7. <u>Henry</u> broke Samantha's <u>heart</u>.

8. Ashley is <u>holding</u> a very big <u>hammer</u>.

9. Brenda puts green <u>herbs</u> in the <u>hummus</u>.

10. The <u>hacker</u> accessed <u>Harry's</u> email account.

hacker	hammer	Harry's
heart	heavy	Henry
herbs	high	holding
	hummus	

Learn To Read English With Directions In Spanish

Homework

 Name: _____ Date: ___/___/_____ Score: _____

Lesson 8.2

Reading Words with the Letter "h" Combinations:
"sh," "wh," "ch," "th," "rh," "ph" and "gh"

✓ Lesson Check Point

 Directions: Read the target words in the word box. Identify the words with the following letter combinations: "sh," "wh," "ch," "th," "rh," "ph" and "gh." Write the word on the line that shows the position of the letter combination: beginning, within or end.

Direksyons: Li mo objektif yo ki nan ti bwat mo a. Idantifye mo yo ki genyen konbinezon lèt sa yo: "sh," "wh," "ch," "th," "rh," "ph" ak "gh". Ekri mo a sou liy ki montre pozisyon konbinezon lèt la: kòmansman, ladan oubyen finisman.

Target Word Box				
white	myrrh	phonics	echo	laughed
birthday	shake	letterhead	triumph	rich
rhetoric	chorus	theme	north	tough
flywheel	finish	telephone	ghetto	wishes

	Beginning	Within	End
sh	1. shake	2. wishes	3. finish
wh	4. white	5. flywheel	
ch	6. chorus	7. echo	8. rich
th	9. theme	10. birthday	11. north
rh	12. rhetoric	13. letterhead	14. myrrh
ph	15. phonics	16. telephone	17. triumph
gh	18. ghetto	19. laughed	20. tough

Homework

L. Name: _____ Date: ___/___/_____ Score: _____

Lesson 8.2

Reading Words with the Letter "h" Combinations: "sh," "wh," "ch," "th," "rh," "ph," "gh" and "sch"

✓ **Lesson Check Point**

Directions: Read the target words in the word box. Identify the words with the following letter combinations: "sh," "wh," "ch," "th," "rh," "ph," "gh" and "sch." Write the target word that correctly completes each sentence on the line.

Direksyons: Li mo objektif yo ki nan ti bwat mo a. Idantifye mo yo ki genyen konbinezon lèt sa yo: "sh," "wh," "ch," "th," "rh," "ph," "gh"ak "sch". Ekri mo objektif la ki konplete chak fraz korèkteman sou liy lan.

Target Word Box		
shower	Ghana	Children
Whales	theater	through
phones		Chemicals
school		rhombus

1. My family and I saw a big ___elephant___ at the circus.

2. My science ___teacher___ wrote three facts on the board.

3. Sharon wore her new ___white___ shoes to school.

4. My parents bought me three notebooks for ___school___.

5. The diamond-shaped figure is called a ___rhombus___.

6. The cruise ___ship___ sailed from New York to Florida.

7. Everyone ___laughed___ at Grandma's funny jokes.

8. The children walked ___through___ the rain without umbrellas.

9. Alexandria is unable to sync her ___phone___ to the computer.

10. The bakers baked ___shortbread___ cookies with three ingredients.

Name: _____ Date: ___/___/_____ Score: _____

Homework

Lesson 8.3

Reading Words with a Silent Letter "h"

✓ **Lesson Check Point**

Directions: Read the target words in the word box. Write the words that have a silent letter "h" in the first column. Write the words that do not have a silent letter "h" in the second column.

Direksyons: Li mo objektif yo ki nan ti bwat mo a. Ekri mo yo ki genyen lèt "h" ki pa pwononse a nan premye kolòn nan. Ekri mo yo ki pa genyen lèt "h" ki pa pwononse a nan dezyèm kolòn nan.

Target Word Box				
manhood	behind	honest	prohibit	ought
overhaul	whisk	honorarium	inherit	helpful
bought	right	spaghetti	houses	manhole
shorthand	heirs	rehearse	exhume	rhyme

Letter "h" is silent

- heirs
- right
- ought
- whisk
- honest
- rhyme
- bought
- exhume
- spaghetti
- honorarium

Letter "h" has the /h/ sound

- helpful
- behind
- houses
- inherit
- prohibit
- overhaul
- rehearse
- manhole
- manhood
- shorthand

Homework

 Name: _____ Date: ___/___/_____ Score: _____

The Reading Challenge

Lesson 8.4

Reading Multisyllable Words

✓ Lesson Check Point

 Directions: Read and divide each target word into syllables. Write each word and place a hyphen (-) between the syllables in the second column. Write the number of syllables in the third column. Use a dictionary or the Internet to check your answers.

Direksyons: Li epi divize chak mo objektif an silab. Ekri chak mo epi mete yon tirè (-) ant silab yo nan dezyèm kolòn nan. Ekri kantite silab ke yo genyen an nan twazyèm kolòn nan. Itilize yon diksyonè oubyen entènèt pou tcheke repons ou yo.

Target Words	Words Divided into Syllables	Number of Syllables
1. hibernate	hi-ber-nate	3
2. hallway	hall-way	2
3. helicopter	hel-i-cop-ter	4
4. holdover	hold-o-ver	3
5. headstrong	head-strong	2
6. hazardous	haz-ard-ous	3
7. historic	his-tor-ic	3
8. humorous	hu-mor-ous	3
9. heartbroken	heart-bro-ken	3
10. homework	home-work	2

Homework

 Name: _____ Date: ___/___/_____ Score: _____

The Reading Challenge

Lesson 8.4

Reading Multisyllable Words

✓ **Lesson Check Point**

 Directions: Read each target word. Circle the word in the row that is divided correctly into syllables. Use a dictionary or the Internet to check your answers.

Direksyons: Li chak mo objektif. Antoure mo a ki nan ranje a ki divize an silab korèkteman yo. Itilize yon diksyonè oubyen entènèt pou tcheke repons ou yo.

Model

heroic	a. he-roi-c	b. her-o-ic	c. he-ro-ic ⭕
1. histogram	a. his-to-gram ⭕	b. hi-sto-gram	c. his-tog-ram
2. hab-i-tat	a. ha-bi-tat	b. ha-bit-at	c. hab-i-tat ⭕
3. hospital	a. hos-pi-tal ⭕	b. hos-pit-al	c. ho-spi-tal
4. hamburger	a. ham-burg-er ⭕	b. hamb-urg-er	c. hamb-ur-ger
5. habitual	a. hab-it-ual	b. hab-i-tual	c. ha-bit-u-al ⭕
6. handicap	a. hand-i-cap ⭕	b. han-di-cap	c. hand-ic-ap
7. holiday	a. hol-i-day ⭕	b. ho-lid-ay	c. ho-li-day
8. humorous	a. hum-or-ous	b. hum-o-rous	c. hu-mor-ous ⭕

Learn To Read English With Directions In Haitian Creole

Homework

Name: _____ Date:___/___/_____ Score:_____

Lesson 8.5

Reading and Writing

Proper and Common Nouns and Adjectives

Directions: Read the words in the word box. Put an (X) on the line next to each word that is written incorrectly. Remember that all proper nouns and proper adjectives are capitalized. Use a dictionary or the Internet to check your answers.

Direksyons: Li chak mo yo ki nan bwat mo a. Met yon (X) sou ti trè a ki bò kote mo ki pa kri byen yo. Sonje ke tout non pwòp ak adjektif pwop ekri avèk yon lèt majiskil nan kòmansman yo. Itilize yon diksyonè oubyen entènèt pou tcheke repons ou yo.

Word Box					
__	Haiti	__	hawk	X	Hotel
X	Horizon	X	House	__	herself
__	Heather	X	holland	__	horses
X	hinduism	__	Hannah	X	honduras

Directions: Read each unedited sentence and underline the word that is written incorrectly. Write each sentence correctly on the line.

Direksyons: Li chak fraz ki pa edite yo epi soulinye mo ki pa ekri byen an. Ekri chak fraz korèkteman sou liy lan.

Model
Mr. Hitt has a big house on <u>hope</u> Avenue.
<u>Mr. Hitt has a big house on Hope Avenue.</u>

1. Hadia and Henry are standing in the <u>Hallway</u>.
<u>Hadia and Henry are standing in the hallway.</u>

2. The best <u>Hamburgers</u> are sold at Harpo's Diner.
<u>The best hamburgers are sold at Harpo's Diner.</u>

3. Hollywood is producing a movie entitled, "The <u>house</u> of Hearts."
<u>Hollywood is producing a movie entitled, "The House of Hearts."</u>

4. The <u>Hacker</u> broke into Hartford Hospital's computer database.
<u>The hacker broke into Hartford Hospital's computer database.</u>

Homework

 Name: _____ Date: ___/___/_____ Score: _____

Lesson 9.1

Reading Words with the Letter I/i

✓ Lesson Check Point

 Directions: Read each target word. Find the letter "i" and put a check (✓) in the column that identifies its position: beginning, within or end.
Direksyons: Li chak mo objektif. Jwenn lèt "i" a epi mete yon tchèck (✓) nan kolòn ki idantifye pozisyon li an: nan kòmansman, ladan oubyen nan finisman.

Target Words	Beginning (First Letter)	Within	End (Last Letter)
1. blink		✓	
2. octopi			✓
3. certify		✓	
4. iceberg	✓		
5. alumni			✓

 Directions: Read each target word. Read the words in the row and circle the word that has a different vowel "i" sound.
Direksyons: Li chak mo objektif. Li mo yo ki nan ranje a epi antoure mo a ki bay yon son vwayèl "i" ki diferan an.

Target Words				
6. pink	fib	did	him	(like)
7. ring	(bride)	kid	bit	fig
8. gift	jig	blip	(drive)	hint
9. fish	flit	(lime)	brim	hid
10. pick	(cite)	kit	fill	silk

Homework

 Name: _____ Date:___/___/_____ Score: _____

Lesson 9.2

Reading Words with the Short Vowel "i" Sound

✓ **Lesson Check Point**

 Directions: Read the words in the four boxes. Circle two words with the short vowel /ĭ/ sound. The anchor word for the short vowel /ĭ/ sound is <u>insect</u>.

Direksyons: Li mo yo ki nan kat ti bwat yo. Antoure de mo ki genyen son vwayèl kout /ĭ/ a. Mo referans pou son vwayel kout /ĭ/ a se mo, <u>insect</u>.

| ripe | (did) | (wish) | (link) | (click) | vice |
| lid | five | fine | dime | wipe | (bring) |

| wide | size | (dish) | (wing) | (sing) | dive |
| (stick) | (flint) | miles | wild | dine | (limp) |

 Directions: Read the words in the four boxes. Circle two words that rhyme. Rhyming words have the same ending sound, such as <u>hip</u> and <u>dip</u>.

Direksyons: Li mo yo ki nan kat ti bwat yo. Antoure de mo ki rime. De mo oubyen plizyè mo ki rime genyen menm son nan finisman yo, tankou <u>hip</u> ak <u>dip</u>.

| (trim) | fire | hive | (grip) | tire | pipe |
| tide | (brim) | tile | (trip) | (skip) | (ship) |

| (flip) | (snip) | (swim) | dice | file | (gift) |
| wire | pile | (skim) | ride | (lift) | hire |

Unit I Lesson 9.2

Homework

⌶ Name: _____ Date: ___/___/_____ Score: _____

Lesson 9.2

Reading & Writing Words with the Short Vowel "i" Sound

✓ **Lesson Check Point**

Directions: Read each sentence and underline three words with the short vowel /ĭ/ sound. Then, write the underlined words on the lines below. The anchor word for the short vowel /ĭ/ sound is <u>insect</u>.

Direksyons: Li chak fraz epi soulinye twa mo ki genyen son vwayèl kout /ĭ/ a. Answit, ekri mo soulinye yo sou trè sa yo ki anba. Mo referans pou son vwayèl kout /ĭ/ a se mo, <u>insect</u>.

Model

<u>Jim</u> placed a <u>big</u> cup of ice on the <u>windowsill</u>.

      Jim   big   windowsill
   _____   _____   _____

1. <u>Gil's</u> white shirt <u>did</u> not <u>fit</u>.

      Gil's   did   fit

2. Isaac <u>drinks</u> white <u>skim</u> <u>milk</u>.

    drinks   skim   milk

3. <u>Jim</u> likes to <u>sit</u> on top of the <u>hill</u>.

     Jim   sit   hill

4. <u>Will</u> you <u>miss</u> the five <u>kids</u> from Iceland?

     Will   miss   kids

5. My friends, Irene and <u>Tim</u>, ate <u>six</u> tortilla <u>chips</u>.

     Tim   six   chips

Learn To Read English With Directions In Haitian Creole

Homework

 Name: _____ Date: ___/___/_____ Score: _____

Lesson 9.3

Reading Words with the Long Vowel "i" Sound

✓ Lesson Check Point

 Directions: Read the words in the four boxes. Circle two words with the long vowel /ī/ sound. The anchor word for the long vowel /ī/ sound is <u>ice</u>.

Direksyons: Li mo yo ki nan kat ti bwat yo. Antoure de mo ki genyen son vwayèl long /ī/ a. Mo referans pou son vwayel long /ī/ a se mo, <u>ice</u>.

(tile)	wing		cling	(dine)		trick	milk
(side)	grill		chain	(cite)		(hide)	(lime)

(rite)	(lice)		(price)	click		(hive)	(item)
main	brick		disk	(pile)		sink	Spain

 Directions: Read the words in the four boxes. Circle two words that rhyme. Rhyming words have the same ending sound, such as <u>rice</u> and <u>nice</u>.

Direksyons: Li mo yo ki nan kat ti bwat yo. Antoure de mo ki rime. De mo oubyen plizyè mo ki rime genyen menm son nan finisman yo, tankou <u>rice</u> ak <u>nice</u>.

(file)	stick		(wide)	lint		mist	rink
clip	(mile)		(side)	mill		(mice)	(dice)

trip	(tile)		(nice)	wish		limb	skip
(pile)	king		ski	(vice)		(pipe)	(ripe)

Homework

Name: _____ Date:___/___/_____ Score:_____

Lesson 9.3

Reading & Writing Words with the Long Vowel "i" Sound

✓ Lesson Check Point

Directions: Read each sentence and underline three words with the long vowel /ī/ sound. Then, write the underlined words on the lines below. The anchor word for the long vowel /ī/ sound is ice.

Direksyons: Li chak fraz epi soulinye twa mo ki genyen son vwayèl long /ī/ a. Answit, ekri mo soulinye yo sou trè sa yo ki anba. Mo referans pou son vwayèl long /ī/ a se mo, ice.

Model

David and I flew our big, white kite along the riverbank.

I	white	kite

1. The child likes to hide in the old mill.

child	likes	hide

2. At night, Jim drives his car for miles.

night	drives	miles

3. He will win a prize for the ninth time.

prize	ninth	time

4. At five o'clock, the bride simply smiled at William.

five	bride	smiled

5. His wife admires the six firefighters for their bravery.

wife	admires	firefighters

Learn To Read English With Directions In Haitian Creole

Homework

Name: _____ Date: ___/___/_____ Score: _____

Review Lessons 9.2 & 9.3

Reading Short Vowel and Long Vowel Words

Directions: Read the target words in the word box. In the first column, write the words that have the short vowel /ĭ/ sound, as in the word <u>insect</u>. In the second column, write the words that have the long vowel /ī/ sound, as in the word <u>ice</u>.

Direksyons: Li mo objektif yo ki nan bwat mo a. Nan premye kolòn nan, ekri mo ki bay son vwayèl kout /ĭ/ yo, tankou li ye nan mo <u>insect</u> la. Nan dezyèm kolòn nan, ekri mo ki bay son vwayèl long /ī/ yo, tankou li ye nan mo <u>ice</u> la.

Target Word Box				
lion	blimp	hike	mild	lie
dill	tiger	bring	tried	fine
fish	miss	king	fried	ring
dice	fiber	cinch	spring	click

Letter "i" has the /ĭ/ sound as in the word <u>insect</u>

- dill
- fish
- blimp
- miss
- bring
- king
- cinch
- spring
- ring
- click

Letter "i" has the /ī/ sound as in the word <u>ice</u>

- lion
- dice
- tiger
- fiber
- hike
- mild
- tried
- fried
- lie
- fine

Homework

 Name: _____ Date: ___/___/_____ Score: _____

Lesson 9.4

Reading Words with Letter "i" Vowel Pairs

✓ Lesson Check Point

   Directions: Read each target word. Circle the word in the column that has the same vowel "ia," "ie," "io" or "iu" sound(s) as the target word.
Direksyons: Li chak mo objektif. Antoure mo a ki nan kolòn nan ki bay menm son "ia," "ie," "io" oubyen "iu" la (yo) tankou mo objektif la.

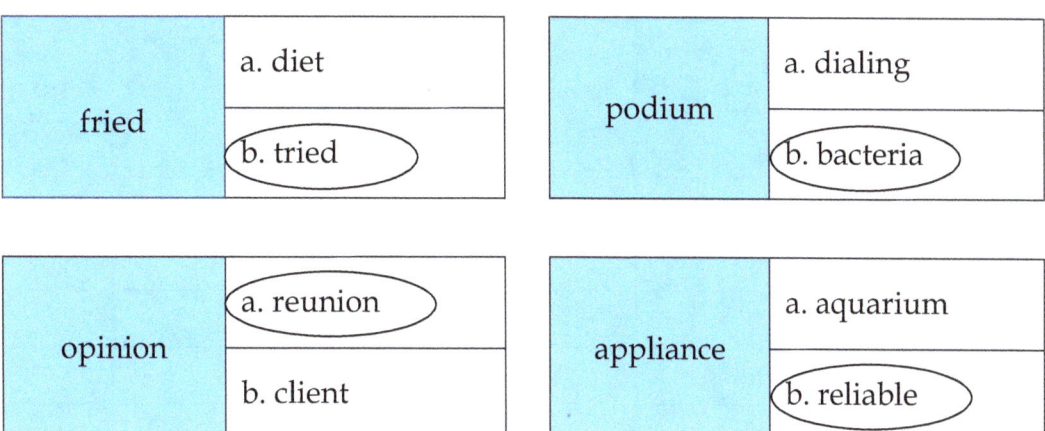

   Directions: Read each target word. Put a check (✓) under the correct column heading.
Direksyons: Li chak mo objektif. Mete yon tchèk (✓) anba antèt kolòn ki kòrèk la.

Target Words	Words have the long "i" sound as in the word <u>dial</u>	Words do not have the long "i" sound
1. fried	✓	
2. podium		✓
3. opinion		✓
4. appliance	✓	

Learn To Read English With Directions In Haitian Creole

Homework

 Name: _____ Date: ___/___/_____ Score: _____

Lesson 9.5

Reading Words with the Final Letter "i"

✓ Lesson Check Point

 Directions: Read each target word. Find the letter "i" and put a check (✓) in the column that identifies its position within the syllable.

Direksyons: Li chak mo objektif. Jwenn lèt "i" a epi mete yon tchèck (✓) nan kolòn nan ki idantifye pozisyon li an nan silab la.

Target Words	"i" is at the end of a one syllable word	"i" is at the end of the first syllable	"i" is at the end of a multi-syllable word
1. I	✓		
2. hi	✓		
3. alibi			✓
4. dinette		✓	
5. bifocal		✓	

 Directions: Read each target word. Put a check (✓) under the correct column heading.

Direksyons: Li chak mo objektif. Mete yon tchèk (✓) anba antèt kolòn ki kòrèk la.

Target Words	"i" has the /ĭ/ sound as in the word insect	"i" has the /ī/ sound as in the word bike	"i" has the /ə/ sound as in the word pencil	"i" is silent as in the word maid
6. raised				✓
7. fashion			✓	
8. lipstick	✓			
9. tiger		✓		
10. uniform			✓	

Homework

 Name: _____ Date: ___/___/_____ Score: _____

Lesson 9.6

Reading Letter "i" Words with the Schwa Vowel Sound

✓ **Lesson Check Point**

 Directions: Read each target word. Circle the word in the column that has the same "i" sound as the target word.
Direksyons: Li chak mo objektif. Antoure mo a ki nan kolòn nan ki bay menm son "i" a tankou mo objektif la.

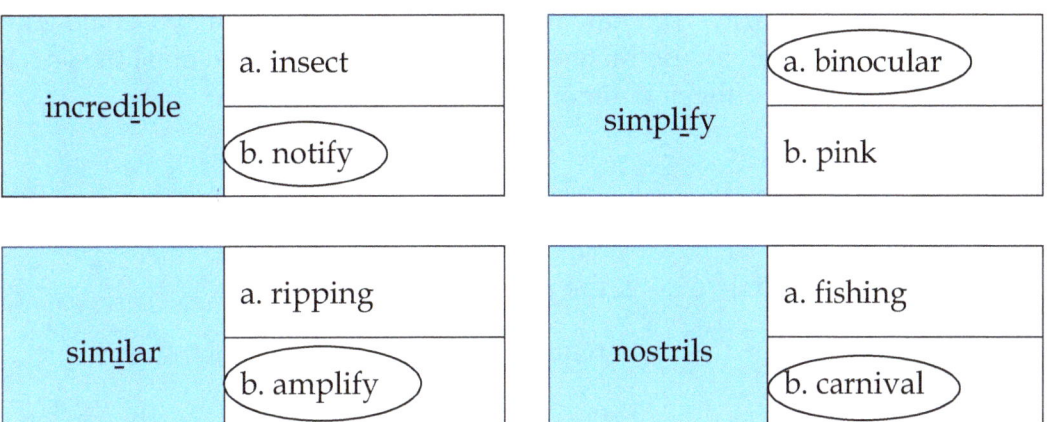

 Directions: Read each sentence and underline the letter "i" word that has the schwa vowel /ə/ sound. The anchor word for the letter "i" schwa vowel sound is <u>pencil</u>.
Direksyons: Li chak fraz epi soulinye mo ki genyen lèt "i" a ki bay son schwa /ə/ a. Mo referans pou son schwa lèt "i" a se mo, <u>pencil</u>.

1. The <u>animals</u> in the zoo are excited.

2. Those five children are simply <u>beautiful</u>.

3. The <u>principal</u> approved the school's signs.

4. Irene and her <u>family</u> like to ski in Iceland.

5. The filing <u>cabinets</u> have important documents.

6. Every student is required to wear the school <u>uniform</u>.

Homework

Name: _____ Date: ___/___/_____ Score: _____

Lesson 9.7

Reading Words with the "ir" Letter Combination

Dictionary Skills/ Vocabulary

✓ **Lesson Check Point**

Directions: Read each target word and its definition. Write the letter of the definition on the line of each target word. Use a dictionary or the Internet to check your answers.

Direksyons: Li chak mo objektif ak definisyon yo chak. Ekri lèt la ki koresponn ak definisyon an sou trè chak mo objektif yo. Itilize yon diksyonè oubyen entènèt pou tcheke repons ou yo.

Target Words	Definitions
1. _b_ thirst	a. the position before the second
2. _e_ squirt	b. having a desire to drink something
3. _c_ dirt	c. the upper, brown layer of the earth; garden soil
4. _a_ first	d. the use of circular motions to mix or blend something
5. _d_ stirred	e. to squeeze liquid out of something

Directions: Read each sentence and write the target word that completes the sentence.

Direksyons: Li chak fraz epi ekri mo objektif ki konplete fraz la kòrèkteman.

6. We planted the seeds deep into the __dirt__.

7. Bertha admires her __first__ grade teacher.

8. Iris __stirred__ low-fat milk into her Spanish coffee.

9. I drank a cold glass of water to quench my __thirst__.

10. She will __squirt__ chocolate syrup on her ice cream.

Name: _____ Date: ___/___/_____ Score: _____

Homework

Lesson 9.8

Reading Letter "i" Words with the Long Vowel "e" Sound

✓ **Lesson Check Point**

 Directions: Read each target word. Circle the word in the column that has the same "i" sound as the target word.

Direksyons: Li chak mo objektif. Antoure mo a ki nan kolòn nan ki bay menm son lèt "i" a tankou mo objektif la.

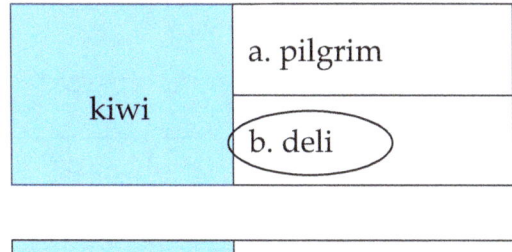
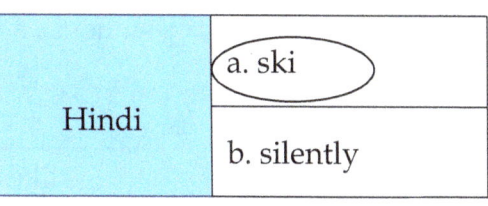
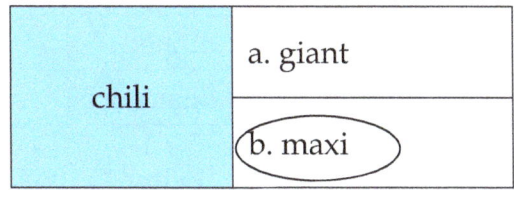
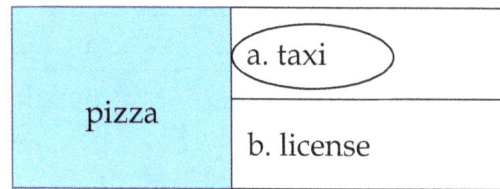

 Directions: Read each sentence and underline the letter "i" word that has the long vowel /ē/ sound. Then, write the word on the line. The anchor word, taxi has a letter "i" that represents the long vowel /ē/ sound.

Direksyons: Li chak fraz epi soulinye mo ki gen lèt "i" a ki bay son vwayèl long /ē/ a. Answit, ekri mo a sou trè a. Mo referans, taxi gen yon lèt "i" ladan li ki bay son vwayèl long /ē/.

1. I plan to ride in a yellow <u>taxicab</u>. ____taxicab____

2. Nick and Jim will join the <u>Marine</u> Corps. ____Marine____

3. In the winter, the Rivers family likes to <u>ski</u>. _____ski_____

4. The African <u>safari</u> ride costs sixty-six dollars. _____safari_____

5. Isaac and Allison ate <u>pepperoni</u> rolls for dinner. ___pepperoni___

6. The chef sprinkled <u>paprika</u> on her stuffed eggs. ____paprika____

Homework

 Name: _____ Date:___/___/_____ Score:_____

Lesson 9.9

Reading Words with a Silent Letter "i"

✓ **Lesson Check Point**

 Directions: Read the target words in the word box. Write the words that have a silent letter "i" in the first column. Write the words that do not have a silent letter "i" in the second column.

Direksyons: Li mo objektif yo ki nan ti bwat mo a. Ekri mo yo ki genyen lèt "i" ki pa pwononse a nan premye kolòn nan. Ekri mo yo ki pa genyen lèt "i" ki pa pwononse a nan dezyèm kolòn nan.

Target Word Box				
vain	likes	pipe	civil	waist
insects	suits	lines	rails	cruise
inside	instant	tails	dinner	obtained
finding	detailed	gripping	Jamaican	attained

Letter "i" is silent

- vain
- tails
- rails
- suits
- waist
- cruise
- attained
- detailed
- obtained
- Jamaican

Letter "i" has a letter /i/ sound

- pipe
- likes
- lines
- civil
- insects
- inside
- dinner
- finding
- instant
- gripping

Homework

 Name: _____ Date: ___/___/_____ Score: _____

Unit Review - I/i

Reading Words with Vowel "i" Sounds: /ĭ/, /ī/, /ə/ & Silent

✓ Lesson Check Point

 Directions: Read each target word. Circle the word in the column that has the same "i" sound as the target word.

Direksyons: Li chak mo objektif. Antoure mo a ki nan kolòn nan ki bay menm son "i" a tankou mo objektif la.

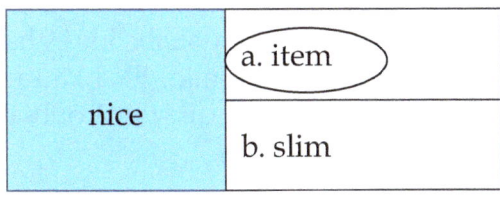
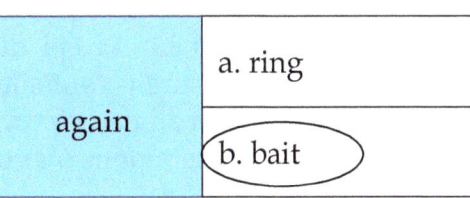
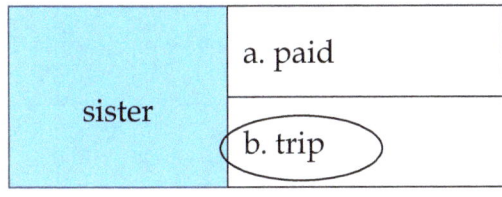
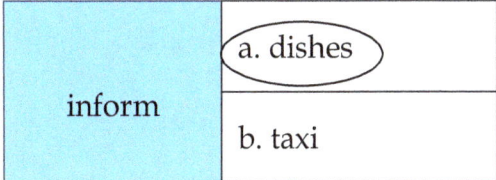

 Directions: Read each target word. Put a check (✓) under the correct column heading.

Direksyons: Li chak mo objektif. Mete yon tchèk (✓) anba antèt kolòn ki kòrèk la.

Target Words	"i" has the /ĭ/ sound as in the word <u>insect</u>	"i" has the /ī/ sound as in the word <u>bike</u>	"i" has the /ə/ sound as in the word <u>pencil</u>	"i" is silent as in the word <u>maid</u>
1. nice		✓		
2. again				✓
3. sister	✓			
4. inform	✓			

Homework

 Name: _____ Date: ___/___/_____ Score: _____

The Reading Challenge

Lesson 9.10

Reading Multisyllable Words

✓ Lesson Check Point

 Directions: Read and divide each target word into syllables. Write each word and place a hyphen (-) between the syllables in the second column. Write the number of syllables in the third column. Use a dictionary or the Internet to check your answers.

Direksyons: Li epi divize chak mo objektif an silab. Ekri chak mo epi mete yon tirè (-) ant silab yo nan dezyèm kolòn nan. Ekri kantite silab ke yo genyen an nan twazyèm kolòn nan. Itilize yon diksyonè oubyen entènèt pou tcheke repons ou yo.

Target Words	Words Divided into Syllables	Number of Syllables
1. tiger	ti-ger	2
2. silently	si-lent-ly	3
3. outsider	out-sid-er	3
4. relief	re-lief	2
5. national	na-tion-al	3
6. wishing	wish-ing	2
7. compiling	com-pil-ing	3
8. regional	re-gion-al	3
9. visionary	vi-sion-a-ry	4
10. graciously	gra-cious-ly	3

Homework

 Name: _____ Date: ___/___/_____ Score: _____

The Reading Challenge

Lesson 9.10

Reading Multisyllable Words

✓ Lesson Check Point

 Directions: Read each target word. Circle the word in the row that is divided correctly into syllables. Use a dictionary or the Internet to check your answers.

Direksyons: Li chak mo objektif. Antoure mo a ki nan ranje a ki divize an silab korèkteman yo. Itilize yon diksyonè oubyen entènèt pou tcheke repons ou yo.

Model

| interesting | a. in-ter-est-ing (circled) | b. int-er-est-ing | c. inte-rest-ing |

1. scientific	a. sci-en-tif-ic (circled)	b. scien-ti-fic	c. sci-en-ti-fic
2. uniform	a. un-i-form	b. u-ni-form (circled)	c. u-nif-orm
3. ingredient	a. in-gre-di-ent (circled)	b. in-gre-dient	c. ing-red-i-ent
4. nutrient	a. nu-tri-ent (circled)	b. nut-ri-ent	c. nut-rie-nt
5. impatient	a. im-pat-ient	b. im-pa-tient (circled)	c. i-mpa-tient
6. tastier	a. tas-ti-er	b. ta-sti-er	c. tast-i-er (circled)
7. position	a. po-si-tion (circled)	b. pos-it-ion	c. pos-i-tion
8. mediate	a. me-di-ate (circled)	b. med-i-ate	c. med-iat-e

Learn To Read English With Directions In Haitian Creole

Homework

Name: _____ Date: ___/___/_____ Score: _____

Lesson 9.11

Reading and Writing

Proper and Common Nouns and Adjectives

Directions: Read the words in the word box. Put an (X) on the line next to each word that is written incorrectly. Remember that all proper nouns and proper adjectives are capitalized. Use a dictionary or the Internet to check your answers.

Direksyons: Li chak mo yo ki nan bwat mo a. Met yon (X) sou ti trè a ki bò kote mo ki pa kri byen yo. Sonje ke tout non pwòp ak adjektif pwop ekri avèk yon lèt majiskil nan kòmansman yo. Itilize yon diksyonè oubyen entènèt pou tcheke repons ou yo.

Word Box					
X	inca	__	India	__	identify
__	Italy	__	index	X	Industry
X	ireland	__	irrigate	X	Ice cream
__	impressive	X	iberian	X	Illusionist

Directions: Read each unedited sentence and underline the word that is written incorrectly. Write each sentence correctly on the line.

Direksyons: Li chak fraz ki pa edite yo epi soulinye mo ki pa ekri byen an. Ekri chak fraz korèkteman sou liy lan.

Model
New Delhi and Indore are beautiful cities in <u>india</u>.
<u>New Delhi and Indore are beautiful cities in India.</u>

1. My friend, Indira, attends Intel <u>institute</u>.
<u>My friend, Indira, attends Intel Institute.</u>

2. The Itla family has an interesting <u>indian</u> heritage.
<u>The Itla family has an interesting Indian heritage.</u>

3. One day, Irwin will <u>Investigate</u> cases in Italy and Indonesia.
<u>One day, Irwin will investigate cases in Italy and Indonesia.</u>

4. Irene wrote a report about the <u>ivory</u> Coast for International Day.
<u>Irene wrote a report about the Ivory Coast for International Day.</u>

Name: _____ Date: ___/___/_____ Score: _____

Homework

Lesson 10.1

Reading Words with the Letter J/j

✓ **Lesson Check Point**

Directions: Read each target word. Find the letter "j" and put a check (✓) in the column that identifies its position: beginning, within or end.

Direksyons: Li chak mo objektif. Jwenn lèt "j" a epi mete yon tchèck (✓) nan kolòn ki idantifye pozisyon li an: nan kòmansman, ladan oubyen nan finisman.

Target Words	Beginning (First Letter)	Within	End (Last Letter)
1. jump	✓		
2. jewel	✓		
3. adjust		✓	
4. rejoice		✓	
5. rejuvenate		✓	

Directions: Read each sentence and underline the words that begin with the letter "j." Write all the underlined words in alphabetical order on the lines below.

Direksyons: Li chak fraz epi soulinye mo ki kòmanse avèk lèt "j" yo. Ekri tout mo ki soulinye yo nan lòd alfabetik sou trè sa yo ki anba.

6. Bob <u>joined</u> the <u>jazz</u> band.

7. <u>Jimmy</u> enjoys eating <u>jellybeans</u>.

8. Mr. Adams has a new <u>job</u> as a <u>janitor</u>.

9. Everyone is <u>joyous</u> at the country <u>jamboree</u>.

10. Gianna's denim <u>jacket</u> has a <u>jaguar</u> on the back.

<u>jacket</u>　　　　　<u>jaguar</u>　　　　　<u>jamboree</u>
<u>janitor</u>　　　　　<u>jazz</u>　　　　　　<u>jellybeans</u>
<u>Jimmy</u>　　　　　<u>job</u>　　　　　　<u>joined</u>
　　　　　　　　　<u>joyous</u>

Homework

 Name: _____ Date:___/___/_____ Score: _____

The Reading Challenge

Lesson 10.2

Reading Multisyllable Words

✓ **Lesson Check Point**

Directions: Read and divide each target word into syllables. Write each word and place a hyphen (-) between the syllables in the second column. Write the number of syllables in the third column. Use a dictionary or the Internet to check your answers.

Direksyons: Li epi divize chak mo objektif an silab. Ekri chak mo epi mete yon tirè (-) ant silab yo nan dezyèm kolòn nan. Ekri kantite silab ke yo genyen an nan twazyèm kolòn nan. Itilize yon diksyonè oubyen entènèt pou tcheke repons ou yo.

Target Words	Words Divided into Syllables	Number of Syllables
1. jingle	jin-gle	2
2. joker	jok-er	2
3. juror	ju-ror	2
4. jaguar	jag-uar	2
5. jersey	jer-sey	2
6. journey	jour-ney	2
7. justice	jus-tice	2
8. jockey	jock-ey	2
9. jumper	jump-er	2
10. jargon	jar-gon	2

Homework

 Name: _____ Date: ___/___/_____ Score: _____

The Reading Challenge

Lesson 10.2

Reading Multisyllable Words

✓ **Lesson Check Point**

 Directions: Read each target word. Circle the word in the row that is divided correctly into syllables. Use a dictionary or the Internet to check your answers.

Direksyons: Li chak mo objektif. Antoure mo a ki nan ranje a ki divize an silab korèkteman yo. Itilize yon diksyonè oubyen entènèt pou tcheke repons ou yo.

Model

| janitor | a. ja-ni-tor | b. jan-it-or | c. (jan-i-tor) |

| 1. jeweler | a. (jew-el-er) | b. jewe-le-r | c. je-wel-er |

| 2. jubilee | a. ju-bil-ee | b. jub-i-lee | c. (ju-bi-lee) |

| 3. joining | a. (join-ing) | b. jo-in-ing | c. jo-ining |

| 4. jeopardy | a. (jeop-ard-y) | b. jeo-pard-y | c. jeop-ar-dy |

| 5. journalist | a. jour-na-list | b. journ-a-list | c. (jour-nal-ist) |

| 6. jovial | a. jov-i-al | b. (jo-vi-al) | c. jovi-al |

| 7. judicial | a. (ju-di-cial) | b. jud-i-cial | c. ju-dic-ial |

| 8. jamboree | a. jamb-o-ree | b. (jam-bo-ree) | c. jam-bor-ee |

Homework

Name: _____ Date: ___/___/_____ Score: _____

Lesson 10.3

Reading and Writing

Proper and Common Nouns and Adjectives

Directions: Read the words in the word box. Put an (X) on the line next to each word that is written incorrectly. Remember that all proper nouns and proper adjectives are capitalized. Use a dictionary or the Internet to check your answers.

Direksyons: Li chak mo yo ki nan bwat mo a. Met yon (X) sou ti trè a ki bò kote mo ki pa kri byen yo. Sonje ke tout non pwòp ak adjektif pwop ekri avèk yon lèt majiskil nan kòmansman yo. Itilize yon diksyonè oubyen entènèt pou tcheke repons ou yo.

Word Box					
_X_	Joke	_X_	july	___	James
_X_	june	___	jargon	___	jewel
___	Japan	_X_	Jungle	_X_	Jigsaw
___	Jordan	_X_	jefferson	___	January

Directions: Read each unedited sentence and underline the word that is written incorrectly. Write each sentence correctly on the line.

Direksyons: Li chak fraz ki pa edite yo epi soulinye mo ki pa ekri byen an. Ekri chak fraz korèkteman sou liy lan.

Model
Joey and his family live in New <u>jersey</u>.
<u>Joey and his family live in New Jersey.</u>

1. The <u>Janitor</u> has a good job.
<u>The janitor has a good job.</u>

2. Joseph and <u>james</u> are going to Japan.
<u>Joseph and James are going to Japan.</u>

3. In Jamaica, people eat <u>Jerk</u> chicken for dinner.
<u>In Jamaica, people eat jerk chicken for dinner.</u>

4. We are taking a <u>Journey</u> along the Jordan River.
<u>We are taking a journey along the Jordan River.</u>

Name: _____ Date: ___/___/_____ Score: _____

Homework

Lesson 11.1

Reading Words with the Letter K/k

✓ **Lesson Check Point**

 Directions: Read each target word. Find the letter "k" and put a check (✓) in the column that identifies its position: beginning, within or end.
Direksyons: Li chak mo objektif. Jwenn lèt "k" a epi mete yon tchèck (✓) nan kolòn ki idantifye pozisyon li an: nan kòmansman, ladan oubyen nan finisman.

Target Words	Beginning (First Letter)	Within	End (Last Letter)
1. shark			✓
2. kitchen	✓		
3. ketchup	✓		
4. folktale		✓	
5. comeback			✓

 Directions: Read each sentence and underline the words that begin with the letter "k." Write all the underlined words in alphabetical order on the lines below.
Direksyons: Li chak fraz epi soulinye mo ki kòmanse avèk lèt "k" yo. Ekri tout mo ki soulinye yo nan lòd alfabetik sou trè sa yo ki anba.

6. <u>Kidney</u> beans taste great with <u>ketchup</u>.

7. The three <u>kids</u> are eating in the <u>kitchen</u>.

8. The five <u>kittens</u> are staying in the <u>kennel</u>.

9. <u>Kelvin's</u> <u>kite</u> is flying high above the trees.

10. The powerful <u>kingdom</u> was guarded by <u>knights</u>.

Kelvin's	kennel	ketchup
Kidney	kids	kingdom
kitchen	kite	kittens
	knights	

Homework

 Name: _____ Date:___/___/_____ Score:_____

Lesson 11.2

Reading Words with the Letter "k" and "ck" Letter Combination

✓ **Lesson Check Point**

 Directions: Read each target word. Put a check (✓) in the second column if the target word has one vowel. Put a check (✓) in the third column if the target word has two vowels.

Direksyons: Li chak mo objektif. Mete yon tchèk (✓) nan dezyèm kolòn nan si mo objektif la genyen yon vwayèl. Mete yon tchèk (✓) nan twazyèm kolòn nan si mo objektif la genyen de vwayèl.

Target Words	Words with 1 Vowel	Words with 2 Vowels
1. rack	✓	
2. take		✓
3. sock	✓	
4. seek		✓
5. lock	✓	

 Directions: Read each target word in the first column and write the number of vowels within the word in the second column. Read each target word in the third column and write the number of vowels within the word in the fourth column.

Direksyons: Li chak mo objektif ki nan premye kolòn nan, epi ekri kantite vwayèl la ki nan mo a nan dezyèm kolòn nan. Li chak mo objektif ki nan twazyèm kolòn nan, epi ekri kantite vwayèl la ki nan mo a nan katryèm kolòn nan.

Target Words	Number of Vowels	Target Words	Number of Vowels
6. back	1	bake	2
7. pick	1	pike	2
8. stoke	2	stock	1
9. stack	1	stake	2
10. make	2	Mack	1

Homework

Name: _____ Date: ___/___/_____ Score: _____

Lesson 11.3

Reading Words with the "kle" Letter Combination

✓ Lesson Check Point

Directions: Read each target word. Find the "kle" letter combination and put a check (✓) in the column that identifies its position: beginning, within or end.

Direksyons: Li chak mo objektif. Jwenn konbinezon lèt "kle" a epi mete yon tchèk (✓) nan kolòn nan ki idantifye pozisyon li an: nan kòmansman, ladan oubyen nan finisman.

Target Words	Beginning (First 3 Letters)	Within	End (Last 3 Letters)
1. shackle			✓
2. anklets		✓	
3. wrinkled		✓	
4. unbuckle			✓
5. kleptomaniac	✓		

Directions: Read each target word. Put a check (✓) in the "yes" column if the "kle" letter combination has the /k/ + /ə/ + /l/ sounds. Put a check (✓) in the "no" column if the "kle" letter combination does not have the /k/ + /ə/ + /l/ sounds.

Direksyons: Li chak mo objektif. Mete yon tchèk (✓) nan kolòn "yes" an si konbinezon lèt "kle" a bay sons /k/ + /ə/ + /l/. Mete yon tchèk (✓) nan kolòn "no" an si konbinezon lèt "kle" a pa bay sons /k/ + /ə/ + /l/.

Target Words	Yes	No
6. shackle	✓	
7. anklets		✓
8. wrinkled	✓	
9. unbuckle	✓	
10. kleptomaniac		✓

Learn To Read English With Directions In Haitian Creole

Homework

 Name: _____ Date: ___/___/_____ Score: _____

Lesson 11.4

Reading Words with a Silent Letter "k"

✓ Lesson Check Point

 Directions: Read the target words in the word box. Write the words that have a silent letter "k" in the first column. Write the words that do not have a silent letter "k" in the second column.

Direksyons: Li mo objektif yo ki nan ti bwat mo a. Ekri mo yo ki genyen lèt "k" ki pa pwononse a nan premye kolòn nan. Ekri mo yo ki pa genyen lèt "k" ki pa pwononse a nan dezyèm kolòn nan.

Target Word Box				
knife	knits	knots	knew	keys
kneel	knish	leaking	knight	know
keeping	kangaroo	kerosene	market	knack
knowledge	breaking	keyboard	forsake	knuckles

Letter "k" is silent

- knew
- know
- kneel
- knits
- knots
- knack
- knife
- knight
- knuckles
- knowledge

Letter "k" has the /k/ sound

- keys
- knish
- forsake
- market
- breaking
- kerosene
- keeping
- leaking
- kangaroo
- keyboard

Homework

 Name: _____ Date: ___/___/_____ Score: _____

The Reading Challenge

Lesson 11.5

Reading Multisyllable Words

✓ Lesson Check Point

 Directions: Read and divide each target word into syllables. Write each word and place a hyphen (-) between the syllables in the second column. Write the number of syllables in the third column. Use a dictionary or the Internet to check your answers.

Direksyons: Li epi divize chak mo objektif an silab. Ekri chak mo epi mete yon tirè (-) ant silab yo nan dezyèm kolòn nan. Ekri kantite silab ke yo genyen an nan twazyèm kolòn nan. Itilize yon diksyonè oubyen entènèt pou tcheke repons ou yo.

Target Words	Words Divided into Syllables	Number of Syllables
1. kazoo	ka-zoo	2
2. kidney	kid-ney	2
3. knocker	knock-er	2
4. kosher	ko-sher	2
5. keycard	key-card	2
6. Kansas	Kan-sas	2
7. kindred	kin-dred	2
8. kinetic	ki-net-ic	3
9. kayak	kay-ak	2
10. keeping	keep-ing	2

Homework

 Name: _____ Date: ___/___/_____ Score: _____

The Reading Challenge

Lesson 11.5

Reading Multisyllable Words

✓ Lesson Check Point

 Directions: Read each target word. Circle the word in the row that is divided correctly into syllables. Use a dictionary or the Internet to check your answers.

Direksyons: Li chak mo objektif. Antoure mo a ki nan ranje a ki divize an silab korèkteman yo. Itilize yon diksyonè oubyen entènèt pou tcheke repons ou yo.

Model

| kangaroo | a. kang-a-roo | b. kan-ga-roo ⬅ | c. kan-gar-oo |

1. kerosene	a. ker-o-sene ⬅	b. ker-os-ene	c. ke-ro-sene
2. kneecap	a. knee-cap ⬅	b. kn-ee-cap	c. kn-eec-ap
3. Korean	a. K-ore-an	b. Kor-e-an	c. Ko-re-an ⬅
4. kneeling	a. kneel-ing ⬅	b. knee-ling	c. kne-eling
5. keeper	a. kee-per	b. keep-er ⬅	c. ke-eper
6. kinship	a. kinsh-ip	b. ki-nship	c. kin-ship ⬅
7. knowing	a. know-ing ⬅	b. kno-wing	c. knowi-ng
8. koala	a. ko-al-a	b. k-oa-la	c. ko-a-la ⬅

Learn To Read English With Directions In Spanish

Homework

Name: _____ Date: ___/___/_____ Score: _____

Lesson 11.6

Reading and Writing

Proper and Common Nouns and Adjectives

Directions: Read the words in the word box. Put an (X) on the line next to each word that is written incorrectly. Remember that all proper nouns and proper adjectives are capitalized. Use a dictionary or the Internet to check your answers.

Direksyons: Li chak mo yo ki nan bwat mo a. Met yon (X) sou ti trè a ki bò kote mo ki pa kri byen yo. Sonje ke tout non pwòp ak adjektif pwop ekri avèk yon lèt majiskil nan kòmansman yo. Itilize yon diksyonè oubyen entènèt pou tcheke repons ou yo.

Word Box					
_X_	korea	_X_	kuwait	___	Korean
___	kennel	_X_	Kicking	___	kitchen
___	Kansas	_X_	Keycard	_X_	key West
___	ketchup	___	Kwanzaa	_X_	Kangaroo

Directions: Read each unedited sentence and underline the word that is written incorrectly. Write each sentence correctly on the line.

Direksyons: Li chak fraz ki pa edite yo epi soulinye mo ki pa ekri byen an. Ekri chak fraz korèkteman sou liy lan.

Model
Helen <u>keller</u> was a kind person.
<u>Helen Keller was a kind person.</u>

1. In <u>kuwait</u>, kids like to kick their soccer balls.
<u>In Kuwait, kids like to kick their soccer balls.</u>

2. The State of <u>kansas</u> is located in America's heartland.
<u>The State of Kansas is located in America's heartland.</u>

3. The Kennedy kids enjoy eating <u>klondike</u> ice cream bars.
<u>The Kennedy kids enjoy eating Klondike ice cream bars.</u>

4. <u>key</u> West and Key Largo are islands off the coast of Florida.
<u>Key West and Key Largo are islands off the coast of Florida.</u>

Learn To Read English With Directions In Haitian Creole

Homework

L. Name: _____ Date: ___/___/_____ Score: _____

Lesson 12.1

Reading Words with the Letter L/l

✓ **Lesson Check Point**

Directions: Read each target word. Find the letter "l" and put a check (✓) in the column that identifies its position: beginning, within or end.
Direksyons: Li chak mo objektif. Jwenn lèt "l" a epi mete yon tchèck (✓) nan kolòn ki idantifye pozisyon li an: nan kòmansman, ladan oubyen nan finisman.

Target Words	Beginning (First Letter)	Within	End (Last Letter)
1. like	✓		
2. curl			✓
3. bowl			✓
4. lunch	✓		
5. helper		✓	

Directions: Read each sentence and underline the words that begin with the letter "l." Write all the underlined words in alphabetical order on the lines below.
Direksyons: Li chak fraz epi soulinye mo ki kòmanse avèk lèt "l" yo. Ekri tout mo ki soulinye yo nan lòd alfabetik sou trè sa yo ki anba.

6. I brought my <u>laptop</u> to the <u>library</u>.

7. David applied a handful of <u>lotion</u> to his <u>legs</u>.

8. Everyone knows Abigail <u>loves</u> to write <u>letters</u>.

9. On Friday, the <u>lawyer</u> wrote a <u>legal</u> document.

10. My family and I had <u>liver</u> and <u>lettuce</u> for dinner.

<u>laptop</u>   <u>lawyer</u>   <u>legal</u>
<u>legs</u>   <u>letters</u>   <u>lettuce</u>
<u>library</u>   <u>liver</u>   <u>lotion</u>
              <u>loves</u>

Homework

 Name: _____ Date: ___/___/_____ Score: _____

Lesson 12.2

Reading Words with the Letter "l" Combinations:
"cl," "fl," "pl" & "sl"

Dictionary Skills/ Vocabulary

✓ Lesson Check Point

 Directions: Read each target word and its definition. Write the target word on the line in front of its meaning. Use a dictionary or the Internet to check your answers.

Direksyons: Li chak mo objektif ak definisyon yo chak. Ekri mo objektif la sou trè ki devan definisyon li an. Itilize yon diksyonè oubyen entènèt pou tcheke repons ou yo.

Target Word Box				
flew	plants	plastic	sleep	slide

1. _plants_   living things that are grown in soil
2. _plastic_   a flexible man-made material that can be shaped
3. _slide_   to move in a downward motion on a slippery surface
4. _flew_   traveled through the air with wings
5. _sleep_   closing eyes and going into a periodic state of rest

 Directions: Read each sentence. Underline the word in the parentheses that correctly completes each sentence. Then, write the underlined word on the line.

Direksyons: Li chak fraz. Soulinye mo a ki nan parantèz yo ki konplete chak fraz kòrèkteman. Answit, ekri mo soulinye a sou trè a.

6. At camp, the campers will __sleep__ on bunk beds. (<u>sleep</u>, flew)

7. Pam loves to __slide__ down the hill with her sled. (plants, <u>slide</u>)

8. Early in the morning, the birds __flew__ over the pond. (<u>flew</u>, plastic)

9. The __plants__ in Grandma's garden are colorful. (slide, <u>plants</u>)

10. Paul's comb is made with a strong __plastic__ material. (sleep, <u>plastic</u>)

Homework

 Name: _____ Date: ___/___/_____ Score: _____

Lesson 12.3

Reading Words with a Silent Letter "l"

✓ Lesson Check Point

 Directions: Read the target words in the word box. Write the words that have a silent letter "l" in the first column. Write the words that do not have a silent letter "l" in the second column.

Direksyons: Li mo objektif yo ki nan ti bwat mo a. Ekri mo yo ki genyen lèt "l" ki pa pwononse a nan premye kolòn nan. Ekri mo yo ki pa genyen lèt "l" ki pa pwononse a nan dezyèm kolòn nan.

Target Word Box				
love	calf	tail	half	yolk
should	hello	balm	chalk	letter
salmon	ladder	dental	closed	would
Lincoln	telephone	laughs	perfectly	lower

Letter "l" is silent

- yolk
- half
- calf
- hello
- balm
- chalk
- would
- should
- Lincoln
- salmon

Letter "l" has the /l/ sound

- tail
- love
- letter
- lower
- dental
- laughs
- ladder
- closed
- perfectly
- telephone

Homework

 Name: _____ Date: ___/___/_____ Score: _____

The Reading Challenge

Lesson 12.4

Reading Multisyllable Words

✓ **Lesson Check Point**

 Directions: Read and divide each target word into syllables. Write each word and place a hyphen (-) between the syllables in the second column. Write the number of syllables in the third column. Use a dictionary or the Internet to check your answers.

Direksyons: Li epi divize chak mo objektif an silab. Ekri chak mo epi mete yon tirè (-) ant silab yo nan dezyèm kolòn nan. Ekri kantite silab ke yo genyen an nan twazyèm kolòn nan. Itilize yon diksyonè oubyen entènèt pou tcheke repons ou yo.

Target Words	Words Divided into Syllables	Number of Syllables
1. linguistic	lin-guis-tic	3
2. laughing	laugh-ing	2
3. lighting	light-ing	2
4. ligament	lig-a-ment	3
5. likely	like-ly	2
6. lexicon	lex-i-con	3
7. lavender	lav-en-der	3
8. leftover	left-o-ver	3
9. lasting	last-ing	2
10. languish	lan-guish	2

Homework

 Name: _____ Date: ___/___/_____ Score: _____

The Reading Challenge

Lesson 12.4

Reading Multisyllable Words

✓ **Lesson Check Point**

 Directions: Read each target word. Circle the word in the row that is divided correctly into syllables. Use a dictionary or the Internet to check your answers.

Direksyons: Li chak mo objektif. Antoure mo a ki nan ranje a ki divize an silab korèkteman yo. Itilize yon diksyonè oubyen entènèt pou tcheke repons ou yo.

Model

| liberty | a. li-ber-ty | (b. lib-er-ty) | c. lib-ert-y |

1. Latino	a. Lat-i-no	b. Lat-in-o	(c. La-ti-no)
2. leverage	a. le-ver-age	b. lev-e-rage	(c. lev-er-age)
3. liberate	a. li-ber-ate	b. lib-e-rate	(c. lib-er-ate)
4. limousine	(a. lim-ou-sine)	b. li-mou-sine	c. lim-o-usine
5. lyrical	(a. lyr-i-cal)	b. ly-ri-cal	c. lyr-ic-al
6. lexicon	a. le-xi-con	b. lex-ic-on	(c. lex-i-con)
7. library	a. lib-rar-y	(b. li-brar-y)	c. li-bra-ry
8. ligament	(a. lig-a-ment)	b. li-ga-ment	c. li-gam-ent

Homework

Name: _____ Date:___/___/_____ Score:_____

Lesson 12.5

Reading and Writing

Proper and Common Nouns and Adjectives

Directions: Read the words in the word box. Put an (X) on the line next to each word that is written incorrectly. Remember that all proper nouns and proper adjectives are capitalized. Use a dictionary or the Internet to check your answers.

Direksyons: Li chak mo yo ki nan bwat mo a. Met yon (X) sou ti trè a ki bò kote mo ki pa kri byen yo. Sonje ke tout non pwòp ak adjektif pwop ekri avèk yon lèt majiskil nan kòmansman yo. Itilize yon diksyonè oubyen entènèt pou tcheke repons ou yo.

Word Box					
__	Lagos	__	Libya	X	lima
X	Lunch	X	Lemonade	__	London
X	Laptop	__	living room	__	landlord
X	License	__	Long Island	X	liverpool

Directions: Read each unedited sentence and underline the word that is written incorrectly. Write each sentence correctly on the line.

Direksyons: Li chak fraz ki pa edite yo epi soulinye mo ki pa ekri byen an. Ekri chak fraz korèkteman sou liy lan.

Model
I am studying <u>latin</u> at Lutheran Life Academy.
<u>I am studying Latin at Lutheran Life Academy.</u>

1. My family ate <u>Lunch</u> at Long Beach, New York.
<u>My family ate lunch at Long Beach, New York.</u>

2. Larry said, "The <u>Largest</u> city in Nigeria is Lagos."
<u>Larry said, "The largest city in Nigeria is Lagos."</u>

3. We visited London and <u>liverpool</u> on the same day.
<u>We visited London and Liverpool on the same day.</u>

4. The <u>labrador</u> Peninsula is a large peninsula in Eastern Canada.
<u>The Labrador Peninsula is a large peninsula in Eastern Canada.</u>

Homework

Name: _____ Date:__/__/____ Score:_____

Lesson 13.1

Reading Words with the Letter M/m

Directions: Read each target word. Find the letter "m" and put a check (✓) in the column that identifies its position: beginning, within or end.
Direksyons: Li chak mo objektif. Jwenn lèt "m" a epi mete yon tchèck (✓) nan kolòn ki idantifye pozisyon li an: nan kòmansman, ladan oubyen nan finisman.

Target Words	Beginning (First Letter)	Within	End (Last Letter)
1. hermit		✓	
2. mother	✓		
3. summer		✓	
4. romance		✓	
5. upstream			✓

Directions: Read each sentence and underline the words that begin with the letter "m." Write all the underlined words in alphabetical order on the lines below.
Direksyons: Li chak fraz epi soulinye mo ki kòmanse avèk lèt "m" yo. Ekri tout mo ki soulinye yo nan lòd alfabetik sou trè sa yo ki anba.

6. His sister, <u>Mercy</u>, wrote a great <u>manuscript</u>.

7. Dr. <u>Mingo's</u> class is reading a book about <u>Mexico</u>.

8. The <u>mail</u> carrier placed the letters in the <u>mailbox</u>.

9. Grandma bought <u>mandarin</u> oranges at the <u>market</u>.

10. Our friend, <u>Max</u>, sailed along the great <u>Mississippi</u> River.

<u>mail   </u>   <u>mailbox   </u>   <u>mandarin </u>
<u>manuscript </u>   <u>market   </u>   <u>Max   </u>
<u>Mercy   </u>   <u>Mexico   </u>   <u>Mingo's   </u>
                           <u>Mississippi   </u>

Homework

 Name: _____ Date: ___/___/_____ Score: _____

Lesson 13.2

Reading Words with a Silent Letter "m"

✓ **Lesson Check Point**

 Directions: Read each target word. Find the letter "m" and put a check (✓) in the column that identifies its position: beginning, within or end.
Direksyons: Li chak mo objektif. Jwenn lèt "m" a epi mete yon tchèk (✓) nan kolòn ki idantifye pozisyon li an: nan kòmansman, ladan oubyen nan finisman.

Target Words	Beginning (First Letter)	Within	End (Last Letter)
1. monkey	✓		
2. immune		✓	
3. symmetry		✓	
4. globalism			✓
5. mnemonic	✓		

 Directions: Read each target word. Put a check (✓) in the "yes" column if the target word has a silent letter "m" Put a check (✓) in the "no" column if the target word does not have a silent letter "m."
Direksyons: Li chak mo objektif. Mete yon tchèk (✓) nan kolòn "yes" an si mo objektif la genyen yon lèt "m" ki pa pwononse. Mete yon tchèk (✓) nan kolòn "no" an si mo objektif la pa genyen yon lèt "m" ki pa pwononse.

Target Words	Yes	No
6. monkey		✓
7. immune	✓	
8. symmetry	✓	
9. globalism		✓
10. mnemonic	✓	

Homework

 Name: _____ Date: ___/___/_____ Score: _____

The Reading Challenge

Lesson 13.3

Reading Multisyllable Words

✓ Lesson Check Point

 Directions: Read and divide each target word into syllables. Write each word and place a hyphen (-) between the syllables in the second column. Write the number of syllables in the third column. Use a dictionary or the Internet to check your answers.

Direksyons: Li epi divize chak mo objektif an silab. Ekri chak mo epi mete yon tirè (-) ant silab yo nan dezyèm kolòn nan. Ekri kantite silab ke yo genyen an nan twazyèm kolòn nan. Itilize yon diksyonè oubyen entènèt pou tcheke repons ou yo.

Target Words	Words Divided into Syllables	Number of Syllables
1. meditate	med-i-tate	3
2. master	mas-ter	2
3. medium	me-di-um	3
4. Mexico	Mex-i-co	3
5. musical	mu-si-cal	3
6. mother	moth-er	2
7. mustard	mus-tard	2
8. mystery	mys-ter-y	3
9. membrane	mem-brane	2
10. multiply	mul-ti-ply	3

Homework

Name: _____ Date: ___/___/_____ Score: _____

The Reading Challenge

Lesson 13.3

Reading Multisyllable Words

✓ Lesson Check Point

Directions: Read each target word. Circle the word in the row that is divided correctly into syllables. Use a dictionary or the Internet to check your answers.

Direksyons: Li chak mo objektif. Antoure mo a ki nan ranje a ki divize an silab korèkteman yo. Itilize yon diksyonè oubyen entènèt pou tcheke repons ou yo.

Model

| magazine | **a. mag-a-zine** (circled) | b. ma-ga-zine | c. mag-az-ine |

1. Milwaukee	a. Mil-wa-ukee	**b. Mil-wau-kee** (circled)	c. Mil-wauk-ee
2. monarchy	**a. mon-ar-chy** (circled)	b. mo-nar-chy	c. mon-archy
3. mediate	**a. me-di-ate** (circled)	b. med-i-ate	c. me-dia-te
4. magnetic	**a. mag-net-ic** (circled)	b. mag-ne-tic	c. magn-et-ic
5. Mercury	a. Merc-u-ry	b. Me-rcu-ry	**c. Mer-cu-ry** (circled)
6. mosquito	**a. mos-qui-to** (circled)	b. mo-squi-to	c. mos-quit-o
7. microwave	a. micr-o-wave	b. mic-ro-wave	**c. mi-cro-wave** (circled)
8. memento	a. mem-en-to	b. mem-e-nto	**c. me-men-to** (circled)

Unit M Lesson 13.3

Homework

Name: _____ Date: ___/___/_____ Score: _____

Lesson 13.4

Reading and Writing

Proper and Common Nouns and Adjectives

Directions: Read the words in the word box. Put an (X) on the line next to each word that is written incorrectly. Remember that all proper nouns and proper adjectives are capitalized. Use a dictionary or the Internet to check your answers.

Direksyons: Li chak mo yo ki nan bwat mo a. Met yon (X) sou ti trè a ki bò kote mo ki pa kri byen yo. Sonje ke tout non pwòp ak adjektif pwop ekri avèk yon lèt majiskil nan kòmansman yo. Itilize yon diksyonè oubyen entènèt pou tcheke repons ou yo.

Word Box					
___	miser	___	Mecca	___	Malta
___	muffins	___	manners	X	Master
X	malaysia	X	Millionaire	X	Monarch
X	massachusetts	X	manchester	___	Mexico

Directions: Read each unedited sentence and underline the word that is written incorrectly. Write each sentence correctly on the line.

Direksyons: Li chak fraz ki pa edite yo epi soulinye mo ki pa ekri byen an. Ekri chak fraz korèkteman sou liy lan.

Model
My son, Mark, is going to attend MIT in <u>massachusetts</u>.
<u>My son, Mark, is going to attend MIT in Massachusetts.</u>

1. Miss Miller will <u>Marry</u> Mr. McShine next month.
<u>Miss Miller will marry Mr. McShine next month.</u>

2. My teacher, <u>mr.</u> Mann, lives in Martha's Vineyard.
<u>My teacher, Mr. Mann, lives in Martha's Vineyard.</u>

3. Every morning, my friend, <u>molly</u>, eats multi-grain cereal.
<u>Every morning, my friend, Molly, eats multi-grain cereal.</u>

4. In the morning, Matthew loves to listen to <u>mozart's</u> music.
<u>In the morning, Matthew loves to listen to Mozart's music.</u>

Homework

 Name: _____ Date: ___/___/_____ Score: _____

Lesson 14.1

Reading Words with the Letter N/n

✓ Lesson Check Point

 Directions: Read each target word. Find the letter "n" and put a check (✓) in the column that identifies its position: beginning, within or end.
Direksyons: Li chak mo objektif. Jwenn lèt "n" a epi mete yon tchèck (✓) nan kolòn ki idantifye pozisyon li an: nan kòmansman, ladan oubyen nan finisman.

Target Words	Beginning (First Letter)	Within	End (Last Letter)
1. freshen			✓
2. noodle	✓		
3. number	✓		
4. transfer		✓	
5. linguistic		✓	

 Directions: Read each sentence and underline the words that begin with the letter "n." Write all the underlined words in alphabetical order on the lines below.
Direksyons: Li chak fraz epi soulinye mo ki kòmanse avèk lèt "n" yo. Ekri tout mo ki soulinye yo nan lòd alfabetik sou trè sa yo ki anba.

6. Jack wrote a <u>note</u> in his blue <u>notebook</u>.

7. Andrew <u>narrated</u> the play entitled, "Our <u>Nation</u>."

8. My grandmother is <u>nibbling</u> on <u>nachos</u> and cheese.

9. <u>Newton</u> wrote the <u>numerator</u> above the denominator.

10. <u>Native</u> Americans <u>navigated</u> their canoes along the Mississippi River.

<u>nachos</u>   <u>narrated</u>   <u>Nation</u>
<u>Native</u>   <u>navigated</u>   <u>Newton</u>
<u>nibbling</u>   <u>note</u>   <u>notebook</u>
                      <u>numerator</u>

Homework

 Name: _____   Date: ___/___/_____   Score: _____

Lesson 14.2

Reading Words with the "ng" Letter Combination

✓ **Lesson Check Point**

 Directions: Read each target word. Circle the word in the column that has the same "ng" sound(s) as the target word.

Direksyons: Li chak mo objektif. Antoure mo a ki nan kolòn nan ki bay menm son "ng" la (yo) tankou mo objektif la.

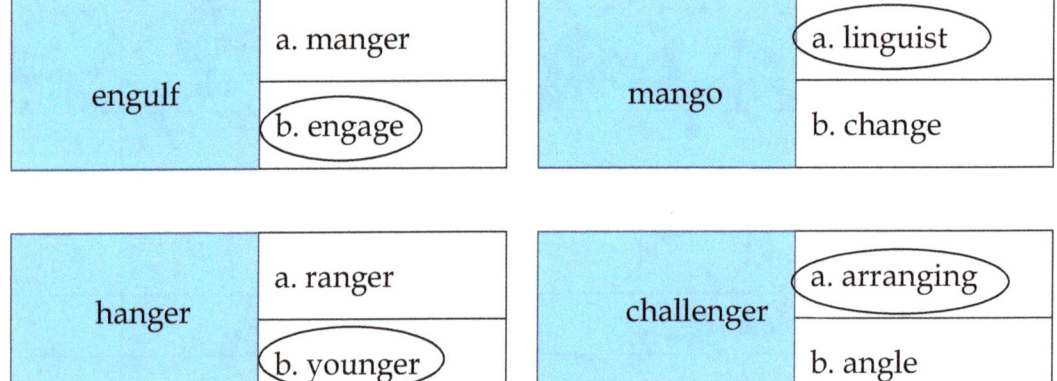

 Directions: Read each target word. Put a check (✓) under the correct column heading.

Direksyons: Li chak mo objektif. Mete yon tchèk (✓) anba antèt kolòn ki kòrèk la.

Target Words	"ng" has the /n/ + /g/ sounds as in the word <u>ingrain</u>	"ng" has the /n/ + /j/ sounds as in the word <u>ginger</u>	"ng" has the /ng/ sound as in the word <u>bang</u>	"ng" has the /ng/ + /g/ sounds as in the word <u>congress</u>
1. engulf	✓			
2. mango				✓
3. hanger			✓	
4. challenger		✓		

Homework

 Name: _____ Date: ___/___/_____ Score: _____

Lesson 14.3

Reading Words with a Silent Letter "n"

✓ **Lesson Check Point**

Directions: Read the target words in the word box. Write the words that have a silent letter "n" in the first column. Write the words that do not have a silent letter "n" in the second column.

Direksyons: Li mo objektif yo ki nan ti bwat mo a. Ekri mo yo ki genyen lèt "n" ki pa pwononse a nan premye kolòn nan. Ekri mo yo ki pa genyen lèt "n" ki pa pwononse a nan dezyèm kolòn nan.

Target Word Box				
inner	needle	hymn	annex	solemn
frozen	bundle	handle	network	expanse
cannon	columns	landmark	chimneys	autumn
condemn	dominate	cinnamon	comments	column

Letter "n" is silent

- inner
- annex
- hymn
- cannon
- solemn
- column
- autumn
- columns
- condemn
- cinnamon

Letter "n" has the /n/ sound

- needle
- frozen
- bundle
- handle
- network
- expanse
- dominate
- chimneys
- landmark
- comments

Homework

Name: _____ Date: ___/___/_____ Score: _____

The Reading Challenge

Lesson 14.4

Reading Multisyllable Words

✓ Lesson Check Point

Directions: Read and divide each target word into syllables. Write each word and place a hyphen (-) between the syllables in the second column. Write the number of syllables in the third column. Use a dictionary or the Internet to check your answers.

Direksyons: Li epi divize chak mo objektif an silab. Ekri chak mo epi mete yon tirè (-) ant silab yo nan dezyèm kolòn nan. Ekri kantite silab ke yo genyen an nan twazyèm kolòn nan. Itilize yon diksyonè oubyen entènèt pou tcheke repons ou yo.

Target Words	Words Divided into Syllables	Number of Syllables
1. nucleus	nu-cle-us	3
2. nobleman	no-ble-man	3
3. nightly	night-ly	2
4. nebula	neb-u-la	3
5. navel	na-vel	2
6. needless	need-less	2
7. ninety	nine-ty	2
8. noodle	noo-dle	2
9. negative	neg-a-tive	3
10. nervously	nerv-ous-ly	3

Homework

Name: _____ Date: ___/___/_____ Score: _____

The Reading Challenge

Lesson 14.4

Reading Multisyllable Words

✓ **Lesson Check Point**

Directions: Read each target word. Circle the word in the row that is divided correctly into syllables. Use a dictionary or the Internet to check your answers.

Direksyons: Li chak mo objektif. Antoure mo a ki nan ranje a ki divize an silab korèkteman yo. Itilize yon diksyonè oubyen entènèt pou tcheke repons ou yo.

Model

| napkin | a. na-pkin | b. napk-in | c. nap-kin (circled) |

1. nephew	a. neph-ew (circled)	b. ne-phew	c. nep-hew
2. nature	a. nat-ure	b. na-ture (circled)	c. natu-re
3. nursery	a. nurse-r-y	b. nurs-er-y (circled)	c. nur-ser-y
4. nominee	a. nom-i-nee (circled)	b. no-mi-nee	c. no-min-ee
5. nitrogen	a. nit-ro-gen	b. ni-tro-gen (circled)	c. nit-rog-en
6. Nevada	a. Nev-ad-a	b. Ne-va-da	c. Ne-vad-a (circled)
7. negative	a. ne-ga-tive	b. neg-a-tive (circled)	c. ne-gat-ive
8. nectarine	a. nec-ta-rine	b. nect-a-rine	c. nec-tar-ine (circled)

Unit N
Lesson 14.4

Homework

Name: _____ Date: ___/___/_____ Score: _____

Lesson 14.5

Reading and Writing

Proper and Common Nouns and Adjectives

Directions: Read the words in the word box. Put an (X) on the line next to each word that is written incorrectly. Remember that all proper nouns and proper adjectives are capitalized. Use a dictionary or the Internet to check your answers.

Direksyons: Li chak mo yo ki nan bwat mo a. Met yon (X) sou ti trè a ki bò kote mo ki pa kri byen yo. Sonje ke tout non pwòp ak adjektif pwop ekri avèk yon lèt majiskil nan kòmansman yo. Itilize yon diksyonè oubyen entènèt pou tcheke repons ou yo.

Word Box					
___	needy	___	nectar	___	negative
___	Nepal	X	Nibble	X	Newscast
X	new York	X	newark	___	New Mexico
X	niagara Falls	X	Neglect	___	New Amsterdam

Directions: Read each unedited sentence and underline the word that is written incorrectly. Write each sentence correctly on the line.

Direksyons: Li chak fraz ki pa edite yo epi soulinye mo ki pa ekri byen an. Ekri chak fraz korèkteman sou liy lan.

Model
Nick and Nancy live in the <u>netherlands</u>.
<u>Nick and Nancy live in the Netherlands.</u>

1. I bought my gold <u>Necklace</u> in Nigeria.
<u>I bought my gold necklace in Nigeria.</u>

2. New York State is next to <u>new</u> Jersey.
<u>New York State is next to New Jersey.</u>

3. The <u>Newspaper</u> article is about Nicaragua.
<u>The newspaper article is about Nicaragua.</u>

4. My <u>Nephew</u>, Nat, navigated his boat along the Nile River.
<u>My nephew, Nat, navigated his boat along the Nile River.</u>

Learn To Read English With Directions In Spanish

Homework

 Name: _____ Date:___/___/_____ Score:_____

Lesson 15.1

Reading Words with the Letter O/o

✓ **Lesson Check Point**

 Directions: Read each target word. Find the letter "o" and put a check (✓) in the column that identifies its position: beginning, within or end.
Direksyons: Li chak mo objektif. Jwenn lèt "o" a epi mete yon tchèck (✓) nan kolòn ki idantifye pozisyon li an: nan kòmansman, ladan oubyen nan finisman.

Target Words	Beginning (First Letter)	Within	End (Last Letter)
1. office	✓		
2. house		✓	
3. turbo			✓
4. object	✓		
5. going		✓	

 Directions: Read each target word. Read the words in the row and circle the word that has a different vowel "o" sound.
Direksyons: Li chak mo objektif. Li mo yo ki nan ranje a epi antoure mo a ki bay yon son vwayèl "o" ki diferan an.

Target Words				
6. most	boat	poke	cope	(mob)
7. doing	(going)	who	to	move
8. colder	bone	no	(dot)	poet
9. chosen	(boxes)	ago	float	hose
10. popping	knock	(roll)	lost	sock

Learn To Read English With Directions In Haitian Creole

Homework

 Name: _____ Date: ___/___/_____ Score: _____

Lesson 15.2

Reading Words with the Short Vowel "o" Sound

✓ **Lesson Check Point**

 Directions: Read the words in the four boxes. Circle two words with the short vowel /ŏ/ or /ô/ sound. The anchor word for the short vowel /ŏ/ and /ô/ sounds is <u>frog</u>.

Direksyons: Li mo yo ki nan kat ti bwat yo. Antoure de mo ki genyen son vwayèl kout /ŏ/ oubyen /ô/ a. Mo referans pou son vwayèl kout /ŏ/ ak /ô/ a se mo, <u>frog</u>.

cone	boast		poem	(jock)		(knock)	cold
(snob)	(mock)		boat	(hog)		bolt	(blotch)

open	(soft)		toll	(frost)		(lot)	almost
(floss)	old		soap	(stock)		fold	(hog)

 Directions: Read the words in the four boxes. Circle two words that rhyme. Rhyming words have the same ending sound, such as <u>hot</u> and <u>not</u>.

Direksyons: Li mo yo ki nan kat ti bwat yo. Antoure de mo ki rime. De mo oubyen plizyè mo ki rime genyen menm son nan finisman yo, tankou <u>hot</u> ak <u>not</u>.

(dot)	(pot)		yolk	(clock)		most	open
cold	cargo		yo-yo	(block)		(pop)	(top)

(log)	so		(box)	(fox)		doc	joke
(fog)	over		scold	token		mold	(wok)

Homework

Name: _____ Date: ___/___/_____ Score: _____

Lesson 15.2

Reading & Writing Words with the Short Vowel "o" Sound

✓ **Lesson Check Point**

Directions: Read each sentence and underline three words with the short vowel /ŏ/ or /ô/ sound. Then, write the underlined words on the lines below. The anchor word for the short vowel /ŏ/ and /ô/ sounds is frog.

Direksyons: Li chak fraz epi soulinye twa mo ki genyen son vwayèl kout /ŏ/ oubyen /ô/ a. Answit, ekri mo soulinye yo sou trè sa yo ki anba. Mo referans pou son vwayèl kout /ŏ/ ak /ô/ a se mo, frog.

Model
Everyone saw the frog hop close to the rock.

    frog   hop   rock

1. Bob will jog around one block.

    Bob   jog   block

2. Owen dropped the hot pot by the oven.

    dropped   hot   pot

3. My boss crossed the street and bought codfish.

    boss   crossed   codfish

4. Odessa tossed the oversized frog back into the pond.

    tossed   frog   pond

5. Tom and Ricardo have three animals: an ox, a cat and a hog.

    Tom   ox   hog

Learn To Read English With Directions In Haitian Creole

Homework

 Name: _____ Date: ___/___/_____ Score: _____

Lesson 15.3

Reading Words with the Long Vowel "o" Sound

✓ **Lesson Check Point**

 Directions: Read the words in the four boxes. Circle two words with the long vowel /ō/ sound. The anchor word for the long vowel /ō/ sound is <u>open</u>.

Direksyons: Li mo yo ki nan kat ti bwat yo. Antoure de mo ki genyen son vwayèl long /ō/ a. Mo referans pou son vwayèl long /ō/ a se mo, <u>open</u>.

note	(stop)	(flop)	loaf	(blond)	roam
(plot)	foam	(soft)	vote	(shock)	lobe

(gloss)	gloat	(lock)	(stock)	(floss)	nose
robe	(doll)	doe	goat	over	(slot)

 Directions: Read the words in the four boxes. Circle two words that rhyme. Rhyming words have the same ending sound, such as <u>hope</u> and <u>soap</u>.

Direksyons: Li mo yo ki nan kat ti bwat yo. Antoure de mo ki rime. De mo oubyen plizyè mo ki rime genyen menm son nan finisman yo, tankou <u>hope</u> ak <u>soap</u>.

chop	(troll)	bond	dome	long	(coal)
toast	(bowl)	(float)	(throat)	mock	(goal)

(soak)	(poke)	rope	most	(hose)	(rose)
hose	moss	(load)	(rode)	cope	dock

Homework

☐ Name: _____   Date: ___/___/_____   Score: _____

Lesson 15.3

Reading & Writing Words with the Long Vowel "o" Sound

✓ **Lesson Check Point**

Directions: Read each sentence and underline three words with the long vowel /ō/ sound. Then, write the underlined words on the lines below. The anchor word for the long vowel /ō/ sound is <u>open</u>.

Direksyons: Li mo yo ki nan kat ti bwat yo. Antoure de mo ki genyen son vwayèl long /ō/ a. Mo referans pou son vwayèl long /ō/ a se mo, <u>open</u>.

Model

We will <u>go</u> to the <u>rodeo</u> and <u>limbo</u> competitions for fun.

    go   rodeo   limbo

1. The <u>motel's</u> lunch <u>combo</u> has two <u>donuts</u> for dessert.

    motel's   combo   donuts

2. The outstanding critic said, "<u>Carlo's</u> company <u>logo</u> is <u>so-so</u>."

    Carlo's   logo   so-so

3. The new apartment <u>condo</u> is <u>going</u> to become available in <u>October</u>.

    condo   going   October

4. The disc jockey will play <u>disco</u> music as we <u>go</u> under the <u>limbo</u> bar.

    disco   go   limbo

5. I read a <u>poem</u> about <u>nomads</u> who traveled along the Atlantic <u>Ocean</u>.

    poem   nomads   Ocean

Learn To Read English With Directions In Haitian Creole

Homework

Name: _____ Date: ___/___/_____ Score: _____

Review Lessons 15.2 & 15.3

Reading Short Vowel and Long Vowel Words

Directions: Read the target words in the word box. In the first column, write the words that have the short vowel /ŏ/ or /ô/ sound, as in the word <u>frog</u>. In the second column, write the words that have the long vowel /ō/ sound, as in the word <u>open</u>.

Direksyons: Li mo objektif yo ki nan bwat mo a. Nan premye kolòn nan, ekri mo yo ki bay son vwayèl kout /ŏ/ oubyen /ô/ a, tankou li ye nan mo <u>frog</u> la. Nan dezyèm kolòn nan, ekri mo yo ki bay son vwayèl long /ō/ a, tankou li ye nan mo <u>open</u> la.

Target Word Box				
close	mom	solar	poster	oval
almost	colder	ocean	boxers	patrol
conflict	hotter	jogging	proceed	doctor
dropping	swollen	stopped	mopping	potting

Letter "o" has the /ŏ/ or /ô/ sound as in the word <u>frog</u>

- conflict
- dropping
- mom
- hotter
- jogging
- stopped
- boxers
- mopping
- doctor
- potting

Letter "o" has the /ō/ sound as in the word <u>open</u>

- close
- almost
- colder
- swollen
- solar
- ocean
- poster
- proceed
- oval
- patrol

Homework

 Name: _____ Date:___/___/_____ Score: _____

Lesson 15.4

Reading Words with Letter "o" Vowel Pairs

✓ Lesson Check Point

   Directions: Read each target word. Circle the word in the column that has the same vowel "oa," "oe," "oo" or "ou" sound(s) as the target word.
Direksyons: Li chak mo objektif. Antoure mo a ki nan kolòn nan ki bay menm son vwayèl "oa," "oe," "oo" oubyen "ou" la (yo) tankou mo objektif la.

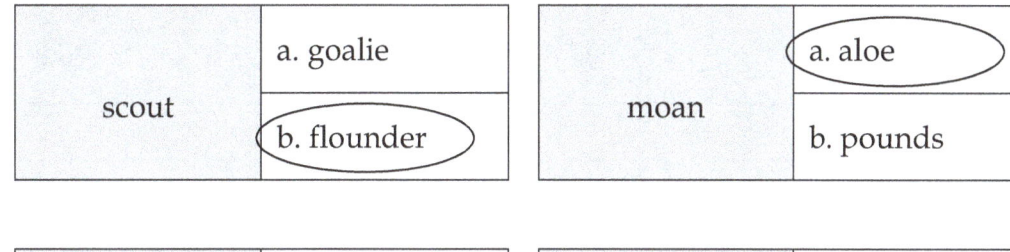

   Directions: Read each target word. Put a check (✓) under the correct column heading.
Direksyons: Li chak mo objektif. Mete yon tchèk (✓) anba antèt kolòn ki kòrèk la.

Target Words	Words have the long "o" sound as in the word coat	Words do not have the long "o" sound
1. scout		✓
2. moan	✓	
3. toast	✓	
4. oboe	✓	

Homework

 Name: _____ Date: ___/___/_____ Score: _____

Lesson 15.5

Reading Words with the Final Letter "o"

✓ **Lesson Check Point**

Directions: Read each target word. Find the letter "o" and put a check (✓) in the column that identifies its position within the syllable.

Direksyons: Li chak mo objektif. Jwenn lèt "o" a epi mete yon tchèck (✓) nan kolòn nan ki idantifye pozisyon li an nan silab la.

Target Words	"o" is at the end of a one syllable word	"o" is at the end of the first syllable	"o" is at the end of a multi-syllable word
1. go	✓		
2. ghetto			✓
3. bravo			✓
4. grocer		✓	
5. hydro			✓

Directions: Read each target word. Put a check (✓) under the correct column heading.

Direksyons: Li chak mo objektif. Mete yon tchèk (✓) anba antèt kolòn ki kòrèk la.

Target Words	"o" has the /ŏ/ sound as in the word <u>frog</u>	"o" has the /ō/ sound as in the word <u>go</u>	"o" has the /ə/ sound as in the word <u>carrot</u>	"o" is silent as in the word <u>people</u>
6. hotel		✓		
7. pocket	✓			
8. leopards				✓
9. complete			✓	
10. wisdom			✓	

 Homework

Name: _____ Date: ___/___/_____ Score: _____

Lesson 15.6

Reading Letter "o" Words with the Schwa Vowel Sound

✓ **Lesson Check Point**

 Directions: Read each target word. Circle the word in the column that has the same "o" sound as the target word.

Direksyons: Li chak mo objektif. Antoure mo a ki nan kolòn nan ki bay menm son "o" a tankou mo objektif la.

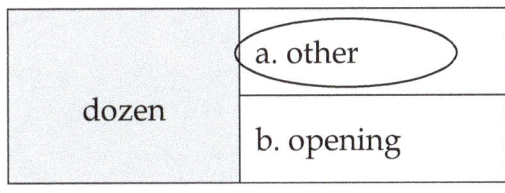
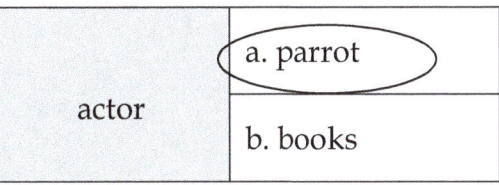
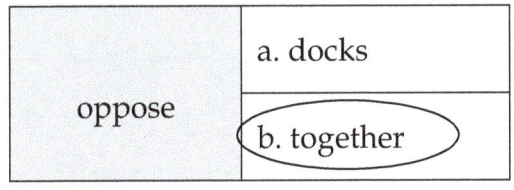
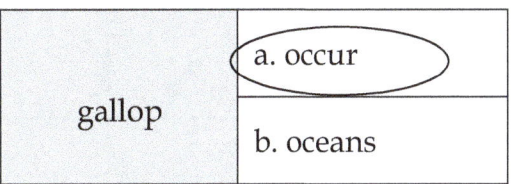

 Directions: Read each sentence and underline the letter "o" word that has the schwa vowel /ə/ sound or short vowel /ŭ/ sound. The anchor word for the letter "o" schwa vowel /ə/ sound is <u>carrot</u> and the letter "o" short vowel /ŭ/ sound is <u>dove</u>.

Direksyons: Li chak fraz epi soulinye mo ki genyen lèt "o" a ki bay son schwa /ə/ oubyen son /ŭ/ a. Mo referans pou son schwa /ə/ lèt "o" a se <u>carrot</u> epi son lèt "o" /ŭ/ kout la se <u>dove</u>.

1. My <u>brother</u> opened two large, orange boxes.

2. <u>Nothing</u> was written in Oscar's new notebooks.

3. Mr. and Mrs. Lopez are going to the <u>Ivory</u> Coast.

4. In the afternoon, Orin drank cold <u>coconut</u> water.

5. My nephew is enrolled in an interesting <u>history</u> class.

6. Early in the morning, the <u>pilot</u> flew over South Africa.

Homework

 Name: _____ Date:___/___/_____ Score:_____

Lesson 15.7

Reading Words with Vowel "o" Sounds: /ŏ/, /ō/ & /o͞o/

✓ Lesson Check Point

Directions: Read each target word. Put a check (✓) under the correct column heading.

Direksyons: Li chak mo objektif. Mete yon tchèk (✓) anba antèt kolòn ki kòrèk la.

Target Words	"o" has the /ŏ/ sound as in the word frog	"o" has the /ō/ sound as in the word go	"o" has the /o͞o/ sound as in the word to
1. total		✓	
2. doing			✓
3. proven			✓
4. holiday	✓		
5. dollars	✓		

Directions: Read each sentence and underline the word that has a letter "o" that has the vowel /o͞o/ sound, as in the word too.
Direksyons: Li chak fraz epi soulinye mo a ki genyen let "o" a ki bay son /o͞o/ an, tankou li ye nan mo too la.

6. <u>Do</u> we have an appointment?

7. Don will return home at <u>two</u> o'clock

8. Ron skillfully <u>proved</u> his answer was correct.

9. I did not <u>lose</u> any money in the stock market.

10. Mrs. Oscar said, "Everyone must <u>move</u> their books."

 Name: _____   Date: ___/___/_____   Score: _____

Homework

Lesson 15.8

Reading Words with the "or" Letter Combination

✓ **Lesson Check Point**

 Directions: Read each target word. Circle the word in the column that has the same "o" + "r" sounds as the target word.
Direksyons: Li chak mo objektif. Antoure mo a ki nan kolòn nan ki bay menm son "o" + "r" yo tankou mo objektif la.

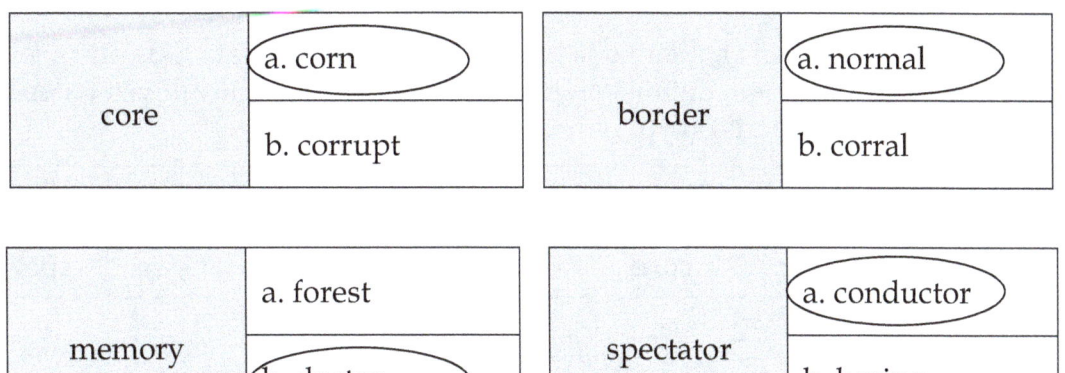

 Directions: Read each target word. Put a check (✓) under the correct column heading.
Direksyons: Li chak mo objektif. Mete yon tchèk (✓) anba antèt kolòn ki kòrèk la.

Target Words	"or" has the /ô/ + /r/ sounds as in the word <u>door</u>	"or" has the /ə/ + /r/ sounds as in the word <u>doctor</u>
1. core	✓	
2. border	✓	
3. memory		✓
4. spectator		✓

Homework

 Name: _____ Date:___/___/_____ Score: _____

Lesson 15.8

Reading Words with the "or" Letter Combination

Dictionary Skills/ Vocabulary

✓ Lesson Check Point

 Directions: Read each target word and its definition. Write the target word on the line in front of its meaning. Use a dictionary or the Internet to check your answers.

Direksyons: Li chak mo objektif ak definisyon yo chak. Ekri mo objektif la sou trè ki devan definisyon li an. Itilize yon diksyonè oubyen entènèt pou tcheke repons ou yo.

Target Word Box				
shortest	corn	horse	poor	sport

1. corn _____ yellow or white grain
2. horse _____ a large four-legged animal
3. shortest _____ measurement that is least in a series
4. sport _____ a physical activity and/or game
5. poor _____ a state of not having money for basic needs

 Directions: Read each sentence and write the target word that correctly completes the sentence.

Direksyons: Li chak fraz epi ekri mo objektif ki konplete fraz la kòrèkteman.

6. Tom's favorite __sport__ is baseball.

7. The __poor__ woman is applying for a job.

8. The __horse__ is eating a pile of hay by the barn.

9. Horace is the __shortest__ boy in Mr. James' class.

10. The farmer has healthy stalks of __corn__ on his farm.

Homework

 Name: _____ Date:___/___/_____ Score: _____

Lesson 15.9

Reading Words with a Silent Letter "o"

✓ **Lesson Check Point**

Directions: Read the target words in the word box. Write the words that have a silent letter "o" in the first column. Write the words that do not have a silent letter "o" in the second column.

Direksyons: Li mo objektif yo ki nan ti bwat mo a. Ekri mo yo ki genyen lèt "o" ki pa pwononse a nan premye kolòn nan. Ekri mo yo ki pa genyen lèt "o" ki pa pwononse a nan dezyèm kolòn nan.

Target Word Box				
total	Rocks	orders	leopard	zero
leopards	Leonard	mouse	popular	people
subpoena	opening	Phoenix	brother	hoping
Phoenician	jeopardy	subpoenas	someone	jeopardize

Letter "o" is silent	Letter "o" has a letter "o" sound
leopard	rocks
jeopardy	zero
leopards	orders
people	total
jeopardize	popular
subpoena	opening
subpoenas	someone
Leonard	mouse
Phoenix	brother
Phoenician	hoping

Homework

 Name: _____ Date: ___/___/_____ Score: _____

Unit Review - O/o

Reading Words with Vowel "o" Sounds: /ŏ/, /ō/, /ə/ & Silent

✓ **Lesson Check Point**

 Directions: Read each target word. Circle the word in the column that has the same "o" sound as the target word.

Direksyons: Li chak mo objektif. Antoure mo a ki nan kolòn nan ki bay menm son "o" a tankou mo objektif la.

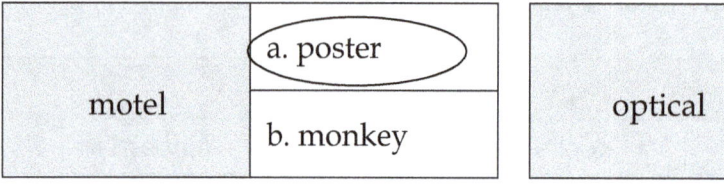

 Directions: Read each target word. Put a check (✓) under the correct column heading.

Direksyons: Li chak mo objektif. Mete yon tchèk (✓) anba antèt kolòn ki kòrèk la.

Target Words	"o" has the /ŏ/ sound as in the word <u>frog</u>	"o" has the /ō/ sound as in the word <u>go</u>	"o" has the /ə/ sound as in the word <u>carrot</u>	"o" is silent as in the word <u>people</u>
1. motel		✓		
2. optical	✓			
3. observe			✓	
4. subpoena				✓

Homework

 Name: _____ Date:___/___/_____ Score:_____

The Reading Challenge

Lesson 15.10

Reading Multisyllable Words

✓ **Lesson Check Point**

 Directions: Read and divide each target word into syllables. Write each word and place a hyphen (-) between the syllables in the second column. Write the number of syllables in the third column. Use a dictionary or the Internet to check your answers.

Direksyons: Li epi divize chak mo objektif an silab. Ekri chak mo epi mete yon tirè (-) ant silab yo nan dezyèm kolòn nan. Ekri kantite silab ke yo genyen an nan twazyèm kolòn nan. Itilize yon diksyonè oubyen entènèt pou tcheke repons ou yo.

Target Words	Words Divided into Syllables	Number of Syllables
1. localize	lo-cal-ize	3
2. total	to-tal	2
3. remote	re-mote	2
4. poetry	po-et-ry	3
5. noble	no-ble	2
6. devoting	de-vot-ing	3
7. pony	po-ny	2
8. morning	morn-ing	2
9. moisture	mois-ture	2
10. pointless	point-less	2

Unit O Lesson 15.10

Learn To Read English With Directions In Haitian Creole

Homework

Name: _____ Date:___/___/_____ Score:_____

The Reading Challenge

Lesson 15.10

Reading Multisyllable Words

✓ **Lesson Check Point**

Directions: Read each target word. Circle the word in the row that is divided correctly into syllables. Use a dictionary or the Internet to check your answers.

Direksyons: Li chak mo objektif. Antoure mo a ki nan ranje a ki divize an silab korèkteman yo. Itilize yon diksyonè oubyen entènèt pou tcheke repons ou yo.

Model

proposal	a. prop-o-sal	b. pro-po-sal	c. pro-pos-al ⭕

1. calculator	a. cal-cul-ator	b. calc-ul-ator	c. cal-cu-la-tor ⭕
2. Yoruba	a. Yo-ru-ba ⭕	b. Yor-u-ba	c. Yor-ub-a
3. reservoir	a. re-ser-voir	b. res-er-voir ⭕	c. res-e-rvoir
4. monitor	a. mon-it-or	b. mon-i-tor ⭕	c. mo-nit-or
5. avocado	a. av-o-ca-do ⭕	b. av-oca-do	c. a-voc-a-do
6. creditor	a. cre-dit-or	b. cred-it-or	c. cred-i-tor ⭕
7. diploma	a. dip-lo-ma	b. di-plo-ma ⭕	c. di-plom-a
8. marigold	a. ma-ri-gold	b. mar-i-gold ⭕	c. ma-rig-old

Learn To Read English With Directions In Spanish

Homework

Name: _____   Date: ___/___/_____   Score: _____

Lesson 15.11

Reading and Writing

Proper and Common Nouns and Adjectives

Directions: Read the words in the word box. Put an (X) on the line next to each word that is written incorrectly. Remember that all proper nouns and proper adjectives are capitalized. Use a dictionary or the Internet to check your answers.

Direksyons: Li chak mo yo ki nan bwat mo a. Met yon (X) sou ti trè a ki bò kote mo ki pa kri byen yo. Sonje ke tout non pwòp ak adjektif pwop ekri avèk yon lèt majiskil nan kòmansman yo. Itilize yon diksyonè oubyen entènèt pou tcheke repons ou yo.

Word Box		
_X_ orion	___ Ohio	___ optical
___ Oxford	___ occupant	_X_ Omnivore
_X_ october	_X_ Octopus	_X_ Ornament
___ observable	_X_ oval Office	___ Ottoman Empire

Directions: Read each unedited sentence and underline the word that is written incorrectly. Write each sentence correctly on the line.

Direksyons: Li chak fraz ki pa edite yo epi soulinye mo ki pa ekri byen an. Ekri chak fraz korèkteman sou liy lan.

Model
At <u>One</u> o'clock, the Owens family went to Onega Bay.
<u>At one o'clock, the Owens family went to Onega Bay.</u>

1. Mr. and Mrs. Oscar bought a house by the <u>Ocean</u>.
<u>Mr. and Mrs. Oscar bought a house by the ocean.</u>

2. Odessa is reading about the origin of the <u>olympics</u>.
<u>Odessa is reading about the origin of the Olympics.</u>

3. The professors at <u>oxford</u> are studying the ozone layer.
<u>The professors at Oxford are studying the ozone layer.</u>

4. <u>our</u> cruise ship, Odyssey, sailed across the Atlantic Ocean.
<u>Our cruise ship, Odyssey, sailed across the Atlantic Ocean.</u>

Homework

L. Name: _____ Date: ___/___/_____ Score: _____

Lesson 16.1

Reading Words with the Letter P/p

✓ **Lesson Check Point**

Directions: Read each target word. Find the letter "p" and put a check (✓) in the column that identifies its position: beginning, within or end.

Direksyons: Li chak mo objektif. Jwenn lèt "p" a epi mete yon tchèck (✓) nan kolòn ki idantifye pozisyon li an: nan kòmansman, ladan oubyen nan finisman.

Target Words	Beginning (First Letter)	Within	End (Last Letter)
1. grip			✓
2. pilot	✓		
3. plain	✓		
4. octopus		✓	
5. complain		✓	

Directions: Read each sentence and underline the words that begin with the letter "p." Write all the underlined words in alphabetical order on the lines below.

Direksyons: Li chak fraz epi soulinye mo ki kòmanse avèk lèt "p" yo. Ekri tout mo ki soulinye yo nan lòd alfabetik sou trè sa yo ki anba.

6. The <u>Perez</u> family is from <u>Peru</u>.

7. I work <u>part-time</u> at a <u>perfume</u> company.

8. The <u>pharmacy</u> is located in Houston <u>Plaza</u>.

9. Jenny has a <u>pencil</u> and five <u>pens</u> in her bag.

10. Dr. Andrew gave me a <u>private</u> <u>physical</u> examination.

<u>part-time</u>	<u>pencil</u>	<u>pens</u>
<u>perfume</u>	<u>Peru</u>	<u>Perez</u>
<u>pharmacy</u>	<u>physical</u>	<u>Plaza</u>
	<u>private</u>	

Homework

 Name: _____   Date: ___/___/_____   Score: _____

Lesson 16.2

Reading Words with the "ph" Letter Combination

✓ **Lesson Check Point**

 Directions: Read each target word. Circle the word in the column that has the same "ph" sound(s) as the target word.

Direksyons: Li chak mo objektif. Antoure mo a ki nan kolòn nan ki bay menm son "ph" la (yo) tankou mo objektif la.

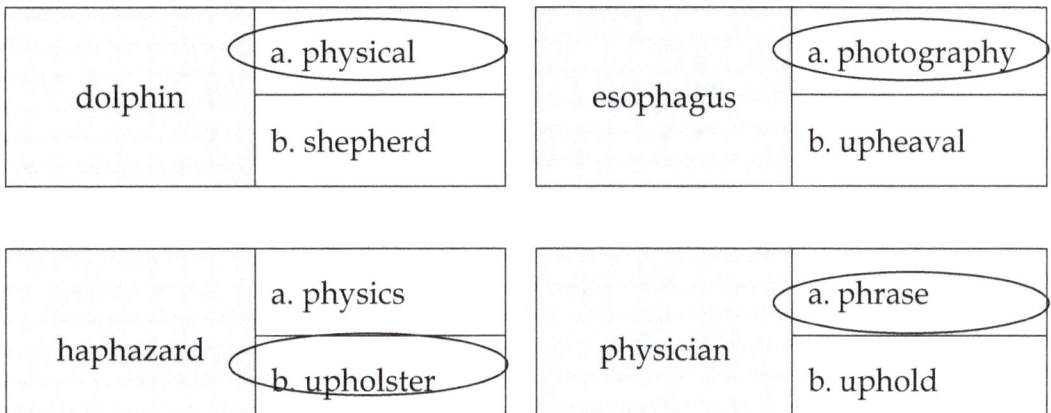

 Directions: Read each target word. Put a check (✓) under the correct column heading.

Direksyons: Li chak mo objektif. Mete yon tchèk (✓) anba antèt kolòn ki kòrèk la.

Target Words	"ph" has the /f/ sound as in the word phone	"ph" has the /p/ + /h/ sounds as in the word uphill
1. dolphin	✓	
2. esophagus	✓	
3. haphazard		✓
4. physician	✓	

Homework

Name: _____ Date: ___/___/_____ Score: _____

Lesson 16.3

Reading Words with the "pr" Letter Combination

Dictionary Skills/ Vocabulary

✓ **Lesson Check Point**

Directions: Read each target word and its definition. Write the letter of the definition on the line of each target word. Use a dictionary or the Internet to check your answers.

Direksyons: Li chak mo objektif ak definisyon yo chak. Ekri lèt la ki koresponn ak definisyon an sou trè chak mo objektif yo. Itilize yon diksyonè oubyen entènèt pou tcheke repons ou yo.

Target Words	Definitions
1. _e_ print	a. the son of a king
2. _b_ profit	b. money earned from the sale of products
3. _a_ prince	c. to do something repeatedly in order to improve
4. _c_ practice	d. state of a woman carrying a baby within her womb
5. _d_ pregnant	e. to produce an image or text on a surface

Directions: Read each sentence and write the target word that correctly completes the sentence.
Direksyons: Li chak fraz epi ekri mo objektif ki konplete fraz la kòrèkteman.

6. Alex has to __practice__ his violin every day.

7. My teacher, Mrs. Primis, is six months __pregnant__.

8. I will __print__ a picture of an artist on my cover page.

9. The king is preparing the __prince__ to become a great ruler.

10. The business owner is planning to make a __profit__ this year.

Homework

Name: _____   Date: ___/___/_____   Score: _____

Lesson 16.4

Reading Words with the "pl" Letter Combination

Dictionary Skills/ Vocabulary

✓ **Lesson Check Point**

Directions: Read each target word and its definition. Write the target word on the line in front of its meaning. Use a dictionary or the Internet to check your answers.

Direksyons: Li chak mo objektif ak definisyon yo chak. Ekri mo objektif la sou trè ki devan definisyon li an. Itilize yon diksyonè oubyen entènèt pou tcheke repons ou yo.

Target Word Box				
planet	play	pliers	plaza	pleaded

1. <u>pliers</u>   a metal or durable plastic tool
2. <u>play</u>   the act of doing something fun
3. <u>pleaded</u>   to have appealed earnestly
4. <u>plaza</u>   a small shopping center within a community
5. <u>planet</u>   sphere shaped, celestial object within the solar system

Directions: Read each sentence. Underline the word in the parentheses that correctly completes each sentence. Then, write the underlined word on the line.

Direksyons: Li chak fraz. Soulinye mo a ki nan parantèz yo ki konplete chak fraz kòrèkteman. Answit, ekri mo soulinye a sou trè a.

6. Earth is the third <u>planet</u> from the sun. (<u>planet</u>, pleaded)

7. The children will <u>play</u> baseball on Saturday. (plaza, <u>play</u>)

8. Paul needs a pair of <u>pliers</u> to fix the bench. (planet, <u>pliers</u>)

9. Peter's pastry shop is in the new shopping <u>plaza</u>. (<u>plaza</u>, play)

10. At court, the plaintiff <u>pleaded</u> with the judge. (<u>pleaded</u>, pliers)

Homework

Name: _____ Date: ___/___/_____ Score: _____

Lesson 16.4

Reading Words with the "ple" Letter Combination

✓ **Lesson Check Point**

Directions: Read each target word. Find the "ple" letter combination and put a check (✓) in the column that identifies its position: beginning, within or end.

Direksyons: Li chak mo objektif. Jwenn konbinezon lèt "ple" a epi mete yon tchèk (✓) nan kolòn nan ki idantifye pozisyon li an: nan kòmansman, ladan oubyen nan finisman.

Target Words	Beginning (First 3 Letters)	Within	End (Last 3 Letters)
1. dimple			✓
2. example			✓
3. pleasant	✓		
4. principle			✓
5. incomplete		✓	

Directions: Read each target word. Put a check (✓) in the "yes" column if the "ple" letter combination has the /p/ + /ə/ + /l/ sounds. Put a check (✓) in the "no" column if the "ple" letter combination does not have the /p/ + /ə/ + /l/ sounds.

Direksyons: Li chak mo objektif. Mete yon tchèk (✓) nan kolòn "yes" an si konbinezon let "ple" a bay sons /p/ + /ə/ + /l/. Mete yon tchèk (✓) nan kolòn "no" an si konbinezon let "ple" a pa bay sons /p/ + /ə/ + /l/.

Target Words	Yes	No
6. dimple	✓	
7. example	✓	
8. pleasant		✓
9. principle	✓	
10. incomplete		✓

Homework

 Name: _____ Date: ___/___/_____ Score: _____

Lesson 16.5

Reading Words with a Silent Letter "p"

✓ Lesson Check Point

 Directions: Read the target words in the word box. Write the words that have a silent letter "p" in the first column. Write the words that do not have a silent letter "p" in the second column.

Direksyons: Li mo objektif yo ki nan ti bwat mo a. Ekri mo yo ki genyen lèt "p" ki pa pwononse a nan premye kolòn nan. Ekri mo yo ki pa genyen lèt "p" ki pa pwononse a nan dezyèm kolòn nan.

Target Word Box				
trips	coup	receipt	rump	jumps
lamp	pseudo	happen	prove	bishop
cupboard	approve	opposite	hamper	pepper
pamphlet	raspberry	trappings	complete	presume

Letter "p" is silent

- coup
- pseudo
- opposite
- approve
- pepper
- happen
- receipt
- raspberry
- trappings
- cupboard

Letter "p" has the /p/ sound

- trips
- lamp
- rump
- prove
- jumps
- bishop
- hamper
- complete
- presume
- pamphlet

Learn To Read English With Directions In Haitian Creole

Homework

 Name: _____ Date: ___/___/_____ Score: _____

The Reading Challenge

Lesson 16.6

Reading Multisyllable Words

✓ **Lesson Check Point**

 Directions: Read and divide each target word into syllables. Write each word and place a hyphen (-) between the syllables in the second column. Write the number of syllables in the third column. Use a dictionary or the Internet to check your answers.

Direksyons: Li epi divize chak mo objektif an silab. Ekri chak mo epi mete yon tirè (-) ant silab yo nan dezyèm kolòn nan. Ekri kantite silab ke yo genyen an nan twazyèm kolòn nan. Itilize yon diksyonè oubyen entènèt pou tcheke repons ou yo.

Target Words	Words Divided into Syllables	Number of Syllables
1. painting	paint-ing	2
2. paragraph	par-a-graph	3
3. pinwheel	pin-wheel	2
4. provoking	pro-vok-ing	3
5. precedent	prec-e-dent	3
6. player	play-er	2
7. pipeline	pipe-line	2
8. peninsula	pen-in-su-la	4
9. pyramid	pyr-a-mid	3
10. program	pro-gram	2

Homework

 Name: _____ Date: ___/___/_____ Score: _____

The Reading Challenge

Lesson 16.6

Reading Multisyllable Words

✓ **Lesson Check Point**

 Directions: Read each target word. Circle the word in the row that is divided correctly into syllables. Use a dictionary or the Internet to check your answers.

Direksyons: Li chak mo objektif. Antoure mo a ki nan ranje a ki divize an silab korèkteman yo. Itilize yon diksyonè oubyen entènèt pou tcheke repons ou yo.

Model

paragraph	a. (par-a-graph)	b. pa-ra-graph	c. par-ag-raph

1. policy	a. po-li-cy	b. (pol-i-cy)	c. polic-y
2. popular	a. (pop-u-lar)	b. po-pu-lar	c. po-pul-ar
3. Pacific	a. Pac-i-fic	b. (Pa-cif-ic)	c. Pa-ci-fic
4. piano	a. pia-n-o	b. (pi-an-o)	c. pi-a-no
5. pajamas	a. paj-a-mas	b. pa-jam-as	c. (pa-ja-mas)
6. president	a. pre-sid-ent	b. (pres-i-dent)	c. pres-id-ent
7. physical	a. (phys-i-cal)	b. phy-si-cal	c. ph-ysic-al
8. politics	a. po-lit-ics	b. po-li-tics	c. (pol-i-tics)

Learn To Read English With Directions In Haitian Creole

Homework

Name: _____ Date: ___/___/_____ Score: _____

Lesson 16.7

Reading and Writing

Proper and Common Nouns and Adjectives

Directions: Read the words in the word box. Put an (X) on the line next to each word that is written incorrectly. Remember that all proper nouns and proper adjectives are capitalized. Use a dictionary or the Internet to check your answers.

Direksyons: Li chak mo yo ki nan bwat mo a. Met yon (X) sou ti trè a ki bò kote mo ki pa kri byen yo. Sonje ke tout non pwòp ak adjektif pwop ekri avèk yon lèt majiskil nan kòmansman yo. Itilize yon diksyonè oubyen entènèt pou tcheke repons ou yo.

Word Box					
__	panda	__	parrot	__	patient
__	partner	X	Person	X	Peacock
X	Parakeet	X	portland	X	portugal
__	Paraguay	X	Paralegal	__	Panama

Directions: Read each unedited sentence and underline the word that is written incorrectly. Write each sentence correctly on the line.

Direksyons: Li chak fraz ki pa edite yo epi soulinye mo ki pa ekri byen an. Ekri chak fraz korèkteman sou liy lan.

Model
The poem, "puddles," was written by Patrick Parker.
<u>The poem, "Puddles," was written by Patrick Parker.</u>

1. The Pouter pigeons flew to Paramount <u>plaza</u>.
<u>The Pouter pigeons flew to Paramount Plaza.</u>

2. The <u>Pilot</u> will land the plane in the Philippines.
<u>The pilot will land the plane in the Philippines.</u>

3. The <u>Passengers</u> are on their way to Poland, Oregon.
<u>The passengers are on their way to Poland, Oregon.</u>

4. The Paterson police officers are trained to protect the <u>People</u>.
<u>The Paterson police officers are trained to protect the people.</u>

Homework

 Name: _____ Date: ___/___/_____ Score: _____

Lesson 17.1

Reading Words with the Letter Q/q

✓ **Lesson Check Point**

Directions: Read each target word. Find the letter "q" and put a check (✓) in the column that identifies its position: beginning, within or end.
Direksyons: Li chak mo objektif. Jwenn lèt "q" a epi mete yon tchèk (✓) nan kolòn ki idantifye pozisyon li an: nan kòmansman, ladan oubyen nan finisman.

Target Words	Beginning (First Letter)	Within	End (Last Letter)
1. conquer		✓	
2. question	✓		
3. quadruplet	✓		
4. disqualified		✓	
5. consequence		✓	

Directions: Read each sentence and underline the words that begin with the letter "q." Write all the underlined words in alphabetical order on the lines below.
Direksyons: Li chak fraz epi soulinye mo ki kòmanse avèk lèt "q" yo. Ekri tout mo ki soulinye yo nan lòd alfabetik sou trè sa yo ki anba.

6. Janice plans to <u>quit</u> her job at the <u>quilting</u> mill.

7. <u>Queenisha</u> and Christopher <u>quibbled</u> over an issue.

8. Recently, the profits at <u>Quantum</u> Inc. have <u>quadrupled</u>.

9. <u>Quincy</u> is a <u>quarterback</u> on the high school's football team.

10. My mother made a beautiful <u>queen-size</u> <u>quilt</u> for her bed.

quadrupled_____   Quantum_____   quarterback_____
Queenisha_____   queen-size_____   quibbled_____
quilt_____   quilting_____   Quincy_____
                    quit_____

Homework

 Name: _____ Date:___/___/_____ Score:_____

Lesson 17.2

Reading Words with the Letter "q" and "qu" Letter Combination

✓ Lesson Check Point

 Directions: Read each target word. Circle the word in the column that has the same "q" or "qu" sound(s) as the target word.

Direksyons: Li chak mo objektif. Antoure mo a ki nan kolòn nan ki bay menm son "q" oubyen "qu" a (yo) tankou mo objektif la.

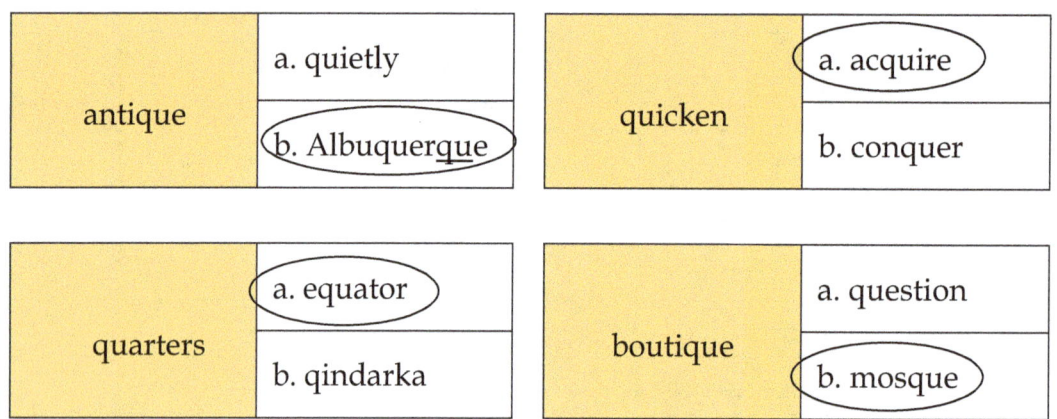

 Directions: Read each target word. Put a check (✓) under the correct column heading.

Direksyons: Li chak mo objektif. Mete yon tchèk (✓) anba antèt kolòn ki kòrèk la.

Target Words	"qu" has the /k/ sound as in the word <u>plaque</u>	"qu" has the /k/ + /w/ sounds as in the word <u>queen</u>
1. antique	✓	
2. quicken		✓
3. quarters		✓
4. boutique	✓	

 Homework

Name: _____ Date: ___/___/_____ Score: _____

Lesson 17.2

Reading Words with the "qu" Letter Combination

✓ **Lesson Check Point**

 Directions: Read each target word. Circle the word in the column that has the same "qu" sound(s) as the target word.

Direksyons: Li chak mo objektif. Antoure mo a ki nan kolòn nan ki bay menm son "qu" a (yo) tankou mo objektif la.

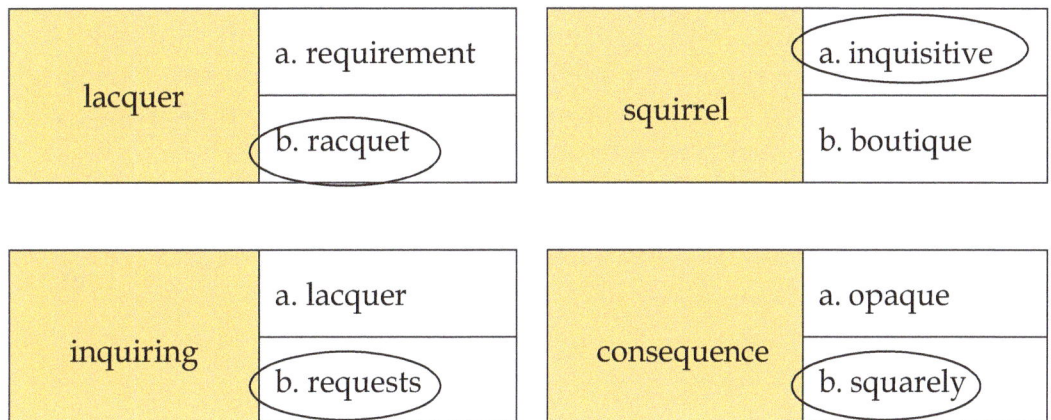

 Directions: Read each target word. Put a check (✓) under the correct column heading.

Direksyons: Li chak mo objektif. Mete yon tchèk (✓) anba antèt kolòn ki kòrèk la.

Target Words	"qu" has the /k/ + /w/ sounds as in the word **queen**	"qu" has the /k/ sound as in the word **plaque**	"qu" is silent as in the word **racquet**
1. lacquer			✓
2. squirrel	✓		
3. inquiring	✓		
4. consequence	✓		

Homework

 Name: _____ Date: ___/___/_____ Score: _____

The Reading Challenge

Lesson 17.3

Reading Multisyllable Words

✓ Lesson Check Point

 Directions: Read and divide each target word into syllables. Write each word and place a hyphen (-) between the syllables in the second column. Write the number of syllables in the third column. Use a dictionary or the Internet to check your answers.

Direksyons: Li epi divize chak mo objektif an silab. Ekri chak mo epi mete yon tirè (-) ant silab yo nan dezyèm kolòn nan. Ekri kantite silab ke yo genyen an nan twazyèm kolòn nan. Itilize yon diksyonè oubyen entènèt pou tcheke repons ou yo.

Target Words	Words Divided into Syllables	Number of Syllables
1. quirky	quirk-y	2
2. quicksand	quick-sand	2
3. quilted	quilt-ed	2
4. questioning	ques-tion-ing	3
5. queasy	quea-sy	2
6. quality	qual-i-ty	3
7. qualitative	qual-i-ta-tive	4
8. quarterly	quar-ter-ly	3
9. qualification	qual-i-fi-ca-tion	5
10. quickening	quick-en-ing	3

Homework

 Name: _____ Date:___/___/_____ Score:_____

The Reading Challenge

Lesson 17.3

Reading Multisyllable Words

✓ **Lesson Check Point**

 Directions: Read each target word. Circle the word in the row that is divided correctly into syllables. Use a dictionary or the Internet to check your answers.

Direksyons: Li chak mo objektif. Antoure mo a ki nan ranje a ki divize an silab korèkteman yo. Itilize yon diksyonè oubyen entènèt pou tcheke repons ou yo.

Model

| quarter | a. quart-er | b. (quar-ter) | c. qu-arter |

1. quarantine	a. (quar-an-tine)	b. qua-rant-ine	c. qua-ran-tine
2. quadruplet	a. qua-drup-let	b. (quad-rup-let)	c. quad-rupl-et
3. qualified	a. qua-lif-ied	b. qua-li-fied	c. (qual-i-fied)
4. quicken	a. (quick-en)	b. qui-cken	c. quic-ken
5. quivering	a. qui-veri-ng	b. (quiv-er-ing)	c. qui-ver-ing
6. quotation	a. quot-a-tion	b. (quo-ta-tion)	c. quot-at-ion
7. quotient	a. (quo-tient)	b. quot-ient	c. qu-otient
8. quotable	a. quo-tab-le	b. quo-ta-ble	c. (quot-a-ble)

Unit Q
Lesson 17.3

Homework

Name: _____   Date:___/___/_____   Score:_____

Lesson 17.4

Reading and Writing

Proper and Common Nouns and Adjectives

Directions: Read the words in the word box. Put an (X) on the line next to each word that is written incorrectly. Remember that all proper nouns and proper adjectives are capitalized. Use a dictionary or the Internet to check your answers.

Direksyons: Li chak mo yo ki nan bwat mo a. Met yon (X) sou ti trè a ki bò kote mo ki pa kri byen yo. Sonje ke tout non pwòp ak adjektif pwop ekri avèk yon lèt majiskil nan kòmansman yo. Itilize yon diksyonè oubyen entènèt pou tcheke repons ou yo.

Word Box					
___	quarterly	___	Quaker	X	qatar
X	Quotient	X	Questions	___	queen
___	quarantine	X	Mrs. quincy	___	quickly
___	Mr. Quinn	X	queen's Park	X	Quiver

Directions: Read each unedited sentence and underline the word that is written incorrectly. Write each sentence correctly on the line.

Direksyons: Li chak fraz ki pa edite yo epi soulinye mo ki pa ekri byen an. Ekri chak fraz korèkteman sou liy lan.

Model
The <u>queen</u> of England was very quiet.
<u>The Queen of England was very quiet.</u>

1. Quinn said, "Yemen and <u>qatar</u> are located on the Arabian Peninsula."
<u>Quinn said, "Yemen and Qatar are located on the Arabian Peninsula."</u>

2. Dr. <u>quinta</u> practices medicine at Queens General Hospital.
<u>Dr. Quinta practices medicine at Queens General Hospital.</u>

3. Mr. Q is qualified for the position at <u>quantum</u> Incorporated.
<u>Mr. Q is qualified for the position at Quantum Incorporated.</u>

4. Pam's <u>Quadruplets</u> are named Queen, Queenie, Quincy and Quinsy.
<u>Pam's quadruplets are named Queen, Queenie, Quincy and Quinsy.</u>

Name: _____   Date: ___/___/_____   Score: _____

Homework

Lesson 18.1

Reading Words with the Letter R/r

✓ Lesson Check Point

 Directions: Read each target word. Find the letter "r" and put a check (✓) in the column that identifies its position: beginning, within or end.
Direksyons: Li chak mo objektif. Jwenn lèt "r" a epi mete yon tchèck (✓) nan kolòn ki idantifye pozisyon li an: nan kòmansman, ladan oubyen nan finisman.

Target Words	Beginning (First Letter)	Within	End (Last Letter)
1. finger			✓
2. radius	✓		
3. carpet		✓	
4. dollar			✓
5. graduation		✓	

 Directions: Read each sentence and underline the words that begin with the letter "r." Write all the underlined words in alphabetical order on the lines below.
Direksyons: Li chak fraz epi soulinye mo ki kòmanse avèk lèt "r" yo. Ekri tout mo ki soulinye yo nan lòd alfabetik sou trè sa yo ki anba.

6. The <u>runners</u> are training for the <u>Riverside</u> Marathon.

7. Gary <u>received</u> a green <u>rocket</u> ship from his favorite aunt.

8. We are <u>returning</u> from a <u>revitalizing</u> tour of the Amazon.

9. Lily and her friends ate chicken and <u>rice</u> at the <u>restaurant</u>.

10. Molly <u>read</u> four nonfiction books about dogs and <u>raccoons</u>.

<u>raccoons</u>　　　　　<u>read</u>　　　　　　<u>received</u>
<u>restaurant</u>　　　　<u>returning</u>　　　　<u>revitalizing</u>
<u>rice</u>　　　　　　　<u>Riverside</u>　　　　<u>rocket</u>
　　　　　　　　　　<u>runners</u>

Homework

Name: _____ Date:___/___/_____ Score: _____

Lesson 18.2

Reading Words with the Letter "r" Combinations:
"br," "cr," "dr," "fr," "gr," "pr" and "tr"

✓ Lesson Check Point

Directions: Read the target words in the word box. Identify the words with the following letter combinations: "br," "cr," "dr," "fr," "gr," "pr" and "tr." Write the target word on the line that correctly completes each sentence.

Direksyons: Li chak mo objektif yo ki nan bwat mo a. Idantifye mo yo ki gen konbinezon lèt: "br," "cr," "dr," "fr," "gr," "pr" ak "tr" yo. Ekri mo objektif la sou liy nan ki konplete korèkteman fraz la.

Target Word Box			
groom	brown	truck	dress
cream	frozen		president
train	cross-examined		cry

1. Francis is eating fresh fruit with vanilla __cream__.

2. The bride and __groom__ are standing on a bridge

3. Frank said, "The block of ice is __frozen__ solid."

4. The __truck__ driver is driving along the highway.

5. Brenda is wearing a pretty __dress__ to the prom.

6. Yesterday, Brad was elected senior class __president__.

7. The colors of the crayons are red, blue and __brown__.

8. The lawyer effectively __cross-examined__ the character witness.

9. All babies __cry__ when they experience hunger.

10. Gare du Lyon is a magnificent __train__ station in France.

Homework

 Name: _____ Date: ___/___/_____ Score: _____

The Reading Challenge

Lesson 18.3

Reading Multisyllable Words

✓ **Lesson Check Point**

 Directions: Read and divide each target word into syllables. Write each word and place a hyphen (-) between the syllables in the second column. Write the number of syllables in the third column. Use a dictionary or the Internet to check your answers.

Direksyons: Li epi divize chak mo objektif an silab. Ekri chak mo epi mete yon tirè (-) ant silab yo nan dezyèm kolòn nan. Ekri kantite silab ke yo genyen an nan twazyèm kolòn nan. Itilize yon diksyonè oubyen entènèt pou tcheke repons ou yo.

Target Words	Words Divided into Syllables	Number of Syllables
1. rocket	rock-et	2
2. rarely	rare-ly	2
3. recalling	re-call-ing	3
4. ratify	rat-i-fy	3
5. recap	re-cap	2
6. ravine	ra-vine	2
7. receiver	re-ceiv-er	3
8. redeeming	re-deem-ing	3
9. raisin	rai-sin	2
10. robotics	ro-bot-ics	3

Homework

Name: _____ Date: ___/___/_____ Score: _____

The Reading Challenge

Lesson 18.3

Reading Multisyllable Words

✓ **Lesson Check Point**

Directions: Read each target word. Circle the word in the row that is divided correctly into syllables. Use a dictionary or the Internet to check your answers.

Direksyons: Li chak mo objektif. Antoure mo a ki nan ranje a ki divize an silab korèkteman yo. Itilize yon diksyonè oubyen entènèt pou tcheke repons ou yo.

Model

| runaway | a. ru-na-way | b. run-a-way ⭕ | c. run-aw-ay |

| 1. recapture | a. re-cap-ture ⭕ | b. re-capt-ure | c. rec-ap-ture |

| 1. romantic | a. rom-an-tic | b. ro-mant-ic | c. ro-man-tic ⭕ |

| 1. rigorous | a. rig-o-rous | b. ri-gor-ous | c. rig-or-ous ⭕ |

| 4. refugee | a. re-fu-gee | b. ref-u-gee ⭕ | c. ref-ug-ee |

| 5. ridicule | a. rid-i-cule ⭕ | b. ri-dic-ule | c. ri-di-cule |

| 6. royalty | a. ro-yal-ty | b. roy-al-ty ⭕ | c. roy-a-lty |

| 7. reversal | a. re-ver-sal ⭕ | b. rev-er-sal | c. re-vers-al |

| 8. recliner | a. recl-i-ner | b. re-clin-er ⭕ | c. rec-li-ner |

Homework

Name: _____ Date: ___/___/_____ Score: _____

Lesson 18.4

Reading and Writing

Proper and Common Nouns and Adjectives

Directions: Read the words in the word box. Put an (X) on the line next to each word that is written incorrectly. Remember that all proper nouns and proper adjectives are capitalized. Use a dictionary or the Internet to check your answers.

Direksyons: Li chak mo yo ki nan bwat mo a. Met yon (X) sou ti trè a ki bò kote mo ki pa kri byen yo. Sonje ke tout non pwòp ak adjektif pwop ekri avèk yon lèt majiskil nan kòmansman yo. Itilize yon diksyonè oubyen entènèt pou tcheke repons ou yo.

Word Box					
_X_	Ranger	___	RSVP	_X_	Raffle
___	reunion	___	royalty	___	realtor
_X_	Raccoon	_X_	roman Empire	_X_	ruthenia
_X_	rio Grande	___	Rhodes scholar	___	riverside

Directions: Read each unedited sentence and underline the word that is written incorrectly. Write each sentence correctly on the line.

Direksyons: Li chak fraz ki pa edite yo epi soulinye mo ki pa ekri byen an. Ekri chak fraz korèkteman sou liy lan.

Model
We saw two <u>Retired</u> racehorses at Richardson Ranch.
<u>We saw two retired racehorses at Richardson Ranch.</u>

1. Roya is <u>Reading</u> her favorite play, "Romeo and Juliet!"
<u>Roya is reading her favorite play, "Romeo and Juliet!"</u>

2. My friend, Rose, bought a nice ring in <u>rio</u> de Janeiro, Brazil.
<u>My friend, Rose, bought a nice ring in Rio de Janeiro, Brazil.</u>

3. Mr. Raymond is studying <u>russian</u> at Russia's best university.
<u>Mr. Raymond is studying Russian at Russia's best university.</u>

4. <u>rita</u> learned that the Nile River provides rich soil for agriculture.
<u>Rita learned that the Nile River provides rich soil for agriculture.</u>

Homework

 Name: _____   Date: ___/___/_____   Score: _____

Lesson 19.1

Reading Words with the Letter S/s

✓ Lesson Check Point

Directions: Read each target word. Find the letter "s" and put a check (✓) in the column that identifies its position: beginning, within or end.
Direksyons: Li chak mo objektif. Jwenn lèt "s" a epi mete yon tchèck (✓) nan kolòn ki idantifye pozisyon li an: nan kòmansman, ladan oubyen nan finisman.

Target Words	Beginning (First Letter)	Within	End (Last Letter)
1. single	✓		
2. seminar	✓		
3. constant		✓	
4. brothers			✓
5. cheeseburger		✓	

Directions: Read each sentence and underline the words that begin with the letter "s." Write all the underlined words in alphabetical order on the lines below.
Direksyons: Li chak fraz epi soulinye mo ki kòmanse avèk lèt "s" yo. Ekri tout mo ki soulinye yo nan lòd alfabetik sou trè sa yo ki anba.

6. You cannot cut a <u>sandwich</u> with <u>scissors</u>.

7. Joy wrote four <u>sentences</u> about <u>sailboats</u>.

8. At college, I am <u>studying</u> computer <u>science</u>.

9. Everyone is <u>saving</u> money for the <u>school</u> trip.

10. We are <u>scheduled</u> to go <u>shopping</u> at one o'clock.

sailboats _____   sandwich _____   saving _____
scheduled _____   school _____   science _____
scissors _____   sentences _____   shopping _____
                       studying _____

Homework

 Name: _____ Date: ___/___/_____ Score: _____

Lesson 19.1

Reading Words with the Letter S/s

✓ **Lesson Check Point**

 Directions: Read each target word. Circle the word in the column that has the same "s" sound as the target word.
Direksyons: Li chak mo objektif. Antoure mo a ki nan kolòn nan ki bay menm son "s" a tankou mo objektif la.

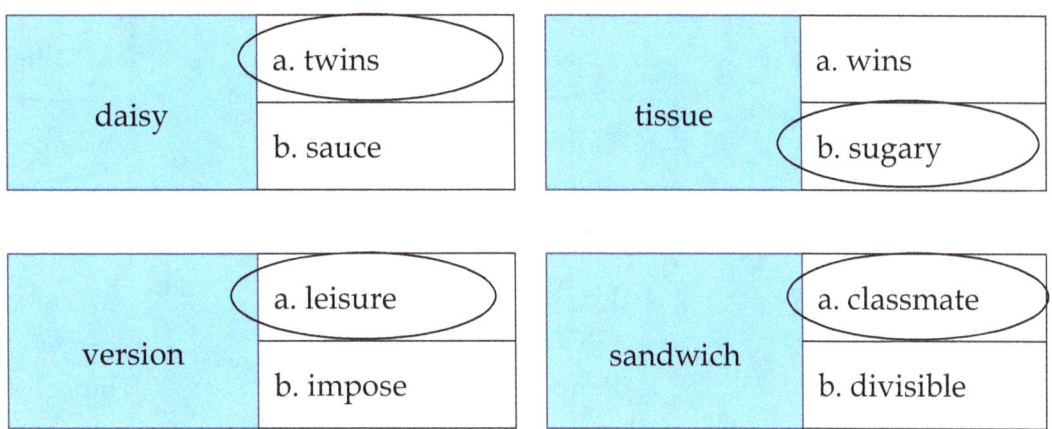

 Directions: Read each target word. Put a check (✓) under the correct column heading.
Direksyons: Li chak mo objektif. Mete yon tchèk (✓) anba antèt kolòn ki kòrèk la.

Target Words	"s" has the /s/ sound as in the word <u>sun</u>	"s" has the /sh/ sound as in the word <u>sugar</u>	"s" has the /z/ sound as in the word <u>his</u>	"s" has the /zh/ sound as in the word <u>vision</u>
1. daisy			✓	
2. tissue		✓		
3. version				✓
4. sandwich	✓			

Homework

 Name: _____ Date:___/___/_____ Score:_____

Lesson 19.2

Reading Words with the "sion," "sial" & "scious" Suffixes

✓ **Lesson Check Point**

 Directions: Read each target word. Circle the word in the column that has the same "sion," "sial" or "scious" sound as the target word.

Direksyons: Li chak mo objektif. Antoure mo a ki nan kolòn nan ki bay menm son "sion", "sial" oubyen "scious" yo tankou mo objektif la.

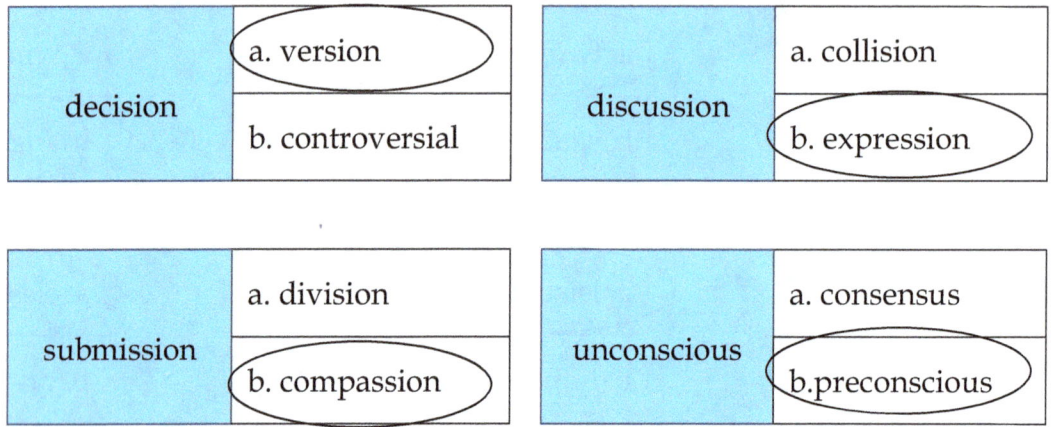

 Directions: Read each target word. Put a check (✓) under the correct column heading.

Direksyons: Li chak mo objektif. Mete yon tchèk (✓) anba antèt kolòn ki kòrèk la.

Target Words	"sion" has the /sh/ +/ə/+/n/ sounds as in the word <u>passion</u>	"sion" has the /zh/ +/ə/+/n/ sounds as in the word <u>vision</u>	"scious" has the /sh/ +/ə/+/s/ sounds as in the word <u>conscious</u>
1. decision		✓	
2. discussion	✓		
3. submission	✓		
4. unconscious			✓

Name: _____ Date: ___/___/_____ Score: _____

Homework

Lesson 19.3

Reading Words with the "sch" Letter Combination

✓ Lesson Check Point

 Directions: Read each target word. Circle the word in the column that has the same "sch" sound(s) as the target word.
Direksyons: Li chak mo objektif. Antoure mo a ki nan kolòn nan ki bay menm son "sch" la (yo) tankou mo objektif la.

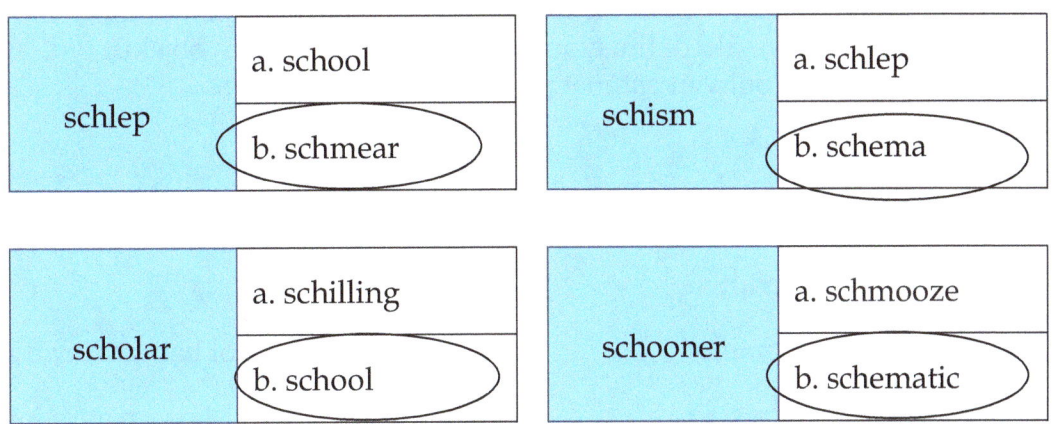

 Directions: Read each target word. Put a check (✓) under the correct column heading.
Direksyons: Li chak mo objektif. Mete yon tchèk (✓) anba antèt kolòn ki kòrèk la.

Target Words	"sch" has the /s/ + /k/ sounds as in the word school	"sch" has the /sh/ sound as in the word schilling
1. schlep		✓
2. schism	✓	
3. scholar	✓	
4. schooner	✓	

Homework

Name: _____ Date: ___/___/_____ Score: _____

Lesson 19.4

Reading Words with the "scr," "shr," "spr" & "str" Letter Combinations

Dictionary Skills/ Vocabulary

✓ Lesson Check Point

Directions: Read each target word and its definition. Write the letter of the definition on the line of each target word. Use a dictionary or the Internet to check your answers.

Direksyons: Li chak mo objektif ak definisyon yo chak. Ekri lèt la ki koresponn ak definisyon an sou trè chak mo objektif yo. Itilize yon diksyonè oubyen entènèt pou tcheke repons ou yo.

Target Words	Definitions
1. **a** script	a. written words of a play
2. **e** sprained	b. an emotional state of being worried
3. **b** stressed	c. to have raised shoulders up and down
4. **c** shrugged	d. to have used a small amount of something
5. **d** scrimped	e. to have had a physical injury to a body part

Directions: Read each sentence. Underline the word in the parentheses that correctly completes each sentence. Then, write the underlined word on the line.

Direksyons: Li chak fraz. Soulinye mo a ki nan parantèz yo ki konplete chak fraz kòrèkteman. Answit, ekri mo soulinye a sou trè a.

6. I __scrimped__ and saved money to buy supplies. (<u>scrimped</u>, shrugged)

7. I am learning to write a __script__ in my English class. (shrugged, <u>script</u>)

8. Jamal is __stressed__ about taking his examinations. (<u>stressed</u>, script)

9. I __sprained__ my ankle during the ball game. (<u>sprained</u>, stressed)

10. He __shrugged__ his shoulders in response to the questions. (scrimped, <u>shrugged</u>)

Homework

Name: _____ Date: ___/___/_____ Score: _____

Lesson 19.5

Reading Words with the "sl" & "sle" Letter Combinations

Dictionary Skills/ Vocabulary

✓ **Lesson Check Point**

Directions: Read each target word and its definition. Write the target word on the line in front of its meaning. Use a dictionary or the Internet to check your answers.

Direksyons: Li chak mo objektif ak definisyon yo chak. Ekri mo objektif la sou trè ki devan definisyon li an. Itilize yon diksyonè oubyen entènèt pou tcheke repons ou yo.

Target Word Box				
slanting	slimy	slippers	slow	slurps

1. __slippers__   backless footwear
2. __slow__   not moving quickly
3. __slimy__   something that feels sticky or slippery
4. __slurps__   making noise while drinking a beverage
5. __slanting__   the position of an object leaning in one direction

Directions: Read each sentence. Underline the word in the parentheses that correctly completes each sentence. Then, write the underlined word on the line.

Direksyons: Li chak fraz. Soulinye mo a ki nan parantèz yo ki konplete chak fraz kòrèkteman. Answit, ekri mo soulinye a sou trè a.

6. The new driver drove in the __slow__ lane. (<u>slow</u>, slimy)

7. Samantha __slurps__ her soda loudly. (<u>slurps</u>, slippers)

8. The __slimy__ fish slipped out of my hands. (slanting, <u>slimy</u>)

9. Mrs. Smith wears her __slippers__ in the kitchen. (slurps, <u>slippers</u>)

10. The people in the painting are __slanting__ to the right. (<u>slanting</u>, slow)

Homework

 Name: _____ Date: ___/___/_____ Score: _____

Lesson 19.5

Reading Words with the "sle" Letter Combination

✓ **Lesson Check Point**

 Directions: Read each target word. Find the "sle" letter combination and put a check (✓) in the column that identifies its position: beginning, within or end.

Direksyons: Li chak mo objektif. Jwenn konbinezon lèt "sle" a epi mete yon tchèk (✓) nan kolòn nan ki idantifye pozisyon li an: nan kòmansman, ladan oubyen nan finisman.

Target Words	Beginning (First 3 Letters)	Within	End (Last 3 Letters)
1. sled	✓		
2. hassle			✓
3. slender	✓		
4. measles		✓	
5. sleeping	✓		

 Directions: Read each target word. Put a check (✓) in the "yes" column if the "sle" letter combination has the /s/ + /ə/ + /l/ or /z/ + /ə/ + /l/ sounds. Put a check (✓) in the "no" column if the "sle" letter combination does not have the /s/ + /ə/ + /l/ or /z/ + /ə/ + /l/ sounds.

Direksyons: Li chak mo objektif. Mete yon tchèk (✓) nan kolòn "yes" an si konbinezon lèt "sle" a bay sons /s/ + /ə/ + /l/ oubyen /z/ + /ə/ + /l/. Mete yon tchèk (✓) nan kolòn "no" an si konbinezon lèt "sle" a pa bay sons /s/ + /ə/ + /l/ oubyen /z/ + /ə/ + /l/.

Target Words	Yes	No
6. sled		✓
7. hassle	✓	
8. slender		✓
9. measles	✓	
10. sleeping		✓

Homework

 Name: _____ Date: ___/___/_____ Score: _____

Lesson 19.6

Reading Words with the "sm" Letter Combination

✓ Lesson Check Point

 Directions: Read each target word. Circle the word in the column that has the same "sm" sounds as the target word.

Direksyons: Li chak mo objektif. Antoure mo a ki nan kolòn nan ki bay menm son "sm" la (yo) tankou mo objektif la.

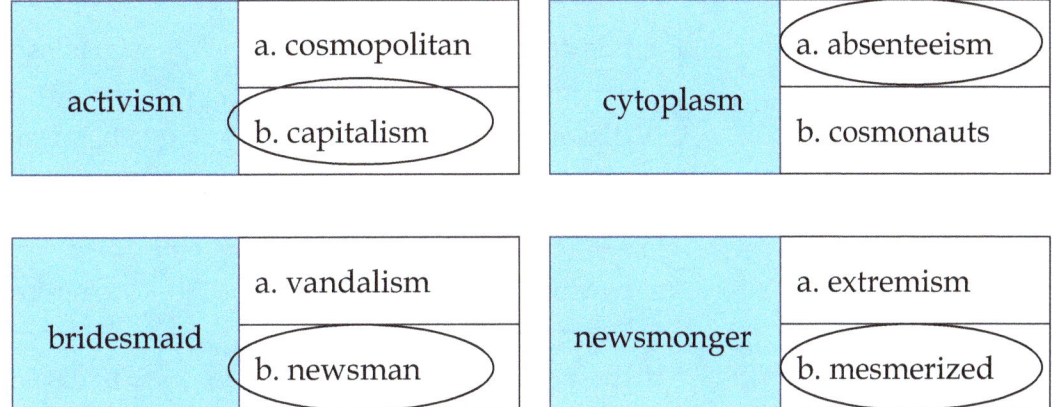

 Directions: Read each target word. Put a check (✓) under the correct column heading.

Direksyons: Li chak mo objektif. Mete yon tchèk (✓) anba antèt kolòn ki kòrèk la.

Target Words	"sm" has the /s/ + /m/ sounds as in the word smell	"sm" has the /z/ + /m/ sounds as in the word cosmic	"sm" has the /z/ + /ə/ + /m/ sounds as in the word autism
1. activism			✓
2. cytoplasm			✓
3. bridesmaid		✓	
4. newsmonger		✓	

Homework

 Name: _____ Date:___/___/_____ Score:_____

Lesson 19.7

Reading Words with the "ss" Letter Combination

✓ Lesson Check Point

 Directions: Read each target word. Circle the word in the column that has the same "ss" sound(s) as the target word.

Direksyons: Li chak mo objektif. Antoure mo a ki nan kolòn nan ki bay menm son "ss" la (yo) tankou mo objektif la.

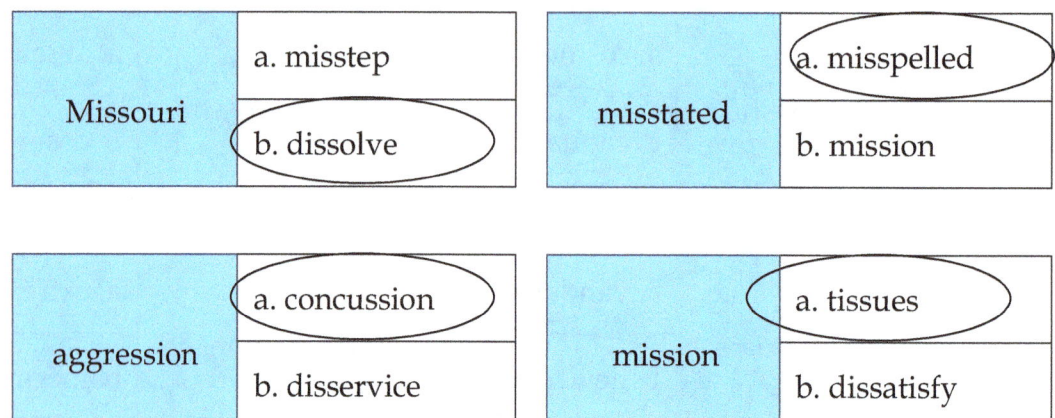

 Directions: Read each target word. Put a check (✓) under the correct column heading.

Direksyons: Li chak mo objektif. Mete yon tchèk (✓) anba antèt kolòn ki kòrèk la.

Target Words	"ss" has the /sh/ sound as in the word <u>tissue</u>	"ss" has the /s/ + /s/ sounds as in the word <u>misspell</u>	"ss" has the /z/ sound as in the word <u>dissolve</u>
1. Missouri			✓
2. misstated		✓	
3. aggression	✓		
4. mission		✓	

Homework

 Name: _____ Date: ___/___/_____ Score: _____

Lesson 19.8

Reading Words with a Silent Letter "s"

✓ Lesson Check Point

Directions: Read the target words in the word box. Write the words that have a silent letter "s" in the first column. Write the words that do not have a silent letter "s" in the second column.

Direksyons: Li mo objektif yo ki nan ti bwat mo a. Ekri mo yo ki genyen lèt "s" ki pa pwononse a nan premye kolòn nan. Ekri mo yo ki pa genyen lèt "s" ki pa pwononse a nan dezyèm kolòn nan.

Target Word Box				
obese	isles	mass	aisle	guess
results	nests	assist	pupils	lesson
island	screen	debris	forsake	stories
Arkansas	humans	exposes	coconuts	blossom

Letter "s" is silent	Letter "s" has the /s/, /z/ or /sh/ sound
mass	nests
isles	obese
aisle	screen
assist	pupils
guess	results
island	exposes
debris	forsake
lesson	stories
blossom	humans
Arkansas	coconuts

Learn To Read English With Directions In Haitian Creole

Unit S Lesson 19.8

Homework

 Name: _____ Date: ___/___/_____ Score: _____

The Reading Challenge

Lesson 19.9

Reading Multisyllable Words

✓ **Lesson Check Point**

 Directions: Read and divide each target word into syllables. Write each word and place a hyphen (-) between the syllables in the second column. Write the number of syllables in the third column. Use a dictionary or the Internet to check your answers.

Direksyons: Li epi divize chak mo objektif an silab. Ekri chak mo epi mete yon tirè (-) ant silab yo nan dezyèm kolòn nan. Ekri kantite silab ke yo genyen an nan twazyèm kolòn nan. Itilize yon diksyonè oubyen entènèt pou tcheke repons ou yo.

Target Words	Words Divided into Syllables	Number of Syllables
1. sentiment	sen-ti-ment	3
2. silver	sil-ver	2
3. shipment	ship-ment	2
4. seventh	sev-enth	2
5. soda	so-da	2
6. sneaker	sneak-er	2
7. shamrock	sham-rock	2
8. secondly	sec-ond-ly	3
9. scheduling	sched-ul-ing	3
10. sewing	sew-ing	2

Homework

 Name: _____ Date: ___/___/_____ Score: _____

The Reading Challenge

Lesson 19.9

Reading Multisyllable Words

✓ Lesson Check Point

 Directions: Read each target word. Circle the word in the row that is divided correctly into syllables. Use a dictionary or the Internet to check your answers.

Direksyons: Li chak mo objektif. Antoure mo a ki nan ranje a ki divize an silab korèkteman yo. Itilize yon diksyonè oubyen entènèt pou tcheke repons ou yo.

Model

| Saturday | a. Sa-tur-day | b. Sat-ur-day ⭕ | c. Sa-turd-ay |

| 1. sectional | a. sec-tion-al ⭕ | b. sect-ion-al | c. se-ction-al |

| 2. solution | a. so-lut-ion | b. sol-ut-ion | c. so-lu-tion ⭕ |

| 3. situate | a. si-tuat-e | b. sit-ua-te | c. sit-u-ate ⭕ |

| 4. slavery | a. sla-ver-y | b. slav-er-y ⭕ | c. sla-ve-ry |

| 5. sisterhood | a. sis-ter-hood ⭕ | b. si-ster-hood | c. sis-terh-ood |

| 6. sodium | a. sod-i-um | b. so-diu-m | c. so-di-um ⭕ |

| 7. scorpion | a. scor-p-ion | b. scor-pi-on ⭕ | c. sco-rpi-on |

| 8. survival | a. sur-viv-al ⭕ | b. sur-vi-val | c. surv-i-val |

Unit S
Lesson 19.9

Homework

Name: _____ Date:___/___/_____ Score:_____

Lesson 19.10

Reading and Writing

Proper and Common Nouns and Adjectives

Directions: Read the words in the word box. Put an (X) on the line next to each word that is written incorrectly. Remember that all proper nouns and proper adjectives are capitalized. Use a dictionary or the Internet to check your answers.

Direksyons: Li chak mo yo ki nan bwat mo a. Met yon (X) sou ti trè a ki bò kote mo ki pa kri byen yo. Sonje ke tout non pwòp ak adjektif pwop ekri avèk yon lèt majiskil nan kòmansman yo. Itilize yon diksyonè oubyen entènèt pou tcheke repons ou yo.

Word Box					
___	Senegal	___	senior	X	sidney
___	seaweed	X	Shelter	X	Seminar
X	Shipyard	___	Saturday	X	saudi Arabia
X	Shepherd	___	Sahara Desert	___	Sierra Leone

Directions: Read each unedited sentence and underline the word that is written incorrectly. Write each sentence correctly on the line.

Direksyons: Li chak fraz ki pa edite yo epi soulinye mo ki pa ekri byen an. Ekri chak fraz korèkteman sou liy lan.

Model
<u>sandy</u> is going to Salt Lake City on Sunday.
Sandy is going to Salt Lake City on Sunday.

1. The students cannot sit in silence for <u>Six</u> minutes.
   The students cannot sit in silence for six minutes.

2. On <u>saturday</u>, Senator Smith made a sensational speech.
   On Saturday, Senator Smith made a sensational speech.

3. The short story entitled, "Seven <u>siblings</u>" has a shocking plot.
   The short story entitled, "Seven Siblings" has a shocking plot.

4. Sidney Elementary School is scheduled to open in <u>september</u>.
   Sidney Elementary School is scheduled to open in September.

Homework

Name: _____ Date:___/___/_____ Score:_____

Lesson 20.1

Reading Words with the Letter T/t

Directions: Read each target word. Find the letter "t" and put a check (✓) in the column that identifies its position: beginning, within or end.
Direksyons: Li chak mo objektif. Jwenn lèt "t" a epi mete yon tchèck (✓) nan kolòn ki idantifye pozisyon li an: nan kòmansman, ladan oubyen nan finisman.

Target Words	Beginning (First Letter)	Within	End (Last Letter)
1. poet			✓
2. rocket			✓
3. liberty		✓	
4. thunder	✓		
5. mustard		✓	

Directions: Read each sentence and underline the words that begin with the letter "t." Write all the underlined words in alphabetical order on the lines below.
Direksyons: Li chak fraz epi soulinye mo yo ki kòmanse avèk lèt "t" a. Ekri tout mo ki souliye yo nan lòd alfabetik sou trè sa yo ki anba.

6. I <u>taped</u> four pages in my <u>textbook</u>.

7. Patrick said, "<u>Tortillas</u> are very <u>tasty</u>."

8. Gina's <u>telephone</u> is <u>tan</u> and dark brown.

9. On Saturday, we will watch <u>television</u> <u>together</u>.

10. My second grade **teacher** read a book about <u>tigers</u>.

tan _____   taped _____   tasty _____
teacher _____   telephone _____   television _____
textbook _____   tigers _____   together _____
                        tortillas _____

Homework

 Name: _____ Date: ___/___/_____ Score: _____

Lesson 20.2

Reading Words with the "thm" Letter Combination

✓ **Lesson Check Point**

 Directions: Read each target word. Circle the word in the column that has the same "thm" sound(s) as the target word.

Direksyons: Li chak mo objektif. Antoure mo a ki nan kolòn nan ki bay menm son "thm" la (yo) tankou mo objektif la.

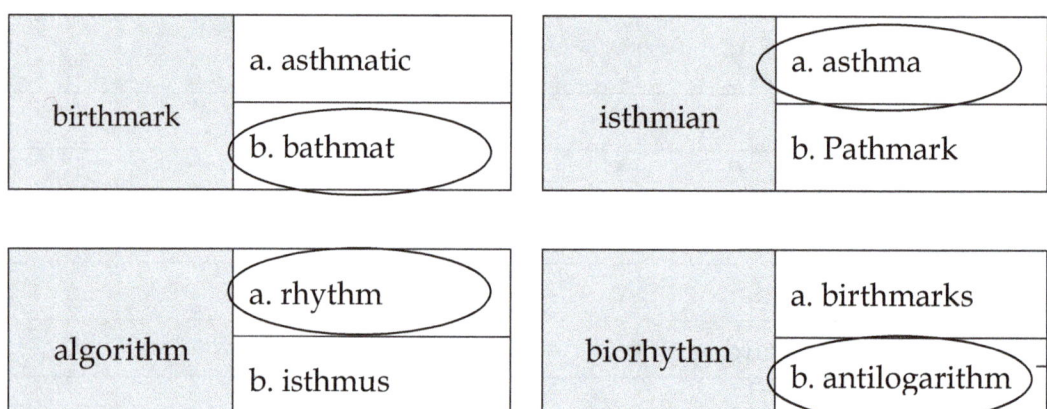

 Directions: Read each target word. Put a check (✓) under the correct column heading.

Direksyons: Li chak mo objektif. Mete yon tchèk (✓) anba antèt kolòn ki kòrèk la.

Target Words	"thm" has the /th/ + /ə/ + /m/ sounds as in the word rhythm	"thm" has the /th/ + /m/ sounds as in the word bathmat	"thm" silent "th" + /m/ sound as in the word asthma
1. birthmark		✓	
2. isthmian			✓
3. algorithm	✓		
4. biorhythm	✓		

Homework

 Name: _____ Date: ___/___/_____ Score: _____

Lesson 20.3

Reading Words with the "tion," "tial" & "tious" Suffixes

✓ **Lesson Check Point**

 Directions: Read each target word. Circle the word in the column that has the same "tion," "tial" or "tious" sound as the target word.

Direksyons: Li chak mo objektif. Antoure mo a ki nan kolòn nan ki bay menm son "tion", "tial" oubyen "tious" yo tankou mo objektif la.

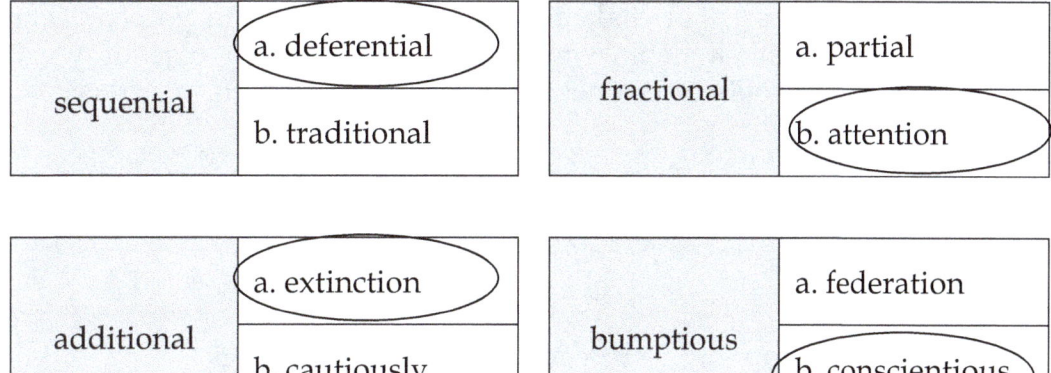

 Directions: Read each target word. Put a check (✓) under the correct column heading.

Direksyons: Li chak mo objektif. Mete yon tchèk (✓) anba antèt kolòn ki kòrèk la.

Target Words	"tion" has the /sh/ +/ə/+/n/ sounds as in the word <u>education</u>	"tial" has the /sh/ +/ə/+/l/ sounds as in the word <u>partial</u>	"tious" has the /sh/ +/ə/+/s/ sounds as in the word <u>ambitious</u>
1. sequential		✓	
2. fractional	✓		
3. additional	✓		
4. bumptious			✓

Homework

Name: _____ Date:___/___/_____ Score:_____

Lesson 20.4

Reading Words with the "tr" Letter Combination

Dictionary Skills/ Vocabulary

✓ Lesson Check Point

Directions: Read each target word and its definition. Write the letter of the definition on the line of each target word. Use a dictionary or the Internet to check your answers.

Direksyons: Li chak mo objektif ak definisyon yo chak. Ekri lèt la ki koresponn ak definisyon an sou trè chak mo objektif yo. Itilize yon diksyonè oubyen entènèt pou tcheke repons ou yo.

Target Words	Definitions
1. _e_ tree	a. a path in a wooden area
2. _b_ trap	b. a device used to catch things
3. _a_ trail	c. to take a trip from one place to another
4. _c_ travel	d. the betrayal of one's country by helping its enemies
5. _d_ treason	e. woody plant with a thick trunk

Directions: Read each sentence. Underline the word in the parentheses that correctly completes each sentence. Then, write the underlined word on the line.

Direksyons: Li chak fraz. Soulinye mo a ki nan parantèz yo ki konplete chak fraz kòrèkteman. Answit, ekri mo soulinye a sou trè a.

6. The mouse was caught in the _____trap_____. (<u>trap</u>, travel)

7. I sat under a shady _____tree_____ in the park. (<u>tree</u>, treason)

8. The traitor was arrested for high _____treason_____. (<u>treason</u>, trap)

9. The toddlers are riding their tricycles along the __trail__. (tree, <u>trail</u>)

10. Today, Troy is scheduled to __travel__ to Tennessee. (trail, <u>travel</u>)

Homework

 Name: _____ Date:___/___/_____ Score:_____

Lesson 20.5

Reading Words with the "tle" Letter Combination

✓ Lesson Check Point

 Directions: Read each target word. Find the "tle" letter combination and put a check in the column that identifies its position: beginning, within or end.

Direksyons: Li chak mo objektif. Jwenn konbinezon lèt "tle" a epi mete yon tchèk (✓) nan kolòn nan ki idantifye pozisyon li an: nan kòmansman, ladan oubyen nan finisman.

Target Words	Beginning (First 3 Letters)	Within	End (Last 3 Letters)
1. beetle			✓
2. rattle			✓
3. bootleg		✓	
4. limitless		✓	
5. effortless		✓	

 Directions: Read each target word. Put a check (✓) in the "yes" column if the "tle" letter combination has the /t/ + /ə/ + /l/ sounds. Put a check (✓) in the "no" column if the "tle" letter combination does not have the /t/ + /ə/ + /l/ sounds.

Direksyons: Li chak mo objektif. Mete yon tchèk (✓) nan kolòn "yes" an si konbinezon let "tle" a bay sons /t/ + /ə/ + /l/. Mete yon tchèk (✓) nan kolòn "no" an si konbinezon let "tle" a pa bay sons /t/ + /ə/ + /l/.

Target Words	Yes	No
6. beetle	✓	
7. rattle	✓	
8. bootleg		✓
9. limitless		✓
10. effortless		✓

Homework

 Name: _____ Date:___/___/_____ Score: _____

Lesson 20.6

Reading Words with the Letter "t" Sounds

✓ **Lesson Check Point**

 Directions: Read each target word. Circle the word in the column that has the same "t" sound as the target word.

Direksyons: Li chak mo objektif. Antoure mo a ki nan kolòn nan ki bay menm son "t" a tankou mo objektif la.

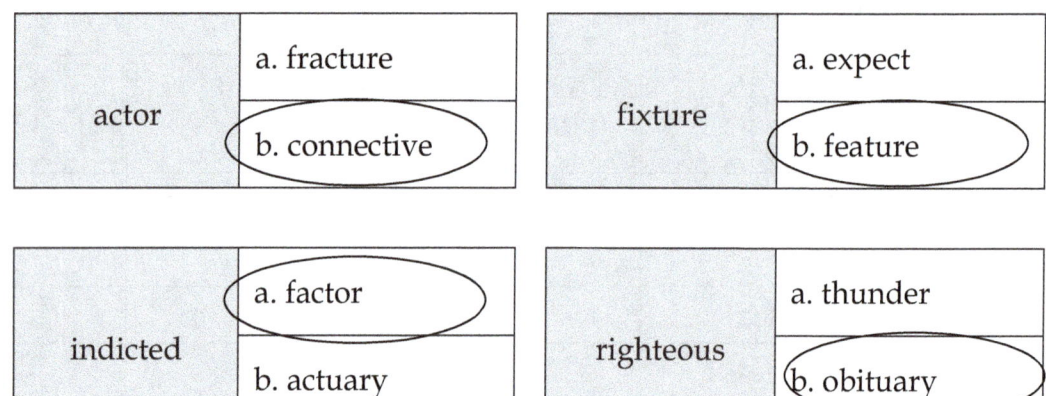

 Directions: Read each target word. Put a check (✓) under the correct column heading.

Direksyons: Li chak mo objektif. Mete yon tchèk (✓) anba antèt kolòn ki kòrèk la.

Target Words	"t" has the /t/ sound as in the word <u>multiply</u>	"t" has the /ch/ sound as in the word <u>picture</u>	"t" has the /sh/ sound as in the word <u>position</u>
1. actor	✓		
2. fixture		✓	
3. indicted	✓		
4. righteous		✓	

Homework

 Name: _____ Date: ___/___/_____ Score: _____

Lesson 20.7

Reading Words with a Silent Letter "t"

✓ **Lesson Check Point**

 Directions: Read the target words in the word box. Write the words that have a silent letter "t" in the first column. Write the words that do not have a silent letter "t" in the second column.

Direksyons: Li mo objektif yo ki nan ti bwat mo a. Ekri mo yo ki genyen lèt "t" ki pa pwononse a nan premye kolòn nan. Ekri mo yo ki pa genyen lèt "t" ki pa pwononse a nan dezyèm kolòn nan.

Target Word Box				
hasten	fault	contract	ballet	digit
educate	debut	buffet	soften	litter
chapter	fainting	fasten	trouble	timely
rapport	tsunami	attach	generate	dustpan

Letter "t" is silent

litter
ballet
buffet
attach
fasten
hasten
debut
soften
rapport
tsunami

Letter "t" has the /t/ sound

digit
fault
chapter
timely
educate
trouble
dustpan
contract
fainting
generate

Homework

 Name: _____ Date: ___/___/_____ Score: _____

The Reading Challenge

Lesson 20.8

Reading Multisyllable Words

✓ **Lesson Check Point**

 Directions: Read and divide each target word into syllables. Write each word and place a hyphen (-) between the syllables in the second column. Write the number of syllables in the third column. Use a dictionary or the Internet to check your answers.

Direksyons: Li epi divize chak mo objektif an silab. Ekri chak mo epi mete yon tirè (-) ant silab yo nan dezyèm kolòn nan. Ekri kantite silab ke yo genyen an nan twazyèm kolòn nan. Itilize yon diksyonè oubyen entènèt pou tcheke repons ou yo.

Target Words	Words Divided into Syllables	Number of Syllables
1. treatment	treat-ment	2
2. tutorial	tu-to-ri-al	4
3. tenderly	ten-der-ly	3
4. today	to-day	2
5. tiger	ti-ger	2
6. thicken	thick-en	2
7. treadmill	tread-mill	2
8. twentieth	twen-ti-eth	3
9. themselves	them-selves	2
10. transported	trans-port-ed	3

Homework

 Name: _____ Date: ___/___/_____ Score: _____

The Reading Challenge

Lesson 20.8

Reading Multisyllable Words

✓ Lesson Check Point

 Directions: Read each target word. Circle the word in the row that is divided correctly into syllables. Use a dictionary or the Internet to check your answers.

Direksyons: Li chak mo objektif. Antoure mo a ki nan ranje a ki divize an silab korèkteman yo. Itilize yon diksyonè oubyen entènèt pou tcheke repons ou yo.

Model

| telephone | a. te-lep-hone | b. tel-e-phone (circled) | c. te-le-phone |

| 1. typify | a. typ-i-fy (circled) | b. ty-pi-fy | c. typ-if-y |

| 2. tropical | a. tro-pi-cal | b. tro-pic-al | c. trop-i-cal (circled) |

| 3. thematic | a. them-at-ic | b. the-m-atic | c. the-mat-ic (circled) |

| 4. tendency | a. ten-denc-y | b. ten-den-cy (circled) | c. tend-en-cy |

| 5. treasury | a. treas-u-ry | b. treas-ur-y (circled) | c. trea-sur-y |

| 6. tragedy | a. trag-e-dy (circled) | b. tra-ged-y | c. trag-ed-y |

| 7. together | a. tog-et-her | b. to-geth-er (circled) | c. to-get-her |

| 8. tricycle | a. tri-cy-cle (circled) | b. tri-cyc-le | c. tric-yc-le |

Unit T
Lesson 20.8

Learn To Read English With Directions In Haitian Creole   201   Copyrighted Material

Homework

Name: _____ Date: ___/___/_____ Score: _____

Lesson 20.9

Reading and Writing

Proper and Common Nouns and Adjectives

Directions: Read the words in the word box. Put an (X) on the line next to each word that is written incorrectly. Remember that all proper nouns and proper adjectives are capitalized. Use a dictionary or the Internet to check your answers.

Direksyons: Li chak mo yo ki nan bwat mo a. Met yon (X) sou ti trè a ki bò kote mo ki pa kri byen yo. Sonje ke tout non pwòp ak adjektif pwop ekri avèk yon lèt majiskil nan kòmansman yo. Itilize yon diksyonè oubyen entènèt pou tcheke repons ou yo.

Word Box					
__	thirst	__	Tibet	__	teapot
X	Tutor	__	triplet	X	Tornado
X	tampa	__	texture	X	Trickster
X	tuesday	X	Tomorrow	__	Tennessee

Directions: Read each unedited sentence and underline the word that is written incorrectly. Write each sentence correctly on the line.

Direksyons: Li chak fraz ki pa edite yo epi soulinye mo ki pa ekri byen an. Ekri chak fraz korèkteman sou liy lan.

Model
On <u>thursday</u>, a tornado destroyed my hometown.
On Thursday, a tornado destroyed my hometown.

1. The <u>Taxicab</u> driver drives all over Trenton, Tennessee.
The taxicab driver drives all over Trenton, Tennessee.

2. <u>the</u> Texas tourism office is located in Town Hall.
The Texas tourism office is located in Town Hall.

3. I quenched my thirst with green tea from <u>thailand</u>.
I quenched my thirst with green tea from Thailand.

4. My English <u>Textbook</u> has a passage about the City of Troy.
My English textbook has a passage about the City of Troy.

Homework

 Name: _____ Date: ___/___/_____ Score: _____

Lesson 21.1

Reading Words with the Letter U/u

✓ Lesson Check Point

Directions: Read each target word. Find the letter "u" and put a check (✓) in the column that identifies its position: beginning, within or end.
Direksyons: Li chak mo objektif. Jwenn lèt "u" a epi mete yon tchèck (✓) nan kolòn ki idantifye pozisyon li an: nan kòmansman, ladan oubyen nan finisman.

Target Words	Beginning (First Letter)	Within	End (Last Letter)
1. Peru			✓
2. south		✓	
3. refuge		✓	
4. umbrella	✓		
5. university	✓		

Directions: Read each target word. Read the words in the row and circle the word that has a different vowel "u" sound.
Direksyons: Li chak mo objektif. Li mo yo ki nan ranje a epi antoure mo a ki bay yon son vwayèl "u" ki diferan an.

Target Words				
6. glum	bug	pub	(dual)	rug
7. dunk	sup	hug	puff	(fluke)
8. lung	puck	(rule)	jug	dug
9. hunch	hub	plug	(flume)	mug
10. umbrella	club	buns	hunting	(quiet)

Learn To Read English With Directions In Haitian Creole

Homework

 Name: _____ Date: ___/___/_____ Score: _____

Lesson 21.2

Reading Words with the Short Vowel "u" Sound

✓ **Lesson Check Point**

   Directions: Read the words in the four boxes. Circle two words with the short vowel /ŭ/ sound. The anchor word for the short vowel /ŭ/ sound is <u>up</u>.

Direksyons: Li mo yo ki nan kat ti bwat yo. Antoure de mo ki genyen son vwayèl kout /ŭ/ a. Mo referans pou son vwayèl kout /ŭ/ a se mo, <u>up</u>.

(gulp)	duke		skull	(chunk)		(munch)	tofu
huge	(stump)		mule	brute		(blush)	cube

(flush)	tube		(hung)	(fuss)		guard	true
(skunk)	fluke		blue	rude		(slush)	(hump)

   Directions: Read the words in the four boxes. Circle two words that rhyme. Rhyming words have the same ending sound, such as <u>just</u> and <u>must</u>.

Direksyons: Li mo yo ki nan kat ti bwat yo. Antoure de mo ki rime. De mo oubyen plizyè mo ki rime genyen menm son nan finisman yo, tankou <u>just</u> ak <u>must</u>.

(rub)	(tub)		(dusk)	quite		(jump)	muse
guess	guide		(tusk)	duo		buy	(pump)

cue	gruel		run	bruise		(hutch)	(Dutch)
(rung)	(sung)		burn	(sun)		prune	hue

Learn To Read English With Directions In Haitian Creole

Homework

L. Name: _____ Date: ___/___/_____ Score: _____

Lesson 21.2

Reading & Writing Words with the Short Vowel "u" Sound

✓ **Lesson Check Point**

Directions: Read each sentence and underline three words with the short vowel /ŭ/ sound. Then, write the underlined words on the lines below. The anchor word for the short vowel /ŭ/ sound is <u>up</u>.

Direksyons: Li chak fraz epi soulinye twa mo ki genyen son vwayèl kout /ŭ/ a. Answit, ekri mo soulinye yo sou trè sa yo ki anba. Mo referans pou son vwayèl kout /ŭ/a se mo, <u>up</u>.

Model
Ulysses, the <u>drummer</u>, <u>jumps</u> when he plays the <u>drums</u>.

    drummer   jumps   drums

1. At <u>lunchtime</u>, Sue said, "Do not <u>run</u> in the <u>hut</u>!"

    lunchtime   run   hut

2. The baby <u>cubs</u> used to <u>jump</u> on the tree <u>stumps</u>.

    cubs   jump   stumps

3. The <u>truck</u> driver had a huge <u>lunch</u> at the <u>clubhouse</u>.

    truck   lunch   clubhouse

4. The cute <u>bugs</u> look like they are having <u>fun</u> in the <u>mud</u>.

    bugs   fun   mud

5. Bruce's new album is entitled, "<u>Running</u> in the Hot <u>Summer</u> <u>Sun</u>."

    Running   Summer   Sun

Learn To Read English With Directions In Haitian Creole

Homework

 Name: _____ Date:___/___/_____ Score:_____

Lesson 21.3

Reading Words with the Long Vowel "u" Sound

✓ Lesson Check Point

 Directions: Read the words in the four boxes. Circle two words with the long vowel /yo͞o/ or /o͞o/ sound. The anchor word for the long vowel /yo͞o/ and /o͞o/ sounds is <u>tube</u>.

Direksyons: Li mo yo ki nan kat ti bwat yo. Antoure de mo ki genyen son vwayèl long /yo͞o/ oubyen /o͞o/ a. Mo referans pou son vwayèl long /yo͞o/ ak /o͞o/ es la palabra, <u>tube</u>.

(tribute)	dune	much	(used)	(produce)	nullify
hump	puff	rusty	(defuse)	hunch	(exclude)

(intrude)	rung	(pollute)	jaguar	liquid	guess
(huge)	plumber	guitar	(spruce)	(dual)	visual

 Directions: Read the words in the four boxes. Circle two words that rhyme. Rhyming words have the same ending sound, such as <u>rule</u> and <u>mule</u>.

Direksyons: Li mo yo ki nan kat ti bwat yo. Antoure de mo ki rime. De mo oubyen plizyè mo ki rime genyen menm son nan finisman yo, tankou <u>rule</u> ak <u>mule</u>.

rung	(tube)	hung	(true)	hunter	truck
(cube)	hush	(issue)	blushing	(tissue)	(argue)

husky	(duke)	dusty	lunch	slum	(blue)
bumper	(fluke)	(cute)	(brute)	brush	(cue)

Homework

📖 Name: _____ Date: ___/___/_____ Score: _____

Lesson 21.3

Reading & Writing Words with the Long Vowel "u" Sound

✓ **Lesson Check Point**

Directions: Read each sentence and underline three words with the long vowel /yōō/ or /ōō/ sound. Then, write the underlined words on the lines below. The anchor word for the long vowel /yōō/ and /ōō/ sounds is <u>tube</u>.

Direksyons: Li chak fraz epi soulinye twa mo ki genyen son vwayèl long /yōō/ oubyen /ōō/ yo. Answit, ekri mo soulinye yo sou trè sa yo ki anba. Mo referans pou son vwayèl long /yōō/ ak /ōō/ es la palabra, <u>tube</u>.

Model

<u>Bruce</u> is going to play the <u>tuba</u> and drums in <u>Uganda</u>.

  Bruce   tuba   Uganda
  _____   _____   _____

1. The <u>students</u> are studying about <u>producers</u> and <u>consumers</u>.

  students   producers   consumers
  _____   _____   _____

2. The <u>truants</u> did not <u>graduate</u> because of their acts of <u>truancy</u>.

  truants   graduate   truancy
  _____   _____   _____

3. The <u>students</u> living on Hunter <u>Avenue</u> will <u>graduate</u> in August.

  students   Avenue   graduate
  _____   _____   _____

4. In <u>June</u>, I will take a fun-filled vacation to <u>Peru</u> and <u>Yugoslavia</u>.

  June   Peru   Yugoslavia
  _____   _____   _____

5. In <u>July</u>, the drummer <u>argued</u> about our <u>contractual</u> agreement.

  July   argued   contractual
  _____   _____   _____

Homework

Name: _____ Date: ___/___/_____ Score: _____

Review Lessons 21.2 & 21.3

Reading Short Vowel and Long Vowel Words

Directions: Read the target words in the word box. In the first column, write the words that have the short vowel /ŭ/ sound, as in the word <u>up</u>. In the second column, write the words that have the long vowel /yōō/ or /ōō/ sound, as in the word <u>tube</u>.

Direksyons: Li mo yoobjektif yo ki nan bwat mo a. Nan premye kolòn nan, ekri mo ki bay son vwayèl kout /ŭ/ yo, tankou li ye nan mo <u>up</u> la. Nan dezyèm kolòn nan, ekri mo ki bay son vwayèl long /yōō/ oubyen /ōō/, yo, tankou li ye nan mo <u>tube</u> la.

Target Word Box				
husky	true	lunch	argue	salute
Dutch	rusty	visual	drunk	chunky
confuse	reduce	flushing	strung	annual
pollute	execute	blushing	graduate	brushing

Letter "u" has the /ŭ/ sound as in the word <u>up</u>

- husky
- Dutch
- rusty
- lunch
- flushing
- blushing
- drunk
- strung
- chunky
- brushing

Letter "u" has the /yōō/ or /ōō/ sound as in the word <u>tube</u>

- confuse
- pollute
- true
- reduce
- execute
- argue
- salute
- visual
- annual
- graduate

Homework

 Name: _____ Date: ___/___/_____ Score: _____

Lesson 21.4

Reading Words with Letter "u" Vowel Pairs

 Lesson Check Point

Directions: Read each target word. Circle the word in the column that has the same vowel "ua," "ue" or "ui" sound(s) as the target word.

Direksyons: Li chak mo objektif. Antoure mo a ki nan kolòn nan ki bay menm son vwayèl "ua," "ue" oubyen "ui" la (yo) tankou mo objektif la.

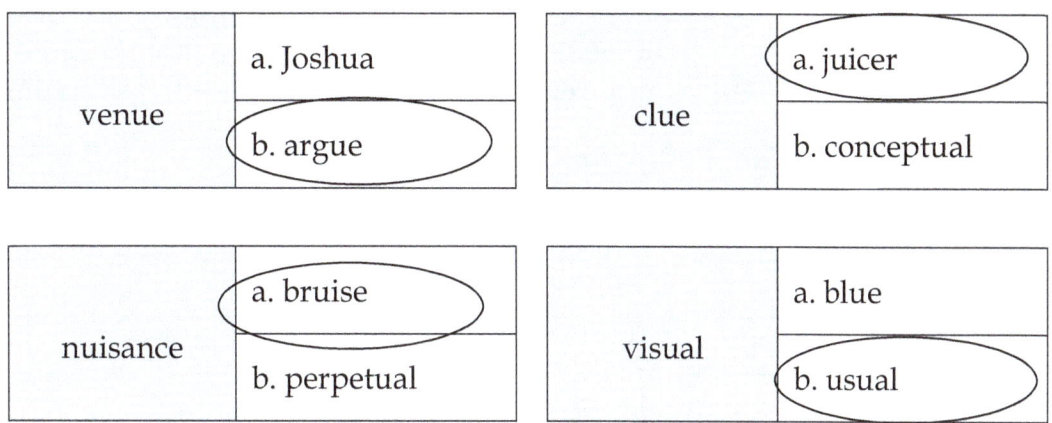

 Directions: Read each target word. Put a check (✓) under the correct column heading.

Direksyons: Li chak mo objektif. Mete yon tchèk (✓) anba antèt kolòn ki kòrèk la.

Target Words	Words have the long "u" sound as in the word <u>blue</u>	Words do not have the long "u" sound
1. due	✓	
2. suite		✓
3. factual	✓	
4. continue	✓	

Homework

 Name: _____ Date: ___/___/_____ Score: _____

Lesson 21.5

Reading Words with the Final Letter "u"

✓ **Lesson Check Point**

 Directions: Read each target word. Find the letter "u" and put a check (✓) in the column that identifies its position within the syllable.

Direksyons: Li chak mo objektif. Jwenn lèt "u" a epi mete yon tchèck (✓) nan kolòn nan ki idantifye pozisyon li an nan silab la.

Target Words	"u" is at the end of a one syllable word	"u" is at the end of the first syllable	"u" is at the end of a multi-syllable word
1. flu	✓		
2. Peru			✓
3. menu			✓
4. humor		✓	
5. tubercle		✓	

 Directions: Read each target word. Put a check (✓) under the correct column heading.

Direksyons: Li chak mo objektif. Mete yon tchèk (✓) anba antèt kolòn ki kòrèk la.

Target Words	"u" has the /ŭ/ sound as in the word <u>tub</u>	"u" has the /yōō/ sound as in the word <u>tube</u>	"u" has the /ə/ sound as in the word <u>circus</u>	"u" is silent as in the word <u>build</u>
6. argue		✓		
7. built				✓
8. sunny	✓			
9. particular			✓	
10. vaguely				✓

Homework

 Name: _____   Date:___/___/_____   Score: _____

Lesson 21.6

Reading Letter "u" Words with the Schwa Vowel Sound

✓ Lesson Check Point

  Directions: Read each target word. Circle the word in the column that has the same "u" sound as the target word.

Direksyons: Li chak mo objektif. Antoure mo a ki nan kolòn nan ki bay menm son "u" a tankou mo objektif la.

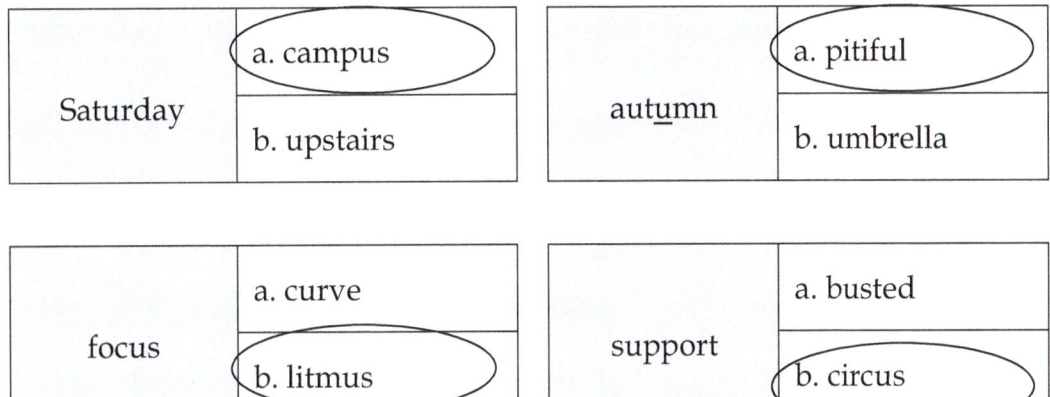

 Directions: Read each sentence and underline the letter "u" word that has the schwa vowel /ə/ sound. The anchor word for the letter "u" schwa vowel sound is campus.

Direksyons: Li chak fraz epi soulinye mo ki genyen lèt "u" a ki bay son schwa /ə/. Mo referans pou son schwa lèt "u" a se mo, campus.

1. <u>Porcupines</u> are mammals with a coat of sharp quills.

2. Eugene is having <u>difficulty</u> completing his assignment.

3. My students are learning to <u>subtract</u> two-digit numbers.

4. Today, the <u>faculty</u> members received their course outline.

5. On Sunday, my uncle drank a <u>medium</u> glass of plum juice.

6. At the <u>circus</u>, the students looked up and saw the acrobats.

Homework

 Name: _____ Date:___/___/_____ Score:_____

Lesson 21.7

Reading Words with the "ur" Letter Combination

Dictionary Skills/ Vocabulary

✓ Lesson Check Point

 Directions: Read each target word and its definition. Write the letter of the definition on the line of each target word. Use a dictionary or the Internet to check your answers.

Direksyons: Li chak mo objektif ak definisyon yo chak. Ekri lèt la ki koresponn ak definisyon an sou trè chak mo objektif yo. Itilize yon diksyonè oubyen entènèt pou tcheke repons ou yo.

Target Words	Definitions
1. _b_ curly	a. someone who steals things
2. _c_ curtain	b. description of something twisted into coils
3. _a_ burglar	c. fabric that hangs by a window
4. _e_ hurricane	d. to have designed a place with furniture
5. _d_ furnished	e. a cyclone with strong winds and heavy rain

 **Directions:** Read each sentence and write the target word on the line that correctly completes the sentence.
Direksyons: Li chak fraz epi ekri mo objektif ki konplete fraz la kòrèkteman.

6. Susan tied the gifts with red __curly__ ribbons.

7. The tropical storm was upgraded to a __hurricane__.

8. The living room __curtain__ is designed to block the sun.

9. The __burglar__ was arrested for robbing the jewelry store.

10. David __furnished__ his apartment with expensive antiques.

Homework

 Name: _____ Date:___/___/_____ Score: _____

Lesson 21.8

Reading Words with a Silent Letter "u"

✓ Lesson Check Point

 Directions: Read the target words in the word box. Write the words that have a silent letter "u" in the first column. Write the words that do not have a silent letter "u" in the second column.

Direksyons: Li mo objektif yo ki nan ti bwat mo a. Ekri mo yo ki genyen lèt "u" ki pa pwononse a nan premye kolòn nan. Ekri mo yo ki pa genyen lèt "u" ki pa pwononse anan dezyèm kolòn nan.

Target Word Box				
Peru	buildings	butcher	disguise	league
guilty	numerous	laughter	rubbing	intrigue
biscuits	pudding	puppy	perfume	musical
salute	vogue	summer	guess	Guinea

Letter "u" is silent	Letter "u" has a letter "u" sound
guilty	Peru
guess	salute
vogue	puppy
league	butcher
Guinea	rubbing
intrigue	pudding
biscuits	musical
disguise	perfume
laughter	summer
buildings	numerous

Learn To Read English With Directions In Haitian Creole

Homework

 Name: _____ Date: ___/___/_____ Score: _____

Unit Review - U/u

Reading Words with Vowel "u" Sounds: /ŭ/, /o͞o/, /ə/ & Silent

✓ **Lesson Check Point**

 Directions: Read each target word. Circle the word in the column that has the same "u" sound as the target word.

Direksyons: Li chak mo objektif. Antoure mo a ki nan kolòn nan ki bay menm son vwayèl "u" atankou mo objektif la.

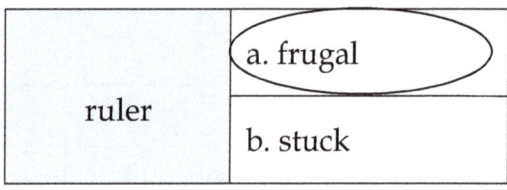
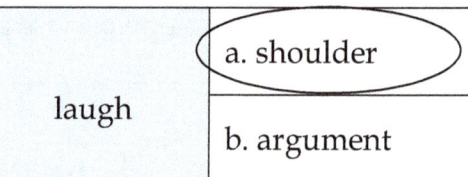
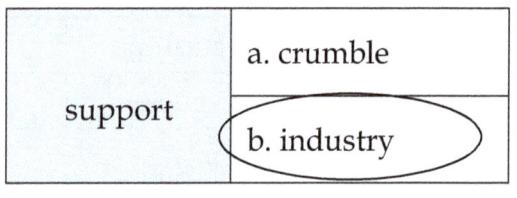
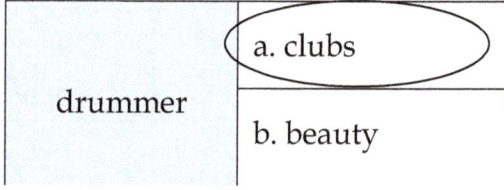

 Directions: Read each target word. Put a check (✓) under the correct column heading.

Direksyons: Li chak mo objektif. Mete yon tchèk (✓) anba antèt kolòn ki kòrèk la.

Target Words	"u" has the /ŭ/ sound as in the word <u>tub</u>	"u" has the /o͞o/ sound as in the word <u>tube</u>	"u" has the /ə/ sound as in the word <u>circus</u>	"u" is silent as in the word <u>build</u>
1. ruler		✓		
2. laugh				✓
3. support			✓	
4. drummer	✓			

Homework

 Name: _____ Date:___/___/_____ Score:_____

The Reading Challenge

Lesson 21.9

Reading Multisyllable Words

✓ **Lesson Check Point**

 Directions: Read and divide each target word into syllables. Write each word and place a hyphen (-) between the syllables in the second column. Write the number of syllables in the third column. Use a dictionary or the Internet to check your answers.

Direksyons: Li epi divize chak mo objektif an silab. Ekri chak mo epi mete yon tirè (-) ant silab yo nan dezyèm kolòn nan. Ekri kantite silab ke yo genyen an nan twazyèm kolòn nan. Itilize yon diksyonè oubyen entènèt pou tcheke repons ou yo.

Target Words	Words Divided into Syllables	Number of Syllables
1. jumpers	jump-ers	2
2. cushion	cush-ion	2
3. brushing	brush-ing	2
4. fullest	full-est	2
5. eluding	e-lud-ing	3
6. butcher	butch-er	2
7. volume	vol-ume	2
8. defusing	de-fus-ing	3
9. customer	cus-tom-er	3
10. arguing	ar-gu-ing	3

Learn To Read English With Directions In Haitian Creole

Homework

Name: _____ Date: ___/___/_____ Score: _____

The Reading Challenge

Lesson 21.9

Reading Multisyllable Words

✓ **Lesson Check Point**

Directions: Read each target word. Circle the word in the row that is divided correctly into syllables. Use a dictionary or the Internet to check your answers.

Direksyons: Li chak mo objektif. Antoure mo a ki nan ranje a ki divize an silab korèkteman yo. Itilize yon diksyonè oubyen entènèt pou tcheke repons ou yo.

Model

| visualize | a. vis-ua-lize | **b. vi-su-al-ize** (circled) | c. vis-u-a-lize |

| 1. execute | **a. ex-e-cute** (circled) | b. ex-ec-ute | c. e-xec-ute |

| 2. absolute | **a. ab-so-lute** (circled) | b. abs-o-lute | c. ab-sol-ute |

| 3. punctual | a. pun-ctu-al | **b. punc-tu-al** (circled) | c. pu-nctu-al |

| 4. resuming | a. res-u-ming | **b. re-sum-ing** (circled) | c. re-sumi-ng |

| 5. included | a. incl-u-ded | **b. in-clud-ed** (circled) | c. inc-lud-ed |

| 6. refusing | a. ref-u-sing | **b. re-fus-ing** (circled) | c. ref-us-ing |

| 7. gradual | a. grad-ual | b. gra-du-al | **c. grad-u-al** (circled) |

| 8. consuming | **a. con-sum-ing** (circled) | b. cons-u-ming | c. con-su-ming |

Homework

Name: _____ Date: ___/___/_____ Score: _____

Lesson 21.10

Reading and Writing

Proper and Common Nouns and Adjectives

Directions: Read the words in the word box. Put an (X) on the line next to each word that is written incorrectly. Remember that all proper nouns and proper adjectives are capitalized. Use a dictionary or the Internet to check your answers.

Direksyons: Li chak mo yo ki nan bwat mo a. Met yon (X) sou ti trè a ki bò kote mo ki pa kri byen yo. Sonje ke tout non pwòp ak adjektif pwop ekri avèk yon lèt majiskil nan kòmansman yo. Itilize yon diksyonè oubyen entènèt pou tcheke repons ou yo.

Word Box					
X	utah	__	usually	__	USA
X	Uproar	X	ural River	X	Ugliest
__	UNICEF	X	ursa Minor	__	upgrade
__	United Kingdom	__	Uzbekistan	X	Utterance

Directions: Read each unedited sentence and underline the word that is written incorrectly. Write each sentence correctly on the line.

Direksyons: Li chak fraz ki pa edite yo epi soulinye mo ki pa ekri byen an. Ekri chak fraz korèkteman sou liy lan.

Model
Mrs. Ubangi usually has union meetings at a local <u>University</u>.
<u>Mrs. Ubangi usually has union meetings at a local university.</u>

1. Last year, university students hiked <u>Up</u> the Ural Mountains.
<u>Last year, university students hiked up the Ural Mountains.</u>

2. The UNICEF volunteers are helping <u>Underprivileged</u> children.
<u>The UNICEF volunteers are helping underprivileged children.</u>

3. Mr. Udell enjoys reading <u>Unusual</u> books about UFO sightings.
<u>Mr. Udell enjoys reading unusual books about UFO sightings.</u>

4. The students from <u>uzbekistan</u> are on our university's honor roll.
<u>The students from Uzbekistan are on our university's honor roll.</u>

Homework

Name: _____ **Date:** ___/___/_____ **Score:** _____

Lesson 22.1

Reading Words with the Letter V/v

✓ **Lesson Check Point**

Directions: Read each target word. Find the letter "v" and put a check (✓) in the column that identifies its position: beginning, within or end.
Direksyons: Li chak mo objektif. Jwenn lèt "v" a epi mete yon tchèck (✓) nan kolòn ki idantifye pozisyon li an: nan kòmansman, ladan oubyen nan finisman.

Target Words	Beginning (First Letter)	Within	End (Last Letter)
1. travail		✓	
2. savings		✓	
3. Vikings	✓		
4. volcanic	✓		
5. Yugoslav			✓

Directions: Read each sentence and underline the words that begin with the letter "v." Write all the underlined words in alphabetical order on the lines below.
Direksyons: Li chak fraz epi soulinye mo ki kòmanse avèk lèt "v" yo. Ekri tout mo ki soulinye yo nan lòd alfabetik sou trè sa yo ki anba.

6. My <u>visor</u> blocks the <u>vivid</u> rays of the sun.

7. Our new <u>vitamins</u> taste like <u>vanilla</u> cream.

8. I used the computer to enter a <u>virtual</u> <u>volcano</u>.

9. During the tour, I had a clear <u>view</u> of <u>Victoria</u> Falls.

10. The <u>villagers</u> <u>voted</u> for an entirely new government.

vanilla	Victoria	view
villagers	virtual	visor
vitamins	vivid	volcano
	voted	

Homework

 Name: _____ Date: ___/___/_____ Score: _____

The Reading Challenge

Lesson 22.2

Reading Multisyllable Words

✓ Lesson Check Point

 Directions: Read and divide each target word into syllables. Write each word and place a hyphen (-) between the syllables in the second column. Write the number of syllables in the third column. Use a dictionary or the Internet to check your answers.

Direksyons: Li epi divize chak mo objektif an silab. Ekri chak mo epi mete yon tirè (-) ant silab yo nan dezyèm kolòn nan. Ekri kantite silab ke yo genyen an nan twazyèm kolòn nan. Itilize yon diksyonè oubyen entènèt pou tcheke repons ou yo.

Target Words	Words Divided into Syllables	Number of Syllables
1. veto	ve-to	2
2. voiceless	voice-less	2
3. vaulting	vault-ing	2
4. version	ver-sion	2
5. video	vid-e-o	3
6. vascular	vas-cu-lar	3
7. vividly	viv-id-ly	3
8. versus	ver-sus	2
9. viruses	vi-rus-es	3
10. vigorous	vig-or-ous	3

Homework

Name: _____ Date: ___/___/_____ Score: _____

The Reading Challenge

Lesson 22.2

Reading Multisyllable Words

✓ **Lesson Check Point**

Directions: Read each target word. Circle the word in the row that is divided correctly into syllables. Use a dictionary or the Internet to check your answers.

Direksyons: Li chak mo objektif. Antoure mo a ki nan ranje a ki divize an silab korèkteman yo. Itilize yon diksyonè oubyen entènèt pou tcheke repons ou yo.

Model

| volcano | a. vo-lcan-o | b. vol-can-o | c. vol-ca-no ⬭ |

| 1. violin | a. vi-ol-in | b. vi-o-lin ⬭ | c. vio-li-n |

| 2. verbalize | a. ver-bali-ze | b. verb-al-ize | c. ver-bal-ize ⬭ |

| 3. vanity | a. van-i-ty ⬭ | b. va-ni-ty | c. van-it-y |

| 4. vocable | a. vo-cab-le | b. vo-c-able | c. vo-ca-ble ⬭ |

| 5. virtual | a. virt-u-al | b. vir-tu-al ⬭ | c. vir-tua-l |

| 6. venison | a. ve-nis-on | b. ven-i-son ⬭ | c. ven-is-on |

| 7. Vietnam | a. Vi-et-nam ⬭ | b. Vie-t-nam | c. Vi-etna-m |

| 8. vestibule | a. ves-ti-bule ⬭ | b. ves-tib-ule | c. vest-i-bule |

Unit V
Lesson 22.2

Learn To Read English With Directions In Haitian Creole

Homework

Name: _____ Date: ___/___/_____ Score: _____

Lesson 22.3

Reading and Writing

Proper and Common Nouns and Adjectives

Directions: Read the words in the word box. Put an (X) on the line next to each word that is written incorrectly. Remember that all proper nouns and proper adjectives are capitalized. Use a dictionary or the Internet to check your answers.

Direksyons: Li chak mo yo ki nan bwat mo a. Met yon (X) sou ti trè a ki bò kote mo ki pa kri byen yo. Sonje ke tout non pwòp ak adjektif pwop ekri avèk yon lèt majiskil nan kòmansman yo. Itilize yon diksyonè oubyen entènèt pou tcheke repons ou yo.

Word Box					
__	version	X	venus	__	vertex
__	vocal cord	X	venice	X	Vessel
X	victoria Falls	X	virginia	__	vocabulary
__	Volcano Island	__	Vanessa	X	valentine's Day

Directions: Read each unedited sentence and underline the word that is written incorrectly. Write each sentence correctly on the line.

Direksyons: Li chak fraz ki pa edite yo epi soulinye mo ki pa ekri byen an. Ekri chak fraz korèkteman sou liy lan.

Model
In the fall, the leaves in <u>vermont</u> have vibrant colors.
In the fall, the leaves in Vermont have vibrant colors.

1. The <u>vikings</u> made many treacherous ocean voyages.
The Vikings made many treacherous ocean voyages.

2. <u>vinny</u> received five African violet plants on Valentine's Day.
Vinny received five African violet plants on Valentine's Day.

3. We are scheduled to play four <u>Volleyball</u> games in Virginia.
We are scheduled to play four volleyball games in Virginia.

4. In November, I plan to <u>Vacation</u> in the British Virgin Islands.
In November, I plan to vacation in the British Virgin Islands.

Homework

Name: _____ Date: ___/___/_____ Score: _____

Lesson 23.1

Reading Words with the Letter W/w

✓ **Lesson Check Point**

Directions: Read each target word. Find the letter "w" and put a check (✓) in the column that identifies its position: beginning, within or end.
Direksyons: Li chak mo objektif. Jwenn lèt "w" a epi mete yon tchèck (✓) nan kolòn ki idantifye pozisyon li an: nan kòmansman, ladan oubyen nan finisman.

Target Words	Beginning (First Letter)	Within	End (Last Letter)
1. answer		✓	
2. washing	✓		
3. somehow			✓
4. tomorrow			✓
5. crossword		✓	

Directions: Read each sentence and underline the words that begin with the letter "w." Write all the underlined words in alphabetical order on the lines below.
Direksyons: Li chak fraz epi soulinye mo ki kòmanse avèk lèt "w" yo. Ekri tout mo ki soulinye yo nan lòd alfabetik sou trè sa yo ki anba.

6. I ate <u>white</u> fish and rice at Adrienne's <u>wedding</u>.

7. The man in the <u>wheelchair</u> is a <u>wealthy</u> businessman.

8. My college professor is <u>writing</u> a <u>wonderful</u> new book.

9. Joan bought her hair extensions at <u>Western</u> <u>Wig</u> Store.

10. During the summer, Brenda likes to <u>walk</u> in the <u>wilderness</u>.

walk _____   wealthy _____   wedding _____

Western _____ wheelchair _____ white _____

Wig _____   wilderness _____ wonderful _____

                    writing _____

Name: _____   Date: ___/___/_____   Score: _____

Lesson 23.2

Reading Words with a Vowel before the Letter "w"

✓ **Lesson Check Point**

 Directions: Read each target word. Circle the word in the column that has the same "aw," "ew" or "ow" sound as the target word.
Direksyons: Li chak mo objektif. Antoure mo a ki nan kolòn nan ki bay menm son vwayèl "aw," "ew" oubyen "ow" la (yo) tankou mo objektif la.

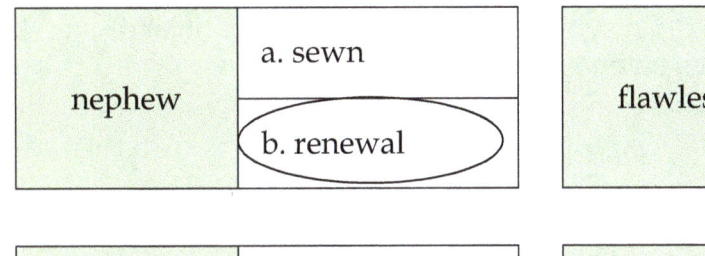
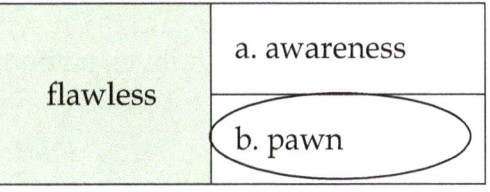
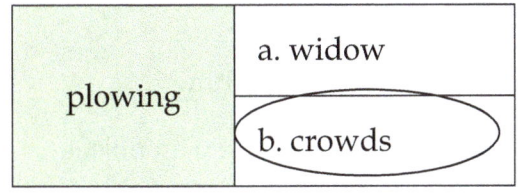
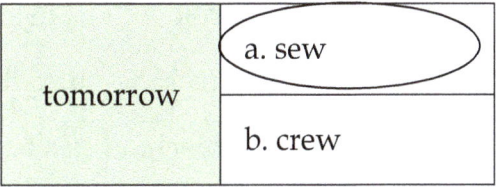

 Directions: Read each target word. Put a check (✓) under the correct column heading.
Direksyons: Li chak mo objektif. Mete yon tchèk (✓) anba antèt kolòn ki kòrèk la.

Target Words	Underlined letters have /oo/ sound as in the word **few**	Underlined letters have /ô/ sound as in the word **law**	Underlined letters have /ō/ sound as in the word **sew**	Underlined letters have /ou/ sound as in the word **cow**
1. neph<u>ew</u>	✓			
2. fl<u>aw</u>less		✓		
3. pl<u>ow</u>ing				✓
4. tomorr<u>ow</u>			✓	

Homework

Name: _____ Date: ___/___/_____ Score: _____

Lesson 23.3

Reading Words with a Silent "w" and "wr" Letter Combination

Dictionary Skills/ Vocabulary

✓ **Lesson Check Point**

Directions: Read each target word and its definition. Write the letter of the definition on the line of each target word. Use a dictionary or the Internet to check your answers.

Direksyons: Li chak mo objektif ak definisyon yo chak. Ekri lèt la ki koresponn ak definisyon an sou trè chak mo objektif yo. Itilize yon diksyonè oubyen entènèt pou tcheke repons ou yo.

Target Words	Definitions
1. _e_ wrote	a. in an incorrect manner
2. _b_ wreck	b. to destroy or damage something
3. _c_ wrench	c. a tool used to tighten or loosen an object
4. _a_ wrongly	d. a material used to wrap something
5. _d_ wrapping	e. to have communicated by forming letters on paper

Directions: Read each sentence. Underline the word in the parentheses that correctly completes each sentence. Then, write the underlined word on the line.

Direksyons: Li chak fraz. Soulinye mo a ki nan parantèz yo ki konplete chak fraz kòrèkteman. Answit, ekri mo soulinye a sou trè a.

6. Wanda __wrote__ a long business letter. (wrecked, <u>wrote</u>)

7. The storm __wrecked__ the fishing fleet. (<u>wrecked</u>, wrongly)

8. Wendell was __wrongly__ accused of a crime. (wrapping, <u>wrongly</u>)

9. I used a hammer and a __wrench__ to fix the chair. (wrote, <u>wrench</u>)

10. Remove the plastic __wrapping__ before eating the sandwich. (<u>wrapping</u>, wrench)

Homework

 Name: _____ Date: ___/___/_____ Score: _____

Lesson 23.3

Reading Words with a Silent Letter "w"

✓ Lesson Check Point

 Directions: Read the target words in the word box. Write the words that have a silent letter "w" in the first column. Write the words that do not have a silent letter "w" in the second column.

Direksyons: Li mo objektif yo in an ti bwat mo a. Ekri mo yo ki genyen lèt "w" ki pa pwononse a nan premye kolòn nan. Ekri mo yo ki pa genyen lèt "w" ki pa pwononse anan dezyèm kolòn nan.

Target Word Box				
wrong	two	pillow	writes	wrap
answer	wrench	earwax	writings	widow
backward	wrinkle	freeway	earthworm	winter
driftwood	doorway	dwindle	Wednesday	firewood

Letter "w" is silent

two
wrap
writes
widow
wrong
pillow
answer
wrench
wrinkle
writings

Letter "w" has the /w/ sound

winter
earwax
freeway
dwindle
doorway
firewood
driftwood
backward
earthworm
Wednesday

Learn To Read English With Directions In Haitian Creole

Homework

 Name: _____ Date: ___/___/_____ Score: _____

The Reading Challenge

Lesson 23.4

Reading Multisyllable Words

✓ **Lesson Check Point**

 Directions: Read and divide each target word into syllables. Write each word and place a hyphen (-) between the syllables in the second column. Write the number of syllables in the third column. Use a dictionary or the Internet to check your answers.

Direksyons: Li epi divize chak mo objektif an silab. Ekri chak mo epi mete yon tirè (-) ant silab yo nan dezyèm kolòn nan. Ekri kantite silab ke yo genyen an nan twazyèm kolòn nan. Itilize yon diksyonè oubyen entènèt pou tcheke repons ou yo.

Target Words	Words Divided into Syllables	Number of Syllables
1. winterize	win-ter-ize	3
2. worldly	world-ly	2
3. windy	wind-y	2
4. weather	weath-er	2
5. watchman	watch-man	2
6. wetland	wet-land	2
7. walnut	wal-nut	2
8. wrinkle	wrin-kle	2
9. welcoming	wel-com-ing	3
10. window	win-dow	2

Homework

 Name: _____ Date: ___/___/_____ Score: _____

The Reading Challenge

Lesson 23.4

Reading Multisyllable Words

✓ Lesson Check Point

 Directions: Read each target word. Circle the word in the row that is divided correctly into syllables. Use a dictionary or the Internet to check your answers.

Direksyons: Li chak mo objektif. Antoure mo a ki nan ranje a ki divize an silab korèkteman yo. Itilize yon diksyonè oubyen entènèt pou tcheke repons ou yo.

Model

| wonderful | a. wo-nder-ful | b. won-der-ful ⬭ | c. won-derf-ul |

| 1. waterfall | a. wa-ter-fall ⬭ | b. wat-er-fall | c. wa-terf-all |

| 2. weathering | a. wea-ther-ing | b. weath-e-ring | c. weath-er-ing ⬭ |

| 3. wolverine | a. wol-ver-ine ⬭ | b. wol-ve-rine | c. wolv-er-ine |

| 4. westernize | a. we-stern-ize | b. west-ern-ize ⬭ | c. west-er-nize |

| 5. whatever | a. wha-tev-er | b. whate-v-er | c. what-ev-er ⬭ |

| 6. webpage | a. web-page ⬭ | b. web-pa-ge | c. we-bpa-ge |

| 7. washable | a. wa-sha-ble | b. wa-shab-le | c. wash-a-ble ⬭ |

| 8. westerly | a. wes-ter-ly | b. west-er-ly ⬭ | c. we-ster-ly |

Homework

Name: _____ Date: ___/___/_____ Score: _____

Lesson 23.5

Reading and Writing

Proper and Common Nouns and Adjectives

Directions: Read the words in the word box. Put an (X) on the line next to each word that is written incorrectly. Remember that all proper nouns and proper adjectives are capitalized. Use a dictionary or the Internet to check your answers.

Direksyons: Li chak mo yo ki nan bwat mo a. Met yon (X) sou ti trè a ki bò kote mo ki pa kri byen yo. Sonje ke tout non pwòp ak adjektif pwop ekri avèk yon lèt majiskil nan kòmansman yo. Itilize yon diksyonè oubyen entènèt pou tcheke repons ou yo.

Word Box					
__	witness	__	woman	X	Weasel
X	Wetland	X	wakayama	__	wellness
X	Workout	X	wednesday	__	Waterbury
	woodcutter	__	West Indian	X	Waterfront

Directions: Read each unedited sentence and underline the word that is written incorrectly. Write each sentence correctly on the line.

Direksyons: Li chak fraz ki pa edite yo epi soulinye mo ki pa ekri byen an. Ekri chak fraz korèkteman sou liy lan.

Model

We walked along the winding path that led to the <u>Waterfalls</u>.
<u>We walked along the winding path that led to the waterfalls.</u>

1. A factory in <u>wisconsin</u> made Wendell's wristwatch.
<u>A factory in Wisconsin made Wendell's wristwatch.</u>

2. In the West Indies, I ate delicious fish with <u>White</u> sauce.
<u>In the West Indies, I ate delicious fish with white sauce.</u>

3. <u>wendy</u> said, "South America is in the Western Hemisphere."
<u>Wendy said, "South America is in the Western Hemisphere."</u>

4. In my opinion, Woody <u>woodpecker</u> is a wonderful character.
<u>In my opinion, Woody Woodpecker is a wonderful character.</u>

Homework

 Name: _____ Date: ___/___/_____ Score: _____

Lesson 24.1

Reading Words with the Letter X/x

✓ Lesson Check Point

 Directions: Read each target word. Find the letter "x" and put a check (✓) in the column that identifies its position: beginning, within or end.
Direksyons: Li chak mo objektif. Jwenn lèt "x" a epi mete yon tchèck (✓) nan kolòn ki idantifye pozisyon li an: nan kòmansman, ladan oubyen nan finisman.

Target Words	Beginning (First Letter)	Within	End (Last Letter)
1. annex			✓
2. fixate		✓	
3. explore		✓	
4. complex			✓
5. xylophone	✓		

 Directions: Read each sentence and underline the words that begin with the letter "x." Write all the underlined words in alphabetical order on the lines below.
Direksyons: Li chak fraz epi soulinye mo ki kòmanse avèk lèt "x" yo. Ekri tout mo ki soulinye in an lòd alfabetik sou trè in a ki anba.

6. <u>Xander</u> attends <u>xylophone</u> lessons every Tuesday.

7. During my vacation to China, I will visit <u>Xian</u> and <u>Xining</u>.

8. I am reading the biographies of Malcolm <u>X</u> and Francis <u>Xavier</u>.

9. Dr. <u>Xerxes</u> used the surgical instrument, <u>xyster</u>, to scrape bones.

10. <u>X-linked</u> refers to a trait controlled by genes on the <u>X-chromosome</u>.

<u>X</u>_____   <u>X-chromosome</u>_____   <u>X-linked</u>_____

<u>Xander</u>_____   <u>Xavier</u>_____   <u>Xerxes</u>_____

<u>Xian</u>_____   <u>Xining</u>_____   <u>xylophone</u>_____

                          <u>xyster</u>_____

Homework

 Name: _____ Date: _____/____/_____ Score: _____

Lesson 24.1

Reading Words with the Letter X/x

✓ Lesson Check Point

 Directions: Read each target word. Circle the word in the column that has the same "x" sound(s) as the target word.
Direksyons: Li chak mo objektif. Antoure mo a ki nan kolòn nan ki bay menm son "x" yo tankou mo objektif la.

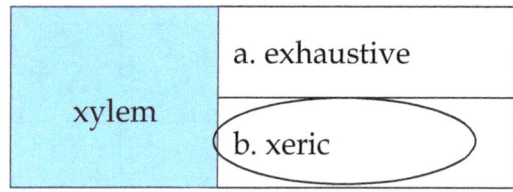
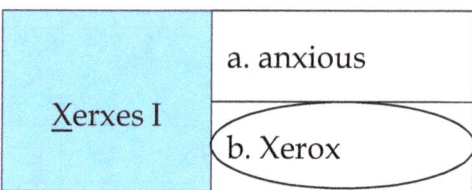
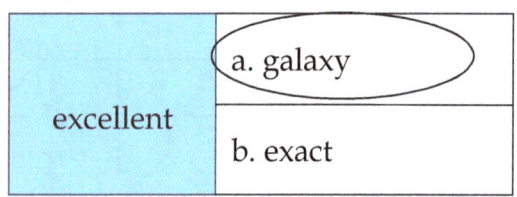
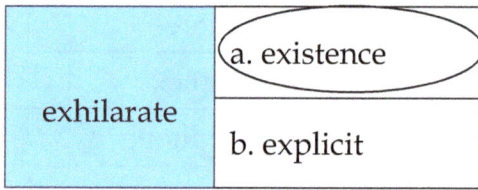

 Directions: Read each target word. Put a check (✓) under the correct column heading.
Direksyons: Li chak mo objektif. Mete yon tchèk (✓) anba antèt kolòn ki kòrèk la.

Target Words	"x" has the /k/ + /s/ sounds as in the word <u>box</u>	"x" has the /z/ sound as in the word <u>xylophone</u>	"x" has the /g/ + /z/ sounds as in the word <u>exhibit</u>	"x" has the /k/ + /sh/ sounds as in the word <u>anxious</u>
1. xylem		✓		
2. Xerxes I		✓		
3. excellent	✓			
4. exhilarate			✓	

Homework

 Name: _____ Date: ___/___/_____ Score: _____

The Reading Challenge

Lesson 24.2

Reading Multisyllable Words

✓ Lesson Check Point

 Directions: Read and divide each target word into syllables. Write each word and place a hyphen (-) between the syllables in the second column. Write the number of syllables in the third column. Use a dictionary or the Internet to check your answers.

Direksyons: Li epi divize chak mo objektif an silab. Ekri chak mo epi mete yon tirè (-) ant silab yo nan dezyèm kolòn nan. Ekri kantite silab ke yo genyen an nan twazyèm kolòn nan. Itilize yon diksyonè oubyen entènèt pou tcheke repons ou yo.

Target Words	Words Divided into Syllables	Number of Syllables
1. xylophone	xy-lo-phone	3
2. oxide	ox-ide	2
3. fixture	fix-ture	2
4. extracting	ex-tract-ing	3
5. example	ex-am-ple	3
6. oxygen	ox-y-gen	3
7. textile	tex-tile	2
8. waxing	wax-ing	2
9. taxation	tax-a-tion	3
10. exercise	ex-er-cise	3

Homework

Name: _____ Date: ___/___/_____   Score: _____

The Reading Challenge

Lesson 24.2

Reading Multisyllable Words

✓ **Lesson Check Point**

Directions: Read each target word. Circle the word in the row that is divided correctly into syllables. Use a dictionary or the Internet to check your answers.

Direksyons: Li chak mo objektif. Antoure mo a ki nan ranje a ki divize an silab korèkteman yo. Itilize yon diksyonè oubyen entènèt pou tcheke repons ou yo.

Model

| oxidized | **a. ox-i-dized** ⭕ | b. oxi-d-ized | c. o-xi-dized |

1. extremely	a. ex-tremel-y	b. ex-tre-mely	**c. ex-treme-ly** ⭕
2. deoxidize	a. de-oxi-dize	**b. de-ox-i-dize** ⭕	c. deo-xi-dize
3. exactly	**a. ex-act-ly** ⭕	b. e-xact-ly	c. ex-a-ctly
4. xenoliths	**a. xen-o-liths** ⭕	b. xe-noli-ths	c. xe-nolit-hs
5. expanding	a. exp-an-ding	**b. ex-pand-ing** ⭕	c. exp-and-ing
6. vexation	a. vex-at-ion	**b. vex-a-tion** ⭕	c. ve-xat-ion
7. xerophytes	**a. xer-o-phytes** ⭕	b. xe-rophy-tes	c. xero-phytes
8. oxygen	a. oxy-g-en	b. o-xyg-en	**c. ox-y-gen** ⭕

Unit X Lesson 24.2

Learn To Read English With Directions In Haitian Creole

Homework

Name: _____ Date: ___/___/_____ Score: _____

Lesson 24.3

Reading and Writing

Proper and Common Nouns and Adjectives

Directions: Read the words in the word box. Put an (X) on the line next to each word that is written incorrectly. Remember that all proper nouns and proper adjectives are capitalized. Use a dictionary or the Internet to check your answers.

Direksyons: Li chak mo yo ki nan bwat mo a. Met yon (X) sou ti trè a ki bò kote mo ki pa kri byen yo. Sonje ke tout non pwòp ak adjektif pwop ekri avèk yon lèt majiskil nan kòmansman yo. Itilize yon diksyonè oubyen entènèt pou tcheke repons ou yo.

Word Box					
_X_	xuzhou	___	xebec	___	Xenon
___	xylocaine	___	xylems	___	Xavier
___	xylophone	_X_	xanthus	_X_	xerxes I
_X_	Xylography	_X_	Xenophobia	_X_	xenophobes

Directions: Read each unedited sentence and underline the word that is written incorrectly. Write each sentence correctly on the line.

Direksyons: Li chak fraz ki pa edite yo epi soulinye mo ki pa ekri byen an. Ekri chak fraz korèkteman sou liy lan.

Model
Xia said, "The population of <u>xankandi</u> is 33,000 people."
<u>Xia said, "The population of Xankandi is 33,000 people."</u>

1. <u>xian's</u> mother bought her a new xylophone.
<u>Xian's mother bought her a new xylophone.</u>

2. The greatest King of Persia was King <u>xerxes</u> I.
<u>The greatest King of Persia was King Xerxes I.</u>

3. I am convinced that <u>Xylocaine</u> numbs the pain.
<u>I am convinced that xylocaine numbs the pain.</u>

4. Dr. Xavier was gentle as he scraped his patient's bones with a <u>Xyster</u>.
<u>Dr. Xavier was gentle as he scraped his patient's bones with a xyster.</u>

Homework

 Name: _____ Date: ___/___/_____ Score: _____

Lesson 25.1

Reading Words with the Letter Y/y

✓ **Lesson Check Point**

 Directions: Read each target word. Find the letter "y" and put a check (✓) in the column that identifies its position: beginning, within or end.
Direksyons : Li chak mo objektif. Jwenn lèt "y" a epi mete yon tchèck (✓) nan kolòn ki idantifye pozisyon li an: nan kòmansman, ladan oubyen nan finisman.

Target Words	Beginning (First Letter)	Within	End (Last Letter)
1. yogurt	✓		
2. money			✓
3. slippery			✓
4. keyboard		✓	
5. yearning	✓		

 Directions: Read each sentence and underline the words that begin with the letter "y." Write all the underlined words in alphabetical order on the lines below.
Direksyons: Li chak fraz epi soulinye mo ki kòmanse avèk lèt "y" yo. Ekri tout mo ki soulinye in an lòd alfabetik sou trè in a ki anba.

6. The <u>yellow</u> <u>yogurt</u> has an artificial lemon flavor.

7. Our <u>yogi</u> practices <u>yoga</u> at least three times a day.

8. The <u>young</u> people are staying at the local <u>youth</u> hostel.

9. Kathy bought a bright orange <u>yo-yo</u> for her <u>younger</u> sister.

10. <u>Yesterday</u>, I drew the <u>y-axis</u> and the x-axis on graph paper.

<u>y-axis</u>_____   <u>yellow</u>_____   <u>Yesterday</u>_____
<u>yoga</u>_____   <u>yogi</u>_____   <u>yogurt</u>_____
<u>yo-yo</u>_____   <u>young</u>_____
                         <u>youth</u>_____

Homework

 Name: _____ Date: ___/___/_____ Score: _____

Lesson 25.1

Reading Words with the Letter Y/y

✓ Lesson Check Point

 Directions: Read each target word. Circle the word in the row that has a different "y" sound than the target word.
Direksyons: Li chak mo objektif. Antoure mo a in an ranje a ki bay yon son vwayèl "y" ki diferan an.

Target Words				
1. yahoo	you'll	youth	(baby)	yours
2. Egypt	typical	symbol	hymn	(yesterday)
3. magnify	typing	(money)	goodbye	styling
4. analysis	catalyst	(rhyming)	calypso	bicycle
5. Wednesday	(younger)	prayer	honey	highway

 Directions: Read the words in the four boxes. Circle two words that have the same "y" sound.
Direksyons: Li mo yo in an kat kat ti bwat yo. Antoure de mo ki bay menm son "y" yo.

baby	(style)
yours	(eyeballs)

(type)	(thyme)
today	mystery

(Kenya)	May
(yield)	typing

candy	gym
(analyze)	(rhyme)

(symptom)	paralyze
yucky	(hypnosis)

(young)	(yogurt)
goodbye	bicycles

Homework

 Name: _____ Date:___/___/_____ Score:_____

Lesson 25.2

Reading Words with a Vowel before the Letter "y"

✓ Lesson Check Point

 Directions: Read each target word. Circle the word in the column that has the same "y" sound as the target word.
Li chak mo objektif. Antoure mo a ki nan kolòn nan ki bay menm son "y" la tankou mo objektif la.

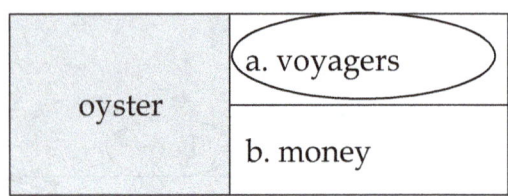
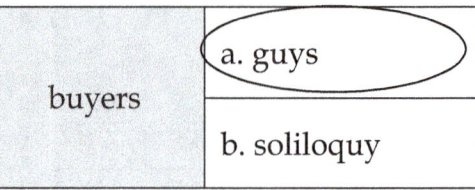
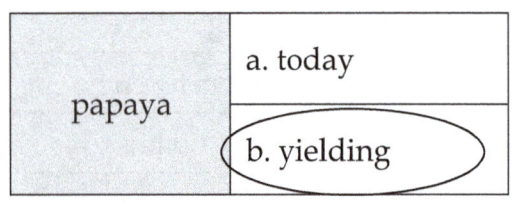
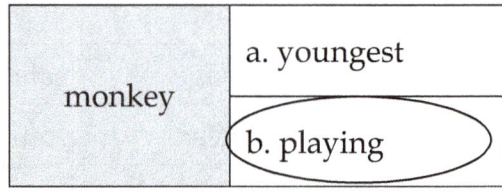

 Directions: Read each target word. Put a check (✓) under the correct column heading.
Direksyons: Li chak mo objektif. Mete yon tchèk (✓) anba antèt kolòn ki kòrèk la.

Target Words	"y" has the /y/ sound as in the word <u>yes</u>	"oy" has the /oi/ sound as in the word <u>boy</u>	"y" has the /ī/ sound as in the word <u>by</u>	"y" is silent as in the word <u>day</u>
1. oyster		✓		
2. buyers			✓	
3. papaya	✓			
4. monkey				✓

Name: _____ Date: ___/___/_____ Score: _____

Homework

Lesson 25.3

Reading Words with the "cy" Letter Combination

✓ **Lesson Check Point**

Directions: Read each target word. Find the "cy" letter combination and put a check (✓) in the column to identify its position in the word: beginning, within or end.

Direksyons: Li chak mo objektif. Jwenn konbinezon lèt "cy" laepi mete yon tchèk (✓) nan kolòn nan ki idantifye pozisyon li an : nan kòmansman, ladan oubyen nan finisman.

Target Words	Beginning (First 2 Letters)	Within	End (Last 2 Letters)
1. cycling	✓		
2. cynical	✓		
3. regency			✓
4. democracy			✓
5. encyclopedia		✓	

Directions: Read each target word. Put a check (✓) under the correct column heading.

Direksyons: Li chak mo objektif. Mete yon tchèk (✓) anba antèt kolòn ki kòrèk la.

Target Words	"cy" has the /s/ + /ĭ/ sounds as in the word <u>cylinder</u>	"cy" has the /s/ + /ī/ sounds as in the word <u>cycle</u>	"cy" has the /s/ + /ē/ sounds as in the word <u>agency</u>
6. cycling		✓	
7. cynical	✓		
8. regency			✓
9. democracy			✓
10. encyclopedia		✓	

Homework

 Name: _____   Date:___/___/_____   Score: _____

Lesson 25.4

Reading Words with the Final Letter "y"

✓ **Lesson Check Point**

 Directions: Read each target word. Find the letter "y" and put a check (✓) in the column that identifies its position within the word.

Direksyons: Li chak mo objektif. Jwenn lèt "y" la epi mete yon tchèck (✓) nan kolòn nan ki idantifye pozisyon li an nan mo a.

Target Words	"y" is at the end of a one syllable word	"y" is at the end of the first syllable	"y" is at the end of a multi-syllable word
1. guy	✓		
2. testify			✓
3. hybrid		✓	
4. comply			✓
5. mommy			✓

 Directions: Read each target word. Put a check (✓) under the correct column heading.

Direksyons: Li chak mo objektif. Mete yon tchèk (✓) anba antèt kolòn ki kòrèk la.

Target Words	"y" has the /ē/ sound as in the word <u>agency</u>	"y" has the /ī/ sound as in the word <u>flying</u>
6. guy		✓
7. testify		✓
8. hybrid		✓
9. comply		✓
10. mommy	✓	

Homework

 Name: _____ Date: ___/___/_____ Score: _____

Lesson 25.5

Reading Words with the "yr" Letter Combination

✓ Lesson Check Point

 Directions: Read each target word. Circle the word in the column that has the same "yr" sounds as the target word.
Direksyons : Li chak mo objektif. Antoure mo a ki nan kolòn nan ki bay menm son "yr" yo tankou mo objektif la.

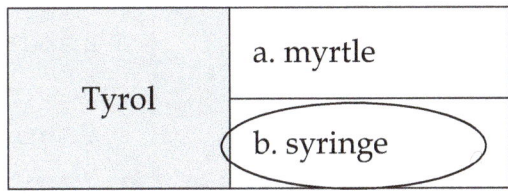
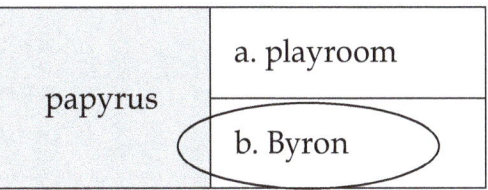
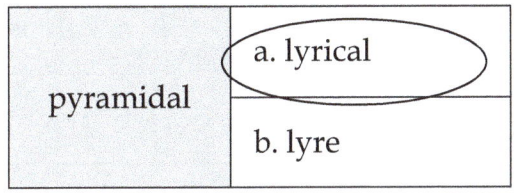
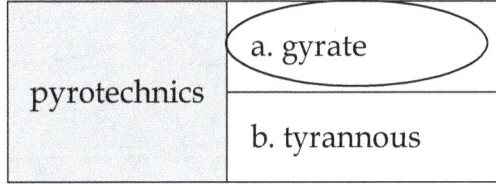

 Directions: Read each target word. Put a check (✓) under the correct column heading.
Direksyons: Li chak mo objektif. Mete yon tchèk (✓) anba antèt kolòn ki kòrèk la.

Target Words	"yr" has the /û/ + /r/ sounds as in the word myrtle	"yr" has the /ĭ/ + /r/ sounds as in the word pyramid	"yr" has the /ī/ + /r/ sounds as in the word gyro	"yr" has the /ə/ + /r/ sounds as in the word martyr
1. myrrh	✓			
2. Cyrus			✓	
3. myriad		✓		
4. syringe				✓

Homework

 Name: _____ Date: ___/___/_____ Score: _____

Lesson 25.6

Reading Letter "y" Words with the Schwa Vowel Sound

✓ **Lesson Check Point**

 Directions: Read each target word. Circle the word in the column that has the same "y" sound as the target word.

Direksyons: Li chak mo objektif. Antoure mo a ki nan kolòn nan ki bay menm son "y" la tankou mo objektif la.

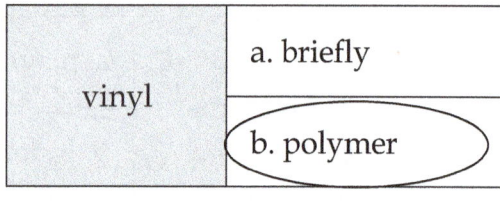

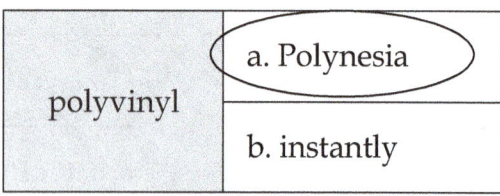

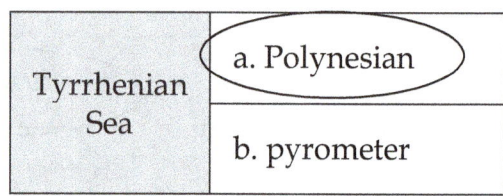

 Directions: Read each target word. Put a check (✓) under the correct column heading.

Direksyons: Li chak mo objektif. Mete yon tchèk (✓) anba antèt kolòn ki kòrèk la.

Target Words	"y" has the /ə/ sound as in the word syringe	"y" does not have the /ə/ sound
1. vinyl	✓	
2. beryl	✓	
3. polyvinyl	✓	
4. Tyrrhenian Sea	✓	

Homework

 Name: _____ Date:___/___/_____ Score: _____

Lesson 25.7

Reading Words with a Silent Letter "y"

✓ Lesson Check Point

 Directions: Read the target words in the word box. Write the words that have a silent letter "y" in the first column. Write the words that do not have a silent letter "y" in the second column.

Direksyons: Li mo objektif yo ki nan ti bwat mo a. Ekri mo yo ki genyen lèt "y" ki pa pwononse a nan premye kolòn nan. Ekri mo yo ki pa genyen lèt "y" ki pa pwononse anan dezyèm kolòn nan.

Target Word Box				
gray	day	yes	sway	essay
yellow	steady	clay	young	Yankee
yardage	needy	prey	journey	academy
Tuesday	honey	yearbook	yardstick	Thursday

Letter "y" is silent

- day
- clay
- prey
- gray
- sway
- essay
- honey
- Tuesday
- journey
- Thursday

Letter "y" has the /y/ or /ē/ sound

- yes
- young
- needy
- steady
- yellow
- Yankee
- yardage
- academy
- yearbook
- yardstick

Homework

 Name: _____ Date: ___/___/_____ Score: _____

The Reading Challenge

Lesson 25.8

Reading Multisyllable Words

✓ **Lesson Check Point**

 Directions: Read and divide each target word into syllables. Write each word and place a hyphen (-) between the syllables in the second column. Write the number of syllables in the third column. Use a dictionary or the Internet to check your answers.

Direksyons: Li epi divize chak mo objektif an silab. Ekri chak mo epi mete yon tirè (-) ant silab yo nan dezyèm kolòn nan. Ekri kantite silab ke yo genyen an nan twazyèm kolòn nan. Itilize yon diksyonè oubyen entènèt pou tcheke repons ou yo.

Target Words	Words Divided into Syllables	Number of Syllables
1. yachting	yacht-ing	2
2. youngsters	young-sters	2
3. Yuletide	Yule-tide	2
4. yahoo	ya-hoo	2
5. yielding	yield-ing	2
6. youthful	youth-ful	2
7. yardstick	yard-stick	2
8. yelping	yelp-ing	2
9. yearly	year-ly	2
10. yardage	yard-age	2

Homework

 Name: _____ Date: ____/____/____ Score: _____

The Reading Challenge

Lesson 25.8

Reading Multisyllable Words

✓ **Lesson Check Point**

 Directions: Read each target word. Circle the word in the row that is divided correctly into syllables. Use a dictionary or the Internet to check your answers.

Direksyons: Li chak mo objektif. Antoure mo a ki nan ranje a ki divize an silab korèkteman yo. Itilize yon diksyonè oubyen entènèt pou tcheke repons ou yo.

Model

| yesterday | a. ye-ster-day | b. yest-er-day | c. yes-ter-day ⭕ |

1. Yoruba	a. Yor-u-ba	b. Yo-ru-ba ⭕	c. Yo-rub-a
2. Yugoslav	a. Yug-o-slav	b. Yu-go-slav ⭕	c. Yu-gos-lav
3. yearly	a. year-ly ⭕	b. ye-ar-ly	c. yearl-y
4. yodeler	a. yo-del-er ⭕	b. yod-e-ler	c. yod-el-er
5. yielding	a. yie-ldi-ng	b. yield-ing ⭕	c. yie-lding
6. yonder	a. yond-er	b. yon-der ⭕	c. yo-nder
7. yourself	a. yo-ur-self	b. your-self ⭕	c. you-rse-lf
8. yoking	a. yo-king	b. yok-ing ⭕	c. yoki-ng

Homework

Name: _____ Date: ____/___/_____ Score: _____

Lesson 25.9

Reading and Writing

Proper and Common Nouns and Adjectives

Directions: Read the words in the word box. Put an (X) on the line next to each word that is written incorrectly. Remember that all proper nouns and proper adjectives are capitalized. Use a dictionary or the Internet to check your answers.

Direksyons: Li chak mo yo ki nan bwat mo a. Met yon (X) sou ti trè a ki bò kote mo ki pa kri byen yo. Sonje ke tout non pwòp ak adjektif pwop ekri avèk yon lèt majiskil nan kòmansman yo. Itilize yon diksyonè oubyen entènèt pou tcheke repons ou yo.

Word Box					
X	Yeast	X	Yoga	__	yeshiva
X	Youth	X	yugoslavia	X	yucatan
__	Yiddish	__	Yokohama	X	Yearbook
__	Yellow River	__	Yogyakarta	__	Yinchuan

Directions: Read each unedited sentence and underline the word that is written incorrectly. Write each sentence correctly on the line.

Direksyons: Li chak fraz ki pa edite yo epi soulinye mo ki pa ekri byen an. Ekri chak fraz korèkteman sou liy lan.

Model
Is the New York <u>yankees</u> your favorite baseball team?
<u>Is the New York Yankees your favorite baseball team?</u>

1. I scheduled two <u>Yoga</u> classes at Yorktown Gym.
<u>I scheduled two yoga classes at Yorktown Gym.</u>

2. Mr. <u>yelp</u> painted his house in Yorktown sunshine yellow.
<u>Mr. Yelp painted his house in Yorktown sunshine yellow.</u>

3. The <u>Yearbook</u> pictures were taken at Yosemite National Park.
<u>The yearbook pictures were taken at Yosemite National Park.</u>

4. All the young people in my class have new, brightly colored <u>Yo-yos</u>.
<u>All the young people in my class have new, brightly colored yo-yos.</u>

Homework

 Name: _____ Date: ___/___/_____ Score: _____

Lesson 26.1

Reading Words with the Letter Z/z

✓ Lesson Check Point

 Directions: Read each target word. Find the letter "z" and put a check (✓) in the column that identifies its position: beginning, within or end.
Direksyons: Li chak mo objektif. Jwenn lèt "z" a epi mete yon tchèk (✓) nan kolòn ki idantifye pozisyon li an: nan kòmansman, ladan oubyen nan finisman.

Target Words	Beginning (First Letter)	Within	End (Last Letter)
1. waltz			✓
2. quartz			✓
3. Zambia	✓		
4. realized		✓	
5. organized		✓	

 Directions: Read each sentence and underline the words that begin with the letter "z." Write all the underlined words in alphabetical order on the lines below.
Direksyons: Li chak fraz epi soulinye mo ki kòmanse avèk lèt "z" yo. Ekri tout mo ki soulinye yo nan lòd alfabetik sou trè sa yo ki anba.

6. The <u>zookeeper's</u> car is in the no parking <u>zone</u>.

7. The <u>zipper</u> on Jenny's <u>zebra</u> print coat is broken.

8. One day, Mr. and Mrs. <u>Zangara</u> will visit <u>Zambia</u>.

9. The interns at the <u>zoo</u> are enrolled in the <u>zoology</u> program.

10. <u>Zeezee</u> said, "<u>Zululand</u> is steeped in ancient history and tradition."

<u>Zambia</u>   <u>Zangara</u>   <u>zebra</u>

<u>Zeezee</u>   <u>zipper</u>   <u>zoo</u>

<u>zookeeper's</u>   <u>zoology</u>   <u>zone</u>

              <u>Zululand</u>

Homework

 Name: _____ Date: ___/___/_____ Score: _____

Lesson 26.1

Reading Words with the Letter Z/z

✓ Lesson Check Point

 Directions: Read each target word. Circle the word in the column that has the same "z" sound as the target word.
Direksyons: Li chak mo objektif. Antoure mo a ki nan kolòn nan ki bay menm son "z" la tankou mo objektif la.

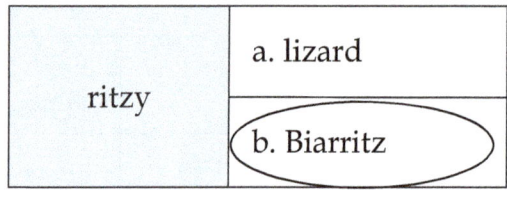
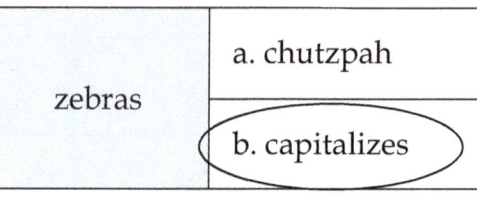
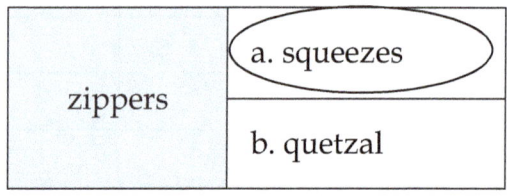
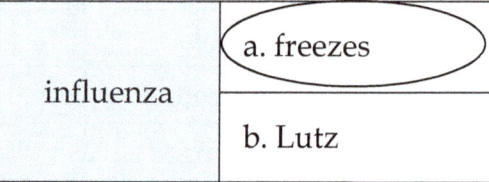

 Directions: Read each target word. Put a check (✓) under the correct column heading.
Direksyons: Li chak mo objektif. Mete yon tchèk (✓) anba antèt kolòn ki kòrèk la.

Target Words	"z" has the /z/ sound as in the word <u>zipper</u>	"z" has the /s/ sound as in the word <u>quartz</u>
1. ritzy		✓
2. zebras	✓	
3. zippers	✓	
4. influenza	✓	

Homework

Name: _____ Date: ___/___/_____ Score: _____

Lesson 26.2

Reading Words with a Silent Letter "z"

Directions: Read the target words in the word box. Write the words that have a silent letter "z" in the first column. Write the words that do not have a silent letter "z" in the second column.

Direksyons: Li mo objektif yo ki nan ti bwat mo a. Ekri mo yo ki genyen lèt "z" ki pa pwononse a nan premye kolòn nan. Ekri mo yo ki pa genyen lèt "z" ki pa pwononse anan dezyèm kolòn nan.

Target Word Box				
lazy	sizzle	grizzly	fizzled	blazed
drizzle	dazzle	hazel	puzzles	sizzling
buzzing	emphasize	lizard	influenza	magnetize
amazement	burglarize	nuzzle	computerize	intermezzo

Letter "z" is silent	Letter "z" has the /z/ or /s/ sound
drizzle	lazy
grizzly	hazel
sizzle	lizard
sizzling	blazed
fizzled	influenza
dazzle	magnetize
nuzzle	burglarize
buzzing	emphasize
puzzles	amazement
intermezzo	computerize

Learn To Read English With Directions In Haitian Creole

Homework

 Name: _____ Date: ___/___/_____ Score: _____

The Reading Challenge

Lesson 26.3

Reading Multisyllable Words

✓ **Lesson Check Point**

Directions: Read and divide each target word into syllables. Write each word and place a hyphen (-) between the syllables in the second column. Write the number of syllables in the third column. Use a dictionary or the Internet to check your answers.

Direksyons: Li epi divize chak mo objektif an silab. Ekri chak mo epi mete yon tirè (-) ant silab yo nan dezyèm kolòn nan. Ekri kantite silab ke yo genyen an nan twazyèm kolòn nan. Itilize yon diksyonè oubyen entènèt pou tcheke repons ou yo.

Target Words	Words Divided into Syllables	Number of Syllables
1. zygote	zy-gote	2
2. zealots	zeal-ots	2
3. zirconium	zir-co-ni-um	4
4. zenith	ze-nith	2
5. zero	ze-ro	2
6. zestful	zest-ful	2
7. Zambia	Zam-bi-a	3
8. Zanzibar	Zan-zi-bar	3
9. zinger	zing-er	2
10. zodiac	zo-di-ac	3

Homework

 Name: _____ Date: ___/___/_____ Score: _____

The Reading Challenge

Lesson 26.3

Reading Multisyllable Words

✓ **Lesson Check Point**

 Directions: Read each target word. Circle the word in the row that is divided correctly into syllables. Use a dictionary or the Internet to check your answers.
Direksyons: Li chak mo objektif. Antoure mo a ki nan ranje a ki divize an silab korèkteman yo. Itilize yon diksyonè oubyen entènèt pou tcheke repons ou yo.

Model

| zoology | a. zo-ol-o-gy ⭕ | b. zoo-lo-gy | c. zool-o-gy |

1. zestful	a. ze-stful	b. zes-tful	c. zest-ful ⭕
2. Zambian	a. Zam-bi-an ⭕	b. Zam-b-ian	c. Zamb-ian
3. Zanzibar	a. Za-nzib-ar	b. Zan-zi-bar ⭕	c. Zanz-i-bar
4. Zealand	a. Ze-aland	b. Zeal-and	c. Zea-land ⭕
5. zealous	a. zeal-ous ⭕	b. zea-lous	c. zeal-ou-s
6. zebra	a. ze-bra ⭕	b. zeb-ra	c. ze-br-a
7. zygote	a. zygo-te	b. zyg-ote	c. zy-gote ⭕
8. zymurgy	a. zy-mur-gy ⭕	b. zym-u-rgy	c. zy-mu-rgy

Homework

Name: _____ Date: ___/___/_____ Score: _____

Lesson 26.4

Reading and Writing

Proper and Common Nouns and Adjectives

Directions: Read the words in the word box. Put an (X) on the line next to each word that is written incorrectly. Remember that all proper nouns and proper adjectives are capitalized. Use a dictionary or the Internet to check your answers.

Direksyons: Li chak mo yo ki nan bwat mo a. Met yon (X) sou ti trè a ki bò kote mo ki pa kri byen yo. Sonje ke tout non pwòp ak adjektif pwop ekri avèk yon lèt majiskil nan kòmansman yo. Itilize yon diksyonè oubyen entènèt pou tcheke repons ou yo.

Word Box					
___	zenith	___	zonal	X	Zealot
___	zucchini	X	Zoology	___	zealous
X	zambezi	X	zululand	X	Zippers
___	Zaragoza	___	zero hour	X	Zebra

Directions: Read each unedited sentence and underline the word that is written incorrectly. Write each sentence correctly on the line.

Direksyons: Li chak fraz ki pa edite yo epi soulinye mo ki pa ekri byen an. Ekri chak fraz korèkteman sou liy lan.

Model
The steep path zigzags through the <u>zagros</u> Mountains.
<u>The steep path zigzags through the Zagros Mountains.</u>

1. Yesterday, I saw three large <u>Zebras</u> at the San Diego Zoo.
<u>Yesterday, I saw three large zebras at the San Diego Zoo.</u>

2. On Friday, the bright sun in <u>zimbabwe</u> rose towards its zenith.
<u>On Friday, the bright sun in Zimbabwe rose towards its zenith.</u>

3. Zola said, "<u>zanzibar</u> is located off the east coast of Africa."
<u>Zola said, "Zanzibar is located off the east coast of Africa."</u>

4. The <u>zambezi</u> River flows from Zambia into the Mozambique Channel.
<u>The Zambezi River flows from Zambia into the Mozambique Channel.</u>

Homework

 Name: _____ Date:___/___/_____ Score:_____

Appendix 1.0

Introduction of the Letter A/a

✓ **Lesson Check Point**

 Directions: Circle the correct letter "a" pair: uppercase and lowercase letters.
Direksyons: Antoure lèt ki kòrèk "a" pè: lèt majiskil ak lèt miniskil.

Ea   Ae   Ao   (Aa)   aZ

 Directions: The uppercase letter "A" is in the first column. Look at the four letters in the row and circle the lowercase letter that matches the uppercase letter "A."
Direksyons: Lèt majiskil "A" se nan premye kolòn nan. Gade kat lèt ki nan ranje a epi antoure lèt miniskil ki koresponn ak lèt majiskil "A".

A	g	(a)	e	o
A	u	e	i	(a)
A	(a)	o	y	e
A	e	c	(a)	q

 Directions: The lowercase letter "a" is in the first column. Look at the four letters in the row and circle the uppercase letter that matches the lowercase letter "a."
Direksyons: Lèt miniskil "a" se nan premye kolòn nan. Gade kat lèt ki nan ranje a epi antoure lèt majiskil ki koresponn ak lèt miniskil "a".

a	C	(A)	E	R
a	X	D	G	(A)
a	(A)	G	D	S
a	O	C	(A)	W

Homework

 Name: _____ Date: ___/___/_____ Score: _____

Appendix 2.0

Introduction of the Letter B/b

✓ **Lesson Check Point**

 Directions: Circle the correct letter "b" pair: uppercase and lowercase letters.
Direksyons: Antoure lèt ki kòrèk "b" pè: lèt majiskil ak lèt miniskil.

    fB   Bq   (bB)   bD   Pb

 Directions: The uppercase letter "B" is in the first column. Look at the four letters in the row and circle the lowercase letter that matches the uppercase letter "B."
Direksyons: Lèt majiskil "B" se nan premye kolòn nan. Gade kat lèt ki nan ranje a epi antoure lèt miniskil ki koresponn ak lèt majiskil "B".

B	p	q	(b)	d
B	f	d	h	(b)
B	m	(b)	f	h
B	k	d	(b)	l

 Directions: The lowercase letter "b" is in the first column. Look at the four letters in the row and circle the uppercase letter that matches the lowercase letter "b."
Direksyons: Lèt miniskil "b" se nan premye kolòn nan. Gade kat lèt ki nan ranje a epi antoure lèt majiskil ki koresponn ak lèt miniskil "b".

b	(B)	M	F	H
b	P	H	(B)	G
b	M	(B)	V	N
b	X	T	(B)	J

Homework

 Name: _____ Date: ___/___/_____ Score: _____

Appendix 2.0

Letter Recognition B/b

Uppercase and Lowercase Letter

✓ **Lesson Check Point**

 Directions: Read each target word. Read the words in the row and circle the word that begins with a different letter.

Direksyons: Li chak mo sib. Li mo ki nan ranje a epi antoure mo ki kòmanse ak yon lèt diferan.

Target Words				
1. buffet	boss	(danger)	bottle	biscuit
2. brain	basket	blank	(pads)	bride
3. brick	behave	beef	big	(demand)
4. butter	(dent)	bank	black	bill
5. brass	blade	bin	bell	(queen)

 Directions: Read the words in the four boxes. Circle two words that start with the uppercase and lowercase letter "b."

Direksyons: Li mo ki nan kat kare yo. Ansèkle de mo ki kòmanse ak lèt majiskil ak lèt miniskil "b".

| (Boy) | Toy |
| (boy) | Soy |

| Ball | hall |
| Hall | (ball) |

| (Book) | Hook |
| (book) | Took |

| Had | had |
| (bad) | (Bad) |

| (Bank) | Tank |
| (bank) | tank |

| (Bread) | head |
| (bread) | Head |

Homework

 Name: _____ Date: ___/___/_____ Score: _____

Appendix 3.0

Introduction of the Letter C/c

✓ Lesson Check Point

Directions: Circle the correct letter "c" pair: uppercase and lowercase letters.
Direksyons: Antoure lèt ki kòrèk "c" pè: lèt majiskil ak lèt miniskil.

Cf   (Cc)   Kc   cD   Co

Directions: The uppercase letter "C" is in the first column. Look at the four letters in the row and circle the lowercase letter that matches the uppercase letter "C."
Direksyons: Lèt majiskil "C" se nan premye kolòn nan. Gade kat lèt ki nan ranje a epi antoure lèt miniskil ki koresponn ak lèt majiskil "C".

C	(c)	g	h	k
C	s	(c)	u	j
C	n	p	d	(c)
C	(c)	v	s	o

Directions: The lowercase letter "c" is in the first column. Look at the four letters in the row and circle the uppercase letter that matches the lowercase letter "c."
Direksyons: Lèt miniskil "c" se nan premye kolòn nan. Gade kat lèt ki nan ranje a epi antoure lèt majiskil ki koresponn ak lèt miniskil "c".

c	K	G	(C)	O
c	H	J	D	(C)
c	Q	G	(C)	V
c	(C)	B	Q	G

Homework

Name: _____ Date: ___/___/_____ Score: _____

Appendix 3.0

Letter Recognition C/c

Uppercase and Lowercase Letter

✓ Lesson Check Point

Directions: Read each target word. Read the words in the row and circle the word that begins with a different letter.

Direksyons: Li chak mo sib. Li mo ki nan ranje a epi antoure mo ki kòmanse ak yon lèt diferan.

Target Words				
1. cart	cry	(oblong)	curtain	city
2. choice	calculate	(queen)	cutter	cycle
3. cherish	(ankle)	chill	comb	cup
4. calcium	(Goat)	circle	choke	caption
5. convert	cherish	career	cell	(boss)

Directions: Read the words in the four boxes. Circle two words that start with the uppercase and lowercase letter "c."

Direksyons: Li mo ki nan kat kare yo. Ansèkle de mo ki kòmanse ak lèt majiskil ak lèt miniskil "c".

(Case)	base		Open	(Cream)		(Castle)	vase
Quiet	(camp)		(cargo)	pool		keep	(coat)

(cream)	(Chase)		jump	(cash)		old	orange
box	grapes		(Child)	food		(cold)	(Crib)

Learn To Read English With Directions In Haitian Creole

Homework

 Name: _____ Date: ___/___/_____ Score: _____

Appendix 4.0

Introduction of the Letter D/d

✓ **Lesson Check Point**

 Directions: Circle the correct letter "d" pair: uppercase and lowercase letters.
Direksyons: Antoure lèt ki kòrèk "d" pè: lèt majiskil ak lèt miniskil.

Db   Fb   (Dd)   Od   Gd

 Directions: The uppercase letter "D" is in the first column. Look at the four letters in the row and circle the lowercase letter that matches the uppercase letter "D."
Direksyons: Lèt majiskil "D" se nan premye kolòn nan. Gade kat lèt ki nan ranje a epi antoure lèt miniskil ki koresponn ak lèt majiskil "D".

D	b	f	h	(d)
D	j	(d)	p	t
D	h	n	(d)	b
D	p	b	(d)	k

 Directions: The lowercase letter "d" is in the first column. Look at the four letters in the row and circle the uppercase letter that matches the lowercase letter "d."
Direksyons: Lèt miniskil "d" se nan premye kolòn nan. Gade kat lèt ki nan ranje a epi antoure lèt majiskil ki koresponn ak lèt miniskil "d".

d	H	(D)	B	K
d	P	J	(D)	B
d	(D)	B	E	R
d	S	K	B	(D)

Homework

Name: _____ Date:___/___/_____ Score:_____

Appendix 4.0

Letter Recognition D/d

Uppercase and Lowercase Letter

✓ Lesson Check Point

Directions: Read each target word. Read the words in the row and circle the word that begins with a different letter.

Direksyons: Li chak mo sib. Li mo ki nan ranje a epi antoure mo ki kòmanse ak yon lèt diferan.

Target Words				
1. dog	dive	dress	dew	(both)
2. due	deal	(place)	date	draw
3. dole	ditch	dome	(bread)	dwarf
4. depth	drop	dish	(prize)	deck
5. drain	(quite)	doze	dream	dodge

Directions: Read the words in the four boxes. Circle two words that start with the uppercase and lowercase letter "d."

Direksyons: Li mo ki nan kat kare yo. Ansèkle de mo ki kòmanse ak lèt majiskil ak lèt miniskil "d".

top	(Dance)
(dear)	ball

(drum)	Open
Pop	(Deck)

(dry)	Queen
(Deer)	Prince

friend	(Due)
Ox	(drink)

Box	(Dress)
(dodge)	boat

Old	Pie
(Dad)	(doubt)

Learn To Read English With Directions In Haitian Creole Copyrighted Material

Homework

 Name: _____ Date: ___/___/_____ Score: _____

Appendix 5.0

Introduction of the Letter E/e

✓ Lesson Check Point

 Directions: Circle the correct letter "e" pair: uppercase and lowercase letters.
Direksyons: Antoure lèt ki kòrèk "e" pè: lèt majiskil ak lèt miniskil.

   eF   (Ee)   Ec   eC   Qe

 Directions: The uppercase letter "E" is in the first column. Look at the four letters in the row and circle the lowercase letter that matches the uppercase letter "E."
Direksyons: Lèt majiskil "E" se nan premye kolòn nan. Gade kat lèt ki nan ranje a epi antoure lèt miniskil ki koresponn ak lèt majiskil "E".

E	c	(e)	s	x
E	a	c	d	(e)
E	(e)	s	c	w
E	v	g	(e)	o

 Directions: The lowercase letter "e" is in the first column. Look at the four letters in the row and circle the uppercase letter that matches the lowercase letter "e."
Direksyons: Lèt miniskil "e" se nan premye kolòn nan. Gade kat lèt ki nan ranje a epi antoure lèt majiskil ki koresponn ak lèt miniskil "e".

e	F	(E)	H	T
e	D	T	(E)	Y
e	(E)	D	R	N
e	X	S	F	(E)

Homework

 Name: _____ Date: ___/___/_____ Score: _____

Appendix 6.0

Introduction of the Letter F/f

✓ Lesson Check Point

 Directions: Circle the correct letter "f" pair: uppercase and lowercase letters.
Direksyons: Antoure lèt ki kòrèk "f" pè: lèt majiskil ak lèt miniskil.

Fd (fF) Yf Ef Bf

 Directions: The uppercase letter "F" is in the first column. Look at the four letters in the row and circle the lowercase letter that matches the uppercase letter "F."
Direksyons: Lèt majiskil "F" se nan premye kolòn nan. Gade kat lèt ki nan ranje a epi antoure lèt miniskil ki koresponn ak lèt majiskil "F".

F	k	(f)	h	t
F	h	t	p	(f)
F	(f)	l	d	h
F	b	k	(f)	t

 Directions: The lowercase letter "f" is in the first column. Look at the four letters in the row and circle the uppercase letter that matches the lowercase letter "f."
Direksyons: Lèt miniskil "f" se nan premye kolòn nan. Gade kat lèt ki nan ranje a epi antoure lèt majiskil ki koresponn ak lèt miniskil "f".

f	B	(F)	E	H
f	E	K	L	(F)
f	(F)	H	M	E
f	J	(F)	E	P

Homework

Name: _____ Date: ___/___/_____ Score: _____

Appendix 6.0

Letter Recognition F/f

Uppercase and Lowercase Letter

✓ Lesson Check Point

Directions: Read each target word. Read the words in the row and circle the word that begins with a different letter.

Direksyons: Li chak mo sib. Li mo ki nan ranje a epi antoure mo ki kòmanse ak yon lèt diferan.

Target Words				
1. fry	(try)	fact	foal	fuse
2. flag	folk	fly	(house)	foam
3. fail	farm	(keep)	flee	five
4. feed	flame	(head)	fish	flew
5. flour	(love)	fox	flesh	fax

Directions: Read the words in the four boxes. Circle two words that start with the uppercase and lowercase letter "f."

Direksyons: Li mo ki nan kat kare yo. Ansèkle de mo ki kòmanse ak lèt majiskil ak lèt miniskil "f".

World	(feel)
(Fawn)	drive

boats	Books
(Flea)	(fit)

(Fit)	breeze
Houses	(flush)

(Fetch)	(fill)
Eggs	dove

fret	Keeps
(Film)	depth

ghost	(Flair)
draw	(flow)

Homework

Name: _____ Date:___/___/_____ Score:_____

Appendix 7.0

Introduction of the Letter G/g

✓ **Lesson Check Point**

 Directions: Circle the correct letter "g" pair: uppercase and lowercase letters.
Direksyons: Antoure lèt ki kòrèk "g" pè: lèt majiskil ak lèt miniskil.

Gj   qG   (Gg)   Jg   Gp

 Directions: The uppercase letter "G" is in the first column. Look at the four letters in the row and circle the lowercase letter that matches the uppercase letter "G."
Direksyons: Lèt majiskil "G" se nan premye kolòn nan. Gade kat lèt ki nan ranje a epi antoure lèt miniskil ki koresponn ak lèt majiskil "G".

G	j	o	(g)	l
G	(g)	y	j	p
G	q	(g)	z	y
G	y	p	q	(g)

 Directions: The lowercase letter "g" is in the first column. Look at the four letters in the row and circle the uppercase letter that matches the lowercase letter "g."
Direksyons: Lèt miniskil "g" se nan premye kolòn nan. Gade kat lèt ki nan ranje a epi antoure lèt majiskil ki koresponn ak lèt miniskil "g".

g	O	(G)	J	L
g	(G)	Q	O	J
g	O	P	Q	(G)
g	Q	F	(G)	O

Learn To Read English With Directions In Haitian Creole — Copyrighted Material

Homework

 Name: _____ Date:___/___/_____ Score: _____

Appendix 7.0

Letter Recognition G/g

Uppercase and Lowercase Letter

✓ Lesson Check Point

 Directions: Read each target word. Read the words in the row and circle the word that begins with a different letter.

Direksyons: Li chak mo sib. Li mo ki nan ranje a epi antoure mo ki kòmanse ak yon lèt diferan.

Target Words				
1. greet	(judge)	grill	gear	glow
2. good	group	glimpse	(paint)	gain
3. gang	give	(boat)	growth	gulf
4. guess	grace	(job)	get	gill
5. grade	gem	grow	girl	(pool)

 Directions: Read the words in the four boxes. Circle two words that start with the uppercase and lowercase letter "g."

Direksyons: Li mo ki nan kat kare yo. Ansèkle de mo ki kòmanse ak lèt majiskil ak lèt miniskil "g".

(get)	jet		Pen	boat		ball	(Gain)
Peach	(Goat)		(Greek)	give		(grow)	jeans

(golf)	(Gray)		place	(good)		(Gift)	pie
plant	deep		jump	(Grant)		(gum)	Ox

Homework

 Name: _____ Date: ___/___/_____ Score: _____

Appendix 8.0

Introduction of the Letter H/h

✓ Lesson Check Point

 Directions: Circle the correct letter "h" pair: uppercase and lowercase letters.
Direksyons: Antoure lèt ki kòrèk "h" pè: lèt majiskil ak lèt miniskil.

(Hh)   bH   Bh   hF   Hk

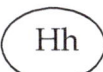 **Directions:** The uppercase letter "H" is in the first column. Look at the four letters in the row and circle the lowercase letter that matches the uppercase letter "H."
Direksyons: Lèt majiskil "H" se nan premye kolòn nan. Gade kat lèt ki nan ranje a epi antoure lèt miniskil ki koresponn ak lèt majiskil "H".

H	l	(h)	g	t
H	(h)	v	l	q
H	t	b	(h)	f
H	f	p	t	(h)

 Directions: The lowercase letter "h" is in the first column. Look at the four letters in the row and circle the uppercase letter that matches the lowercase letter "h."
Direksyons: Lèt miniskil "h" se nan premye kolòn nan. Gade kat lèt ki nan ranje a epi antoure lèt majiskil ki koresponn ak lèt miniskil "h".

h	F	(H)	T	S
h	G	T	(H)	R
h	(H)	D	J	T
h	B	(H)	U	L

Learn To Read English With Directions In Haitian Creole

Homework

L. Name: _____ Date:___/___/_____ Score:_____

Appendix 8.0

Letter Recognition H/h

Uppercase and Lowercase Letter

✓ **Lesson Check Point**

Directions: Read each target word. Read the words in the row and circle the word that begins with a different letter.

Direksyons: Li chak mo sib. Li mo ki nan ranje a epi antoure mo ki kòmanse ak yon lèt diferan.

Target Words				
1. hit	hive	hood	(like)	hub
2. hike	(tape)	health	hall	hook
3. heal	hair	horn	(leaves)	he
4. hard	hole	(bath)	heap	hand
5. hose	(jump)	hang	hence	haul

Directions: Read the words in the four boxes. Circle two words that start with the uppercase and lowercase letter "h."

Direksyons: Li mo ki nan kat kare yo. Ansèkle de mo ki kòmanse ak lèt majiskil ak lèt miniskil "h".

(herb)	tree		pink	teeth		light	(Hand)
brown	(Hoard)		(home)	(Heed)		bath	(hop)

(hair)	(Heal)		look	(Horse)		(Half)	(hot)
keep	true		(hemp)	found		dress	top

Homework

 Name: _____ Date:___/___/_____ Score: _____

Appendix 9.0

Introduction of the Letter I/i

✓ Lesson Check Point

 Directions: Circle the correct letter "i" pair: uppercase and lowercase letters.
Direksyons: Antoure lèt ki kòrèk "i pè: lèt majiskil ak lèt miniskil.

(Ii)　　　Ij　　　iJ　　　Im　　　Ti

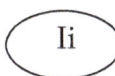 Directions: The uppercase letter "I" is in the first column. Look at the four letters in the row and circle the lowercase letter that matches the uppercase letter "I."
Direksyons: Lèt majiskil "I" se nan premye kolòn nan. Gade kat lèt ki nan ranje a epi antoure lèt miniskil ki koresponn ak lèt majiskil "I".

I	j	(i)	l	y
I	f	j	x	(i)
I	(i)	h	t	v
I	t	d	h	(i)

 Directions: The lowercase letter "i" is in the first column. Look at the four letters in the row and circle the uppercase letter that matches the lowercase letter "i."
Direksyons: Lèt miniskil "i" se nan premye kolòn nan. Gade kat lèt ki nan ranje a epi antoure lèt majiskil ki koresponn ak lèt miniskil "i".

i	K	(I)	T	J
i	(I)	L	H	K
i	D	Y	(I)	L
i	J	G	K	(I)

Homework

 Name: _____ Date: ___/___/_____ Score: _____

Appendix 10.0

Introduction of the Letter J/j

✓ **Lesson Check Point**

 Directions: Circle the correct letter "j" pair: uppercase and lowercase letters.

Direksyons: Antoure lèt ki kòrèk "j" pè: lèt majiskil ak lèt miniskil.

jY   yl   Gj   (Jj)   jL

 Directions: The uppercase letter "J" is in the first column. Look at the four letters in the row and circle the lowercase letter that matches the uppercase letter "J."

Direksyons: Lèt majiskil "J" se nan premye kolòn nan. Gade kat lèt ki nan ranje a epi antoure lèt miniskil ki koresponn ak lèt majiskil "J".

J	y	g	(j)	l
J	(j)	v	y	q
J	p	(j)	g	b
J	g	y	(j)	p

 Directions: The lowercase letter "j" is in the first column. Look at the four letters in the row and circle the uppercase letter that matches the lowercase letter "j."

Direksyons: Lèt miniskil "j" se nan premye kolòn nan. Gade kat lèt ki nan ranje a epi antoure lèt majiskil ki koresponn ak lèt miniskil "j".

j	K	(J)	C	L
j	(J)	O	G	U
j	Q	C	(J)	O
j	G	V	U	(J)

Learn To Read English With Directions In Haitian Creole

Homework

 Name: _____ Date:___/___/_____ Score: _____

Appendix 10.0

Letter Recognition J/j

Uppercase and Lowercase Letter

✓ Lesson Check Point

 Directions: Read each target word. Read the words in the row and circle the word that begins with a different letter.

Direksyons: Li chak mo sib. Li mo ki nan ranje a epi antoure mo ki kòmanse ak yon lèt diferan.

Target Words				
1. jaw	jet	jay	(yes)	joint
2. join	(pie)	jean	junk	jade
3. jump	jazz	(guess)	jar	jog
4. jungle	job	(gem)	judge	jeep
5. January	jail	jug	joke	(years)

 Directions: Read the words in the four boxes. Circle two words that start with the uppercase and lowercase letter "j."

Direksyons: Li mo ki nan kat kare yo. Ansèkle de mo ki kòmanse ak lèt majiskil ak lèt miniskil "j".

(Joke)	Goat
yes	(juice)

just	(Jolt)
prince	your

youth	(June)
(jock)	queen

quest	price
(jog)	(Jam)

young	(Jail)
(jot)	golf

grand	(jump)
press	(Juicy)

Learn To Read English With Directions In Haitian Creole

Homework

 Name: _____ Date:___/___/_____ Score: _____

Appendix 11.0

Introduction of the Letter K/k

✓ Lesson Check Point

 Directions: Circle the correct letter "k" pair: uppercase and lowercase letters.

Direksyons: Antoure lèt ki kòrèk "k" pè: lèt majiskil ak lèt miniskil.

kB   Kl   kt   kY   (Kk)

 Directions: The uppercase letter "K" is in the first column. Look at the four letters in the row and circle the lowercase letter that matches the uppercase letter "K."

Direksyons: Lèt majiskil "K" se nan premye kolòn nan. Gade kat lèt ki nan ranje a epi antoure lèt miniskil ki koresponn ak lèt majiskil "K".

K	l	(k)	y	p
K	b	f	(k)	l
K	p	h	d	(k)
K	(k)	j	l	p

 Directions: The lowercase letter "k" is in the first column. Look at the four letters in the row and circle the uppercase letter that matches the lowercase letter "k."

Direksyons: Lèt miniskil "k" se nan premye kolòn nan. Gade kat lèt ki nan ranje a epi antoure lèt majiskil ki koresponn ak lèt miniskil "k".

k	(K)	L	M	Y
k	M	N	(K)	L
k	J	(K)	H	B
k	V	N	(K)	T

Homework

 Name: _____ Date:___/___/_____ Score:_____

Appendix 11.0

Letter Recognition K/k

Uppercase and Lowercase Letter

✓ Lesson Check Point

 Directions: Read each target word. Read the words in the row and circle the word that begins with a different letter.

Direksyons: Li chak mo sib. Li mo ki nan ranje a epi antoure mo ki kòmanse ak yon lèt diferan.

Target Words				
1. kid	kin	(house)	keel	know
2. knit	keen	knight	king	(lace)
3. kind	kale	(body)	key	keep
4. krill	(hatch)	keg	knock	kick
5. kept	(drop)	kart	knot	kelp

 Directions: Read the words in the four boxes. Circle two words that start with the uppercase and lowercase letter "k."

Direksyons: Li mo ki nan kat kare yo. Ansèkle de mo ki kòmanse ak lèt majiskil ak lèt miniskil "k".

(keep)	house
(Kiss)	Eats

dreams	(Know)
(kind)	friends

jumps	home
(Knock)	(kick)

laughs	(knight)
bounce	(Keys)

(Knit)	(kept)
free	tree

(Knob)	trips
hope	(kale)

Learn To Read English With Directions In Haitian Creole

Homework

 Name: _____ Date: ___/___/_____ Score: _____

Appendix 12.0

Introduction of the Letter L/l

✓ Lesson Check Point

 Directions: Circle the correct letter "l" pair: uppercase and lowercase letters.

Direksyons: Antoure lèt ki kòrèk "l" pè: lèt majiskil ak lèt miniskil.

hL   Lk   lT   (Ll)   lJ

 Directions: The uppercase letter "L" is in the first column. Look at the four letters in the row and circle the lowercase letter that matches the uppercase letter "L."

Direksyons: Lèt majiskil "L" se nan premye kolòn nan. Gade kat lèt ki nan ranje a epi antoure lèt miniskil ki koresponn ak lèt majiskil "L".

L	k	(l)	f	h
L	j	f	(l)	b
L	(l)	h	j	x
L	b	y	k	(l)

 Directions: The lowercase letter "l" is in the first column. Look at the four letters in the row and circle the uppercase letter that matches the lowercase letter "l."

Direksyons: Lèt miniskil "l" se nan premye kolòn nan. Gade kat lèt ki nan ranje a epi antoure lèt majiskil ki koresponn ak lèt miniskil "l".

l	(L)	K	H	V
l	E	F	(L)	K
l	M	V	T	(L)
l	(L)	H	V	E

Homework

 Name: _____ Date:___/___/_____ Score: _____

Appendix 12.0

Letter Recognition L/l

Uppercase and Lowercase Letter

✓ **Lesson Check Point**

 Directions: Read each target word. Read the words in the row and circle the word that begins with a different letter.

Direksyons: Li chak mo sib. Li mo ki nan ranje a epi antoure mo ki kòmanse ak yon lèt diferan.

Target Words				
1. leaf	lack	lush	(town)	land
2. link	(jump)	like	lard	left
3. lead	lift	lance	(brown)	leg
4. late	lunch	(friends)	leek	latch
5. lick	(dreams)	limp	lank	live

 Directions: Read the words in the four boxes. Circle two words that start with the uppercase and lowercase letter "l."

Direksyons: Li mo ki nan kat kare yo. Ansèkle de mo ki kòmanse ak lèt majiskil ak lèt miniskil "l".

trees	(Lend)		boats	Drops		house	(Law)
fruits	(lane)		(Line)	(lash)		(list)	drips

(Less)	(lynch)		(Lots)	home		(Leak)	drive
front	dress		bumps	(lump)		(launch)	found

Homework

 Name: _____ Date: ___/___/_____ Score: _____

Appendix 13.0

Introduction of the Letter M/m

✓ **Lesson Check Point**

 Directions: Circle the correct letter "m" pair: uppercase and lowercase letters.
Direksyons: Antoure lèt ki kòrèk "m" pè: lèt majiskil ak lèt miniskil.

Um   Nm   Mw   Mn   ⟨Mm⟩

 Directions: The uppercase letter "M" is in the first column. Look at the four letters in the row and circle the lowercase letter that matches the uppercase letter "M."
Direksyons: Lèt majiskil "M" se nan premye kolòn nan. Gade kat lèt ki nan ranje a epi antoure lèt miniskil ki koresponn ak lèt majiskil "M".

M	n	⟨m⟩	n	h
M	w	n	u	⟨m⟩
M	u	v	⟨m⟩	n
M	⟨m⟩	u	n	o

 Directions: The lowercase letter "m" is in the first column. Look at the four letters in the row and circle the uppercase letter that matches the lowercase letter "m."
Direksyons: Lèt miniskil "m" se nan premye kolòn nan. Gade kat lèt ki nan ranje a epi antoure lèt majiskil ki koresponn ak lèt miniskil "m".

m	N	U	⟨M⟩	W
m	⟨M⟩	V	X	J
m	V	W	Z	⟨M⟩
m	X	⟨M⟩	U	N

Homework

 Name: _____ Date: ___/___/_____ Score: _____

Appendix 13.0

Letter Recognition M/m

Uppercase and Lowercase Letter

✓ **Lesson Check Point**

 Directions: Read each target word. Read the words in the row and circle the word that begins with a different letter.

Direksyons: Li chak mo sib. Li mo ki nan ranje a epi antoure mo ki kòmanse ak yon lèt diferan.

Target Words				
1. meat	mood	mixed	(were)	might
2. mind	(nail)	mince	much	mean
3. moist	mug	meal	(vote)	miss
4. made	mumps	mouth	mist	(nest)
5. musk	(world)	mall	mock	mint

 Directions: Read the words in the four boxes. Circle two words that start with the uppercase and lowercase letter "m."

Direksyons: Li mo ki nan kat kare yo. Ansèkle de mo ki kòmanse ak lèt majiskil ak lèt miniskil "m".

noise	(moon)
vest	(Main)

write	noon
(most)	(Maid)

(Make)	news
vowel	(mouse)

used	(mane)
(Move)	numb

(Mold)	(milk)
nerve	wrote

(mourn)	nine
(Mail)	cause

Homework

 Name: _____ Date: ___/___/_____ Score: _____

Appendix 14.0

Introduction of the Letter N/n

✓ **Lesson Check Point**

 Directions: Circle the correct letter "n" pair: uppercase and lowercase letters.
Direksyons: Antoure lèt ki kòrèk "n" pè: lèt majiskil ak lèt miniskil.

Nm   Vn   nW   (Nn)   Mn

 Directions: The uppercase letter "N" is in the first column. Look at the four letters in the row and circle the lowercase letter that matches the uppercase letter "N."
Direksyons: Lèt majiskil "N" se nan premye kolòn nan. Gade kat lèt ki nan ranje a epi antoure lèt miniskil ki koresponn ak lèt majiskil "N".

N	v	(n)	u	o
N	y	u	w	(n)
N	(n)	j	m	f
N	u	b	(n)	v

 Directions: The lowercase letter "n" is in the first column. Look at the four letters in the row and circle the uppercase letter that matches the lowercase letter "n."
Direksyons: Lèt miniskil "n" se nan premye kolòn nan. Gade kat lèt ki nan ranje a epi antoure lèt majiskil ki koresponn ak lèt miniskil "n".

n	M	W	(N)	V
n	(N)	C	W	X
n	U	H	X	(N)
n	T	(N)	Z	U

Homework

 Name: _____ Date:___/___/_____ Score:_____

Appendix 14.0

Letter Recognition N/n

Uppercase and Lowercase Letter

✓ Lesson Check Point

 Directions: Read each target word. Read the words in the row and circle the word that begins with a different letter.

Direksyons: Li chak mo sib. Li mo ki nan ranje a epi antoure mo ki kòmanse ak yon lèt diferan.

Target Words				
1. nerve	noon	(right)	news	noun
2. noise	(make)	near	night	need
3. neck	nail	nose	nine	(rope)
4. nine	name	none	(moist)	next
5. name	numb	note	nest	(use)

 Directions: Read the words in the four boxes. Circle two words that start with the uppercase and lowercase letter "n."

Direksyons: Li mo ki nan kat kare yo. Ansèkle de mo ki kòmanse ak lèt majiskil ak lèt miniskil "n".

mall	you
(numb)	(New)

unto	(Name)
house	(nerve)

much	(Near)
(need)	good

(Nap)	mops
ran	(norm)

(Null)	mock
(neat)	vote

(neck)	(Nest)
race	mom

Learn To Read English With Directions In Haitian Creole

Homework

 Name: _____ Date: ___/___/_____ Score: _____

Appendix 15.0

Introduction of the Letter O/o

✓ **Lesson Check Point**

 Directions: Circle the correct letter "o" pair: uppercase and lowercase letters.
Direksyons: Antoure lèt ki kòrèk "o" pè: lèt majiskil ak lèt miniskil.

    Po   Qo   Oc   (Oo)   Co

 Directions: The uppercase letter "O" is in the first column. Look at the four letters in the row and circle the lowercase letter that matches the uppercase letter "O."
Direksyons: Lèt majiskil "O" se nan premye kolòn nan. Gade kat lèt ki nan ranje a epi antoure lèt miniskil ki koresponn ak lèt majiskil "O".

O	(o)	d	g	s
O	c	s	u	(o)
O	g	(o)	c	q
O	d	g	(o)	c

 Directions: The lowercase letter "o" is in the first column. Look at the four letters in the row and circle the uppercase letter that matches the lowercase letter "o."
Direksyons: Lèt miniskil "o" se nan premye kolòn nan. Gade kat lèt ki nan ranje a epi antoure lèt majiskil ki koresponn ak lèt miniskil "o".

o	D	(O)	Q	G
o	C	Q	V	(O)
o	Q	C	(O)	S
o	(O)	H	Q	C

Homework

 Name: _____ Date: ___/___/_____ Score: _____

Appendix 16.0

Introduction of the Letter P/p

✓ **Lesson Check Point**

 Directions: Circle the correct letter "p" pair: uppercase and lowercase letters.
Direksyons: Antoure lèt ki kòrèk "p" pè: lèt majiskil ak lèt miniskil.

Pd   bP   Dp   (Pp)   Bp

 Directions: The uppercase letter "P" is in the first column. Look at the four letters in the row and circle the lowercase letter that matches the uppercase letter "P."
Direksyons: Lèt majiskil "P" se nan premye kolòn nan. Gade kat lèt ki nan ranje a epi antoure lèt miniskil ki koresponn ak lèt majiskil "P".

P	q	b	d	(p)
P	(p)	d	g	j
P	g	(p)	h	f
P	d	g	(p)	b

 Directions: The lowercase letter "p" is in the first column. Look at the four letters in the row and circle the uppercase letter that matches the lowercase letter "p."
Direksyons: Lèt miniskil "p" se nan premye kolòn nan. Gade kat lèt ki nan ranje a epi antoure lèt majiskil ki koresponn ak lèt miniskil "p".

p	R	(P)	Q	B
p	(P)	D	F	D
p	F	K	(P)	Q
p	B	S	G	(P)

Homework

Name: _____ Date: ___/___/_____ Score: _____

Appendix 16.0

Letter Recognition P/p

Uppercase and Lowercase Letter

✓ **Lesson Check Point**

Directions: Read each target word. Read the words in the row and circle the word that begins with a different letter.

Direksyons: Li chak mo sib. Li mo ki nan ranje a epi antoure mo ki kòmanse ak yon lèt diferan.

Target Words				
1. pen	pledge	(quote)	prince	porch
2. play	(years)	plug	park	pear
3. pitch	peer	pinch	(quartz)	pop
4. patch	poise	prompt	place	(bond)
5. praise	(queen)	pain	pile	proof

Directions: Read the words in the four boxes. Circle two words that start with the uppercase and lowercase letter "p."

Direksyons: Li mo ki nan kat kare yo. Ansèkle de mo ki kòmanse ak lèt majiskil ak lèt miniskil "p".

beach	(Peach)
teach	(patch)

fast	(past)
last	(Pearl)

(Pad)	(push)
Bad	Dad

Say	Day
(pay)	(Path)

(Pave)	Dave
(pop)	Have

Deal	meal
(peel)	(Pets)

Homework

 Name: _____ Date: ___/___/_____ Score: _____

Appendix 17.0

Introduction of the Letter Q/q

✓ **Lesson Check Point**

 Directions: Circle the correct letter "q" pair: uppercase and lowercase letters.
Direksyons: Antoure lèt ki kòrèk "q" pè: lèt majiskil ak lèt miniskil.

Pq   Bq   (Qq)   Oq   pQ

 Directions: The uppercase letter "Q" is in the first column. Look at the four letters in the row and circle the lowercase letter that matches the uppercase letter "Q."
Direksyons: Lèt majiskil "Q" se nan premye kolòn nan. Gade kat lèt ki nan ranje a epi antoure lèt miniskil ki koresponn ak lèt majiskil "Q".

Q	p	d	(q)	d
Q	g	(q)	j	b
Q	(q)	f	g	j
Q	j	y	p	(q)

 Directions: The lowercase letter "q" is in the first column. Look at the four letters in the row and circle the uppercase letter that matches the lowercase letter "q."
Direksyons: Lèt miniskil "q" se nan premye kolòn nan. Gade kat lèt ki nan ranje a epi antoure lèt majiskil ki koresponn ak lèt miniskil "q".

q	D	(Q)	S	H
q	O	S	R	(Q)
q	(Q)	D	C	O
q	C	Z	(Q)	S

Homework

Name: _____ Date: ___/___/_____ Score: _____

Appendix 17.0

Letter Recognition Q/q

Uppercase and Lowercase Letter

✓ Lesson Check Point

Directions: Read each target word. Read the words in the row and circle the word that begins with a different letter.

Direksyons: Li chak mo sib. Li mo ki nan ranje a epi antoure mo ki kòmanse ak yon lèt diferan.

Target Words				
1. quiz	(jumps)	quota	quire	quaint
2. quince	quack	quench	quarrel	(guest)
3. queen	quick	(young)	quartz	quit
4. quirk	quote	quest	(puppy)	quack
5. quench	(paints)	queen	quartz	quicken

Directions: Read the words in the four boxes. Circle two words that start with the uppercase and lowercase letter "q."

Direksyons: Li mo ki nan kat kare yo. Ansèkle de mo ki kòmanse ak lèt majiskil ak lèt miniskil "q".

(quite)	peace	(qualm)	(Quality)	puppy	(Quiver)
Jupiter	(Quiet)	Opens	jumps	(quarter)	Cover

Opera	(Quiche)	(qualify)	Over	people	jelly
dance	(quibble)	(Quacks)	person	(Quicken)	(query)

Unit Q
Appendix 17.0

Learn To Read English With Directions In Haitian Creole

Homework

 Name: _____ Date:___/___/_____ Score:_____

Appendix 18.0

Introduction of the Letter R/r

✓ Lesson Check Point

 Directions: Circle the correct letter "r" pair: uppercase and lowercase letters.
Direksyons: Antoure lèt ki kòrèk "r" pè: lèt majiskil ak lèt miniskil.

(rR)   Rv   rX   kR   rP

 Directions: The uppercase letter "R" is in the first column. Look at the four letters in the row and circle the lowercase letter that matches the uppercase letter "R."
Direksyons: Lèt majiskil "R" se nan premye kolòn nan. Gade kat lèt ki nan ranje a epi antoure lèt miniskil ki koresponn ak lèt majiskil "R".

R	x	(r)	f	h
R	g	v	s	(r)
R	(r)	x	z	v
R	j	(r)	a	c

 Directions: The lowercase letter "r" is in the first column. Look at the four letters in the row and circle the uppercase letter that matches the lowercase letter "r."
Direksyons: Lèt miniskil "r" se nan premye kolòn nan. Gade kat lèt ki nan ranje a epi antoure lèt majiskil ki koresponn ak lèt miniskil "r".

r	F	S	T	(R)
r	(R)	F	W	E
r	F	C	A	(R)
r	X	(R)	H	D

Homework

 Name: _____ Date:___/___/_____ Score:_____

Appendix 18.0

Letter Recognition R/r

Uppercase and Lowercase Letter

✓ Lesson Check Point

 Directions: Read each target word. Read the words in the row and circle the word that begins with a different letter.

Direksyons: Li chak mo sib. Li mo ki nan ranje a epi antoure mo ki kòmanse ak yon lèt diferan.

Target Words				
1. role	ride	(nine)	ranch	rope
2. ring	(music)	rose	right	raise
3. rail	ripe	rough	real	(closed)
4. rose	rank	(cream)	rinse	roof
5. run	rhyme	root	(noon)	read

 Directions: Read the words in the four boxes. Circle two words that start with the uppercase and lowercase letter "r."

Direksyons: Li mo ki nan kat kare yo. Ansèkle de mo ki kòmanse ak lèt majiskil ak lèt miniskil "r".

(Roach)	games		march	(rake)		(ring)	(Road)
numb	(rub)		cave	(Round)		need	Peek

Pain	mouth		citizen	(rink)		(Rode)	peer
(Roast)	(race)		(Rent)	Person		(rice)	part

Learn To Read English With Directions In Haitian Creole

Homework

 Name: _____ Date:___/___/_____ Score: _____

Appendix 19.0

Introduction of the Letter S/s

 Lesson Check Point

Directions: Circle the correct letter "s" pair: uppercase and lowercase letters.

Direksyons: Antoure lèt ki kòrèk "s" pè: lèt majiskil ak lèt miniskil.

    Sc   sZ   cS   sX   (sS)

Directions: The uppercase letter "S" is in the first column. Look at the four letters in the row and circle the lowercase letter that matches the uppercase letter "S."

Direksyons: Lèt majiskil "S" se nan premye kolòn nan. Gade kat lèt ki nan ranje a epi antoure lèt miniskil ki koresponn ak lèt majiskil "S".

S	c	(s)	x	z
S	z	o	c	(s)
S	(s)	j	z	t
S	g	c	(s)	k

Directions: The lowercase letter "s" is in the first column. Look at the four letters in the row and circle the uppercase letter that matches the lowercase letter "s."

Direksyons: Lèt miniskil "s" se nan premye kolòn nan. Gade kat lèt ki nan ranje a epi antoure lèt majiskil ki koresponn ak lèt miniskil "s".

s	X	C	T	(S)
s	O	(S)	C	Z
s	G	C	(S)	X
s	(S)	G	O	U

Learn To Read English With Directions In Haitian Creole

Homework

 Name: _____ Date: ___/___/_____ Score: _____

Appendix 19.0

Letter Recognition S/s

Uppercase and Lowercase Letter

✓ Lesson Check Point

 Directions: Read each target word. Read the words in the row and circle the word that begins with a different letter.

Direksyons: Li chak mo sib. Li mo ki nan ranje a epi antoure mo ki kòmanse ak yon lèt diferan.

Target Words				
1. son	since	(cash)	skate	scale
2. snow	sketch	shell	seek	(chick)
3. shape	(zoo)	sell	shrub	soar
4. sheet	smile	save	slip	(mother)
5. search	seem	shade	(corn)	school

 Directions: Read the words in the four boxes. Circle two words that start with the uppercase and lowercase letter "s."

Direksyons: Li mo ki nan kat kare yo. Ansèkle de mo ki kòmanse ak lèt majiskil ak lèt miniskil "s".

court	(Sharp)	(slash)	(Sale)	Zoo	(silk)
grows	(sour)	zipper	Clash	(Share)	clock

house	clowns	(shark)	cord	(show)	vases
(Size)	(sew)	(Snow)	zebra	zero	(Snore)

Name: _____   Date: ___/___/_____   Score: _____

Appendix 20.0

Introduction of the Letter T/t

✓ **Lesson Check Point**

 Directions: Circle the correct letter "t" pair: uppercase and lowercase letters.
Direksyons: Antoure lèt ki kòrèk "t" pè: lèt majiskil ak lèt miniskil.

| Tl | tZ | tJ | (Tt) | Tk |

 Directions: The uppercase letter "T" is in the first column. Look at the four letters in the row and circle the lowercase letter that matches the uppercase letter "T."
Direksyons: Lèt majiskil "T" se nan premye kolòn nan. Gade kat lèt ki nan ranje a epi antoure lèt miniskil ki koresponn ak lèt majiskil "T".

T	j	l	(t)	h
T	l	f	b	(t)
T	(t)	h	f	d
T	j	l	(t)	f

 Directions: The lowercase letter "t" is in the first column. Look at the four letters in the row and circle the uppercase letter that matches the lowercase letter "t."
Direksyons: Lèt miniskil "t" se nan premye kolòn nan. Gade kat lèt ki nan ranje a epi antoure lèt majiskil ki koresponn ak lèt miniskil "t".

t	H	(T)	J	A
t	L	K	L	(T)
t	(T)	A	X	L
t	Y	F	(T)	H

Learn To Read English With Directions In Haitian Creole

Homework

 Name: _____ Date: ___/___/_____ Score: _____

Appendix 20.0

Letter Recognition T/t

Uppercase and Lowercase Letter

✓ Lesson Check Point

 Directions: Read each target word. Read the words in the row and circle the word that begins with a different letter.

Direksyons: Li chak mo sib. Li mo ki nan ranje a epi antoure mo ki kòmanse ak yon lèt diferan.

Target Words				
1. turn	thirst	(fool)	train	thorn
2. tool	touch	trunk	(love)	tent
3. tank	than	tenth	tang	(help)
4. them	tap	tour	(drip)	thank
5. truck	(hope)	tray	third	tare

 Directions: Read the words in the four boxes. Circle two words that start with the uppercase and lowercase letter "t."
Direksyons: Li mo ki nan kat kare yo. Ansèkle de mo ki kòmanse ak lèt majiskil ak lèt miniskil "t".

(Thanks)	(term)
lick	Fine

Phone	(trace)
(Toy)	home

Left	(Tart)
boat	(tint)

(Twirl)	keen
Rain	(tube)

(trail)	leaf
(Tone)	fun

Kind	dock
(Tub)	(take)

Name: _____ Date: ___/___/_____ Score: _____

Homework

Appendix 21.0

Introduction of the Letter U/u

✓ **Lesson Check Point**

 Directions: Circle the correct letter "u" pair: uppercase and lowercase letters.
Direksyons: Antoure lèt ki kòrèk "u" pè: lèt majiskil ak lèt miniskil.

Yu   Uu   Vu   (Ou)   vU

 Directions: The uppercase letter "U" is in the first column. Look at the four letters in the row and circle the lowercase letter that matches the uppercase letter "U."
Direksyons: Lèt majiskil "U" se nan premye kolòn nan. Gade kat lèt ki nan ranje a epi antoure lèt miniskil ki koresponn ak lèt majiskil "U".

U	j	s	(u)	v
U	o	g	h	(u)
U	(u)	k	v	o
U	v	r	o	(u)

 Directions: The lowercase letter "u" is in the first column. Look at the four letters in the row and circle the uppercase letter that matches the lowercase letter "u."
Direksyons: Lèt miniskil "u" se nan premye kolòn nan. Gade kat lèt ki nan ranje a epi antoure lèt majiskil ki koresponn ak lèt miniskil "u".

u	(U)	V	C	X
u	Z	C	(U)	V
u	Y	E	V	(U)
u	T	(U)	N	O

Homework

 Name: _____ Date:____/____/_____ Score:_____

Appendix 22.0

Introduction of the Letter V/v

✓ **Lesson Check Point**

 Directions: Circle the correct letter "v" pair: uppercase and lowercase letters.
Direksyons: Antoure lèt ki kòrèk "v" pè: lèt majiskil ak lèt miniskil.

Cv   Uv   (Vv)   Xv   Vk

 Directions: The uppercase letter "V" is in the first column. Look at the four letters in the row and circle the lowercase letter that matches the uppercase letter "V."
Direksyons: Lèt majiskil "V" se nan premye kolòn nan. Gade kat lèt ki nan ranje a epi antoure lèt miniskil ki koresponn ak lèt majiskil "V".

V	u	(v)	x	y
V	(v)	u	n	s
V	c	b	(v)	x
V	m	(v)	u	z

 Directions: The lowercase letter "v" is in the first column. Look at the four letters in the row and circle the uppercase letter that matches the lowercase letter "v."
Direksyons: Lèt miniskil "v" se nan premye kolòn nan. Gade kat lèt ki nan ranje a epi antoure lèt majiskil ki koresponn ak lèt miniskil "v".

v	X	Y	T	(V)
v	T	(V)	U	M
v	(V)	Y	X	S
v	J	F	(V)	Z

Homework

 Name: _____ Date: ___/___/_____ Score: _____

Appendix 22.0

Letter Recognition V/v

Uppercase and Lowercase Letter

✓ **Lesson Check Point**

 Directions: Read each target word. Read the words in the row and circle the word that begins with a different letter.

Direksyons: Li chak mo sib. Li mo ki nan ranje a epi antoure mo ki kòmanse ak yon lèt diferan.

Target Words				
1. vine	(went)	view	vogue	verb
2. vault	vent	volt	(March)	vague
3. vow	(keys)	vein	vest	vane
4. vamp	valve	(water)	vote	versed
5. voiced	vile	void	vouch	(walk)

 Directions: Read the words in the four boxes. Circle two words that start with the uppercase and lowercase letter "v."

Direksyons: Li mo ki nan kat kare yo. Ansèkle de mo ki kòmanse ak lèt majiskil ak lèt miniskil "v".

mean	(van)
worm	(verse)

(Vase)	sour
root	(veil)

force	(Voice)
(verge)	Wept

(Vain)	apple
(visit)	cost

(veto)	(Vice)
wake	neck

white	raise
(Vex)	(veer)

Homework

 Name: _____ Date: ___/___/_____ Score: _____

Appendix 23.0

Introduction of the Letter W/w

✓ **Lesson Check Point**

 Directions: Circle the correct letter "w" pair: uppercase and lowercase letters.
Direksyons: Antoure lèt ki kòrèk "w" pè: lèt majiskil ak lèt miniskil.

wV   (wW)   Uw   Wv   Yw

 **Directions:** The uppercase letter "W" is in the first column. Look at the four letters in the row and circle the lowercase letter that matches the uppercase letter "W."
Direksyons: Lèt majiskil "W" se nan premye kolòn nan. Gade kat lèt ki nan ranje a epi antoure lèt miniskil ki koresponn ak lèt majiskil "W".

W	v	(w)	x	y
W	u	t	c	(w)
W	(w)	u	v	m
W	n	y	(w)	f

 Directions: The lowercase letter "w" is in the first column. Look at the four letters in the row and circle the uppercase letter that matches the lowercase letter "w."
Direksyons: Lèt miniskil "w" se nan premye kolòn nan. Gade kat lèt ki nan ranje a epi antoure lèt majiskil ki koresponn ak lèt miniskil "w".

w	V	M	(W)	N
w	U	(W)	V	A
w	(W)	X	C	M
w	X	V	Y	(W)

Homework

Name: _____ Date: ___/___/_____ Score: _____

Appendix 23.0

Letter Recognition W/w

Uppercase and Lowercase Letter

✓ Lesson Check Point

Directions: Read each target word. Read the words in the row and circle the word that begins with a different letter.
Direksyons: Li chak mo sib. Li mo ki nan ranje a epi antoure mo ki kòmanse ak yon lèt diferan.

Target Words				
1. what	wedge	wrist	(mugs)	write
2. wire	which	warm	wreck	(voyage)
3. wear	warn	(noon)	wound	went
4. wages	while	wise	weak	(Mouse)
5. wheeze	(vowel)	waist	wipe	wrest

Directions: Read the words in the four boxes. Circle two words that start with the uppercase and lowercase letter "w."
Direksyons: Li mo ki nan kat kare yo.Ansèkle de mo ki kòmanse ak lèt majiskil ak lèt miniskil "w".

(want)	Nail
(Wig)	video

Match	(Where)
(wrong)	None

(With)	(whack)
Merge	Vision

Mud	Verdict
(whim)	(Wart)

Nuts	(wrung)
volcano	(White)

Wool	Volume
Noise	wet

Learn To Read English With Directions In Haitian Creole

Homework

 Name: _____ Date: ___/___/_____ Score: _____

Appendix 24.0

Introduction of the Letter X/x

✓ **Lesson Check Point**

 Directions: Circle the correct letter "x" pair: uppercase and lowercase letters.
Direksyons: Antoure lèt ki kòrèk "x" pè: lèt majiskil ak lèt miniskil.

Xz   Kx   (Xx)   xY   Xk

 Directions: The uppercase letter "X" is in the first column. Look at the four letters in the row and circle the lowercase letter that matches the uppercase letter "X."
Direksyons: Lèt majiskil "X" se nan premye kolòn nan. Gade kat lèt ki nan ranje a epi antoure lèt miniskil ki koresponn ak lèt majiskil "X".

X	(x)	y	z	s
X	v	(x)	k	y
X	u	z	a	(x)
X	(x)	v	k	z

 Directions: The lowercase letter "x" is in the first column. Look at the four letters in the row and circle the uppercase letter that matches the lowercase letter "x."
Direksyons: Lèt miniskil "x" se nan premye kolòn nan. Gade kat lèt ki nan ranje a epi antoure lèt majiskil ki koresponn ak lèt miniskil "x".

x	K	(X)	Z	V
x	B	K	V	(X)
x	(X)	V	U	Y
x	Y	(X)	K	F

Homework

Name: _____ Date: ____/____/_____ Score: _____

Appendix 24.0

Letter Recognition X/x

Uppercase and Lowercase Letter

✓ Lesson Check Point

Directions: Read each target word. Read the words in the row and circle the word that does not contain a letter "x."
Direksyons: Li chak mo sib. Li mo ki nan ranje a epi fè wonn mo ki pa gen yon lèt "x"

Target Words				
1. axed	(vamp)	ox	mixing	annex
2. tax	taxi	waxy	(cooks)	flex
3. max	exit	Texas	(yes)	reflex
4. mix	next	sixth	foxes	(cents)
5. extra	toxic	fax	boxes	(goats)

Directions: Read the words in the four boxes. Circle two words that start with the uppercase and lowercase letter "x."
Direksyons: Li mo ki nan kat kare yo. Ansèkle de mo ki kòmanse ak lèt majiskil ak lèt miniskil "x".

extra	(x-ray)
(Xylan)	vote

cortex	excel
(Xylene)	(xanthate)

kind	(xenon)
vault	(Xerox)

(xeric)	(Xanadu)
kale	nail

(x-axis)	yours
(Xylose)	knit

(Xiphoid)	out
mean	(xanthoma)

Learn To Read English With Directions In Haitian Creole   293   Copyrighted Material

Homework

 Name: _____ Date: ___/___/_____ Score: _____

Appendix 25.0

Introduction of the Letter Y/y

✓ Lesson Check Point

 Directions: Circle the correct letter "y" pair: uppercase and lowercase letters.
Direksyons: Antoure lèt ki kòrèk "y" pè: lèt majiskil ak lèt miniskil.

Yg   (yY)   Jy   Yj   Xy

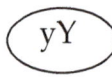 **Directions:** The uppercase letter "Y" is in the first column. Look at the four letters in the row and circle the lowercase letter that matches the uppercase letter "Y."
Direksyons: Lèt majiskil "Y" se nan premye kolòn nan. Gade kat lèt ki nan ranje a epi antoure lèt miniskil ki koresponn ak lèt majiskil "Y".

Y	j	(y)	x	p
Y	(y)	g	j	l
Y	g	q	(y)	j
Y	j	(y)	g	v

 Directions: The lowercase letter "y" is in the first column. Look at the four letters in the row and circle the uppercase letter that matches the lowercase letter "y."
Direksyons: Lèt miniskil "y" se nan premye kolòn nan. Gade kat lèt ki nan ranje a epi antoure lèt majiskil ki koresponn ak lèt miniskil "y".

y	F	G	(Y)	X
y	(Y)	L	M	J
y	B	C	X	(Y)
y	(Y)	L	Z	G

Homework

 Name: _____ Date: ___/___/_____ Score: _____

Appendix 25.0

Letter Recognition Y/y

Uppercase and Lowercase Letter

✓ Lesson Check Point

 Directions: Read each target word. Read the words in the row and circle the word that begins with a different letter.
Direksyons: Li chak mo sib. Li mo ki nan ranje a epi antoure mo ki kòmanse ak yon lèt diferan.

Target Words				
1. yoke	yield	year	(quick)	y-axis
2. yeast	(peace)	yeast	yard	yes
3. yonder	yam	yonder	yak	(great)
4. Yankee	(basket)	yuppie	yolk	yo-yo
5. younger	yap	(group)	yogurt	yonder

 Directions: Read the words in the four boxes. Circle two words that start with the uppercase and lowercase letter "y."
Direksyons: Li mo ki nan kat kare yo. Ansèkle de mo ki kòmanse ak lèt majiskil ak lèt miniskil "y".

(Yacht)	paid
(yes)	glimpse

(yield)	good
jog	(Year)

jean	(yoke)
quit	(Your)

(yeast)	(Yikes)
group	joke

purse	(yoga)
(Yard)	joint

juice	glue
(Yon)	(young)

Homework

Name: _____ Date: ___/___/_____ Score: _____

Appendix 26.0

Introduction of the Letter Z/z

✓ Lesson Check Point

Directions: Circle the correct letter "z" pair: uppercase and lowercase letters.
Direksyons: Antoure lèt ki kòrèk "z" pè: lèt majiskil ak lèt miniskil.

zX   (zZ)   Yz   Zv   zF

Directions: The uppercase letter "Z" is in the first column. Look at the four letters in the row and circle the lowercase letter that matches the uppercase letter "Z."
Direksyons: Lèt majiskil "Z" se nan premye kolòn nan. Gade kat lèt ki nan ranje a epi antoure lèt miniskil ki koresponn ak lèt majiskil "Z".

Z	(z)	c	x	y
Z	x	t	(z)	g
Z	c	g	s	(z)
Z	y	h	(z)	a

Directions: The lowercase letter "z" is in the first column. Look at the four letters in the row and circle the uppercase letter that matches the lowercase letter "z."
Direksyons: Lèt miniskil "z" se nan premye kolòn nan. Gade kat lèt ki nan ranje a epi antoure lèt majiskil ki koresponn ak lèt miniskil "z".

z	D	(Z)	X	C
z	(Z)	C	V	N
z	M	G	B	(Z)
z	(Z)	N	W	X

Homework

 Name: _____ Date:___/__/____ Score:_____

Appendix 26.0

Letter Recognition Z/z

Uppercase and Lowercase Letter

✓ Lesson Check Point

 Directions: Read each target word. Read the words in the row and circle the word that begins with a different letter.
Direksyons: Li chak mo sib. Li mo ki nan ranje a epi antoure mo ki kòmanse ak yon lèt diferan.

Target Words				
1. zero	zillion	zone	zeal	(sold)
2. zebras	zag	(wear)	zip	zygote
3. zinger	(vase)	zodiac	zoo	zipper
4. zenith	zinc	zonal	(suit)	zig
5. zoning	zoom	(school)	zany	zinc

 Directions: Read the words in the four boxes. Circle two words that start with the uppercase and lowercase letter "z."
Direksyons: Li mo ki nan kat kare yo. Ansèkle de mo ki kòmanse ak lèt majiskil ak lèt miniskil "z".

swing	Nose
(Zillion)	(zero)

sugar	(zeal)
wet	(Zebra)

(zinger)	(Zoo)
strive	water

(zig)	stream
(Zebu)	wig

sweet	(Zone)
(zap)	mouse

Never	swan
(Zili)	(zinc)

Learn To Read English With Directions In Haitian Creole

Homework

**Your Next Step:
Learn To Read English Vowels With Directions In Haitian Creole**